WORK HORSE
HANDBOOK

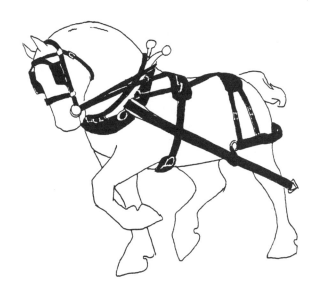

Lynn R. Miller

Publisher
Small Farmer's Journal Inc.
PO Box 1627
325 Barclay Drive
Sisters, Oregon 97759
541-549-2064

Printed in the United States of America
Printer: Parton Press, Redmond, Oregon

Authored, illustrated, edited and designed by Lynn R. Miller

First Edition, Fourteenth Impression
First printing 1981
Subsequent printings 1983, 1985, 1987, 1988, 1990,
1991, 1992, 1993, 1994, 1995, 1996, 1997, 1998

Library of Congress catalog card number -- 81-90515

ISBN 0-9607268-0-2

Also by L. R. Miller

Training Workhorses / Training Teamsters

Buying and Setting Up Your Small Farm or Ranch

Why Farm: Selected Essays and Editorials

Ten Acres Enough: The Small Farm Dream Is Possible

Thought Small: Poems, Prayers, Drawings & Postings

DEDICATION

This book is dedicated to my good friends, Queenie, Goldie, Dick, Bud, Flash, Bobbie, Carol, Sarah, Kedde, Major, Bonnie, Betsy, Ted, Tom, Red, Rob, Rowdy, Lil' Joe, Mel, Penny, Roselle, Tatum, Tip, Bob, and Bud. Some of you are still with me, others in new homes and five of you have passed on. All of you have given me purpose. I can never repay you, but I'll keep trying.

ACKNOWLEDGEMENTS

This book has been a long labor of love. I had to finish it even though it is not done. Perhaps it never will be. It would not have made it, even this far, without the inspiration, forgiving and help of many people. There have been several dozen truly special teamsters that helped me to "see", they inspired me, most often without knowing it. They should remain anonymous but I thank them here.

And my three children, Justin, Juliet and Ian, had to spend less 'precious' time with 'daddy'. But they forgave me in their special way. And my brother, Tony, had to do endless days of farm chores, proof reading and crud work so I could keep doing the book. And there are many others who have forgiven me my excesses in this project.

And then there are those who have 'given' and 'helped'. Topping that list is my very special father who has nurtured me so literally without ever pushing. And Susanne Isom, who typed and corrected an endless stream of words. And Nancy Roberts who took great pictures for years. And Mary Bearden who cared, read and coached. And John Billington who believed in me and dared to be my attorney. And Kristi Gilman for doing a bunch of odd jobs. And Jack Gray for taking on a bunch more work at the Journal office. Thank you all. Here it is. LRM

PREFACE

When the opportunity arose for me to do this preface, it left me in something approaching a state of awe, wonder that this moment had come to me: bemused, I think is the word. Forgive me if I insert a note of personal feeling here; perhaps I can show its relevance.

There are pictures around of this writer perched high up on 'Old Jake', a brown gelding of uncertain ancestry who was dressed for the occasion in his everyday work harness. (Since the photo is a very old one, circa 1918, I was wearing mostly curly hair, short pants and a solemn, if not frightened, expression.) We got rid of our horses a very few years later to my sorrow, and from there on my contacts and use of them was limited to those of my Grandfathers, other relatives and neighbors. I did grow up in an area where the harness horse was in use up until World War II.

A lot of changes occurred as a result of that cataclysm, but aside from the loss of human life, to my mind one of the most devastating was the nearly fatal blow to the use of the harness horse. Right here let me say that I don't really differentiate all that much between the huge draft horses and carriage horses, hackneys or the working ponies. I have a tenderness for them all and I mourned, at least secretly, what I was sure was the certain demise of all those noble animals that had served man so long and well only to be almost literally thrown to the dogs.

When the first stirrings of a revival in such use of horses came to my ears a few years back I hardly dared hope. My delight when it proved true and came close to home was tremendous. I am still moved to be so closely aligned with the revival, even if it is mostly second hand, but then to have even a small part in a book designed to spread the word is a real joy. The sense of awe and bemusement I spoke of is occasioned by my relationship to all this.

In all humility I think I am fitted to introduce the Author; I go back with him to a snowy night in midwinter many years ago. I met him in the arms of the Doctor, an almost amorphous bundle a few minutes old and if you think this forward is colored by the pride his father felt at that moment you may be right. As objective as I try to be, his rapid rise to the position he holds in the horse community leaves me with a feeling of wonderment.

I have been right here near him since he first expressed an interest. I helped him find his first team, encouraged him, cautioned him, watched him and still I find it a little incredible. He was listed in an article in the Smithsonian Magazine as one of three Gurus in the work horse revival in America: On the front page of the Wall Street Journal a story on that movement named him as an acknowledged leader and expert in the field. Writings, speeches, lectures, articles in the Small Farmer's Journal and other publications have added to his stature among horsemen everywhere, but, although he seems to thrive on that attention, he is never so happy as when he is working with his horses on the home farm.

In spite of my own lifelong feeling for horses, I can make no claim to have led him into it. When he started working with them, it was on his own and from scratch. As he indicates in the body of this book, good, clear instruction for the beginning or intermediate horseman was not easy to come by. Early in his use of horses he made it a point to seek out older experienced teamsters. They were of invaluable use, of course, but it was necessary to adapt this advice, varied as it obviously was, to his own practical use. This fact in and of itself gave him insight into the pertinent needs the relative newcomer encounters.

Whatever lack he found in existing writings when he was a novice has been filled in and incorporated along with his own experience and the best of that early advice. In addition to his Editorial hat, he is constantly in contact personally or by letter with people who share his interest or have questions. All this material has been compiled to make it the 'Handbook' that the tyro must have and all others will find helpful.

I don't know how much there can be in predestination or in inherited tendencies for unfulfilled aspirations but along with the harness I started life with a yearning to be involved in the Fine Arts. Although Lynn doesn't make too much of it these days, he did pursue that interest academically and as an avocation up until the time that farming and particularly horses became his dominant pursuit.

Fortunately, publishing and sometimes illustrating a magazine about horses and small farming combines those seemingly varied interests admirably. As the book will make apparent, artistic talent and the eye that accompanies it is a decided advantage in covering a theme of this nature. Not only is he able to diagram and illustrate much of the material presented but the eye trained graphically and to anatomy perceives applications of force, perspectives of design and elements of conformation most conducive to the animal's ability to do the tasks they are bred for. The Farmer and the Artist, far from being antipodes are happily blended to author this work, and from all sides, the practical, the aesthetic, the mundane, the intangible and the interdependence and empathy that has always existed between a man and his equine partners.

Still attempting objectivity, I am struck by the timing of the book. That isn't entirely coincidence, of course; Lynn is totally aware of the demand for such published material because of the swell of interest in the draft horse. Nevertheless, I do see this as a moment that cries out for a definitive work to encourage those who want horses to fill a need in their own lives, to assist those already committed and perhaps to plant a seed in the minds of those only vaguely aware of the possibilities.

The skyrocketing costs of fossil fuel power, the disenchantment with the moil and pollution of mechanically oriented, people-clogged cities, the burgeoning desire to become more self-sufficient, all these things have contributed to the awakening so exciting to those of us who have longed for this day. In addition, there are a growing number of those already farming who are returning to the horse as a practical alternative or a way out of the vicious circle of larger operations with spiraling costs and a constantly dwindling profit margin or outright loss.

None of us expect the horse to replace the combustion powered machines completely but we do see the horse on the way back to a rightful place again. Admittedly the numbers are not great compared to 1914 or in percentage of total population, but put up against 10 or 15 years ago or seen in relation to the wholesale exodus after WW II, the picture is heartening. If this book is instrumental in further turnaround, if it aids those who need help or encouragement, then its primary goal has been achieved. If the present grass roots swell for the return of the harness horse continues this writer's pleasure will be deep and lasting; if the success and prestige of the book's Author increases by its publication this proud parent's satisfaction will increase proportionally . . . . And lastly, if you the reader successfully put these precepts into practice, then I'm certain all of us will have occasion to rejoice in the eventual resurgence of man's willing partner, the horse in harness.

Ralph Miller

TABLE OF CONTENTS

*Working horses allows you to feel alive
and part of the process at hand.*

*Belgian mares belonging to the author.
Photo by Nancy Roberts*

CHAPTER ONE

THE WORK HORSE: CONSIDERATIONS FOR THE BEGINNER

This text is written by one who uses horses in harness for farm work, occassional logging and some highway driving. This author, through experience, believes in the practicality of work horses and hopes to encourage their increased use by providing simple, direct and fairly complete information about what is nearly a lost craft, the art of the teamster.

The decision to depend on horses or mules in harness for farm work, logging or highway work is important and should not be taken lightly. Aside from romantic notions of involvement in a picturesque scene, most of the considerations are serious. This is not to suggest that the romantic notion is negative or in any way detrimental as part of a commitment. Quite the contrary; the prevailing motivation behind a majority of good practicing horse farmers today seems to be just that notion. But without considering all of the practical questions related to "Why use horses?" a person new to the business could very well find himself or herself in either a dangerous, humiliating, confusing or discouraging situation. (It's likely to be a combination of all four.) Make the choice carefully.

Before making the decision to depend on work horses, a person should seek out a good measure of practical information on horses, materials and procedures as well as advantages and limitations. (There is a directory included in this text which will help in locating some of the few publications which carry any information pertaining to work horses.) The single most important source of information is that available person who is doing it or has done it and is willing and capable to communicate his knowledge.

Seek out people who still work horses or who did it in the recent past and talk to them. But first a 'rule' and then a 'warning'. The rule is: Don't settle for "one" source. The warning is: Stand prepared to hear as many different ways and reasons for doing as people you talk to.

Allow yourself the benefit of the doubt by talking to several people and asking them and yourself questions about the differences in methods and approaches you will hear. In the end, you will have to trust your own judgement, so build up a healthy reservoir of information.

Another little suggestion: Be careful of any information you might gather from a meeting of several practitioners. It might be good, but then again . . . . To see first hand what I mean, after you think you have a pretty good grasp of a couple of people's horse thoughts, invite them to meet with you and others at some informal gathering to talk horse. You should be surprised to hear the difference: You will witness some amazing about-faces (and maybe even some rather long silences). So beware of the seminar sources; it seems nobody wants to "look the fool" and the good information often gets set aside.

Hopefully you will discover an intelligent person, with an amazing memory, and a real sensitivity to your need for information, or you will discover a "holdout", someone who is still using horses. Do not, however, disregard someone relatively new at the business. They can make good teachers, because the learning process, with its pitfalls and triumphs, is still fresh to them, and they can communicate this to you. But, remember to seek out as many sources as are available and accept no "one" article, book, person, or magazine as representing the "only way". There is no "only way".

In that context, it should be kept in mind that this text is the work of one man and however complete it may appear, it is as limited and biased as is the author.

If you think you want to work horses, consider these points first:

It is a complex and subtle business of which the teamster must know everything. If he does not, it quickly becomes a dangerous business.

The all-day working speed of a team of draft horses is between 2 and 4 miles per hour. By how most of us are accustomed to living, that is slow. It is, for example, slower to work horses than tractors. If speed is important to you or your operation, horses might prove to be a liability. Modern tillage practices and seasonal work schedules on most farms could not be met satisfactorily by horses. That is not to say that horses cannot get the necessary work done, but it is to say that practices and schedules will have to be modified with the horse in mind.

Fig. 1) It is a complex and subtle business of which the teamster must know everything.

The late Bob Nygren plowing with three abreast.

Fig. 2) Horse drawn equipment in good condition is getting harder to find.

Horses, unlike tractors, must have fuel daily, whether they are working or not. They have to eat. And when working they must be cared for regularly. When the day's field, woods or road work is done, the teamster is not. He must still unharness, feed and curry his horses, looking after anything which needs to be repaired or remedied for the next day's work. A horse farmer must work longer hours, if not as hard, as his tractor counterpart.

In large farming operations (of more than 160 acres) it may become necessary to bring in outside labor to help drive and care for the horses needed. Finding qualified help can be difficult.

The supply of well-broke, draft-type horses suitable for work is limited. The good ones bring healthy prices now. When supply matches or exceeds demand the price should drop some. Until that time, as demand for horses increases, so also will the price.

Consider the availability of harness and equipment. The recent interest in draft animals has pumped some life into the harness-making trade. Due to some international trade pressures, leather prices are high and so new harness is not cheap. However, with proper care it remains an excellent investment choice over old harness. Although there are new harness-makers springing into business, demand still appears to exceed supply. Used harness can be found, but many inexperienced people have had unfortunate, discouraging accidents because important parts of used harness broke at a critical moment. The same holds true for old singletrees and doubletrees as well as neck yokes and poles.

Horse-drawn farm machinery is becoming increasingly hard to find in usable condition. Farm machinery companies no longer build this equipment. However, a handful of small shops do still make a few items, such as plows, but on a very limited basis. So limited, in fact, that they are back-ordered and not bothering to advertise.

The major consideration in favor of horse farming includes the practical economy, the relative independence, and advantages to soil condition. That might not sound like much after the setbacks already discussed but these categories cover a lot of ground.

If comparing the straight-across cost of setting up a working farm with tractors versus horses, horse farming is less expensive. The difference in cost could be dramatic, depending on the particular combination of variables, i.e., crops grown, technology selected, new tractors or purebred breeding stock versus old tractors or grade horses. All these considerations could affect prices by tens of thousands of dollars.

It is also less expensive to operate a farm with true horse-power over tractors. To do an accurate job of accounting actual costs, especially in horse farming, can get complex. For example, horses produce not only net energy converted to work, but also manure (fertilizer) and offspring. These all need to be calculated into the income production of horses. There are also very subtle, almost intangible, values to be derived from the use of horses as they impose certain limitations, which, if accepted as constructive outlines, will account for the development of individual farm systems which are inherently less costly. For example, pasture, hay and grain are the fuel for horses. Horses can be maintained much of the time on grain stubble and pasture that might be made available on marginal areas of the farm. And horses work best as a power source if the cropping practices are mixed and divided between Spring and Fall seasons. Setting up a farm plan to take full advantage of these aspects can reduce out-of-pocket expenses considerably. (A chapter of this book is devoted to the numbers that relate to the cost of using horses.)

If you consider the operations cost for the entire year on the farm, there will be periods when the tractor will not be used and fuel cost will be zero. During those same periods (the horses, because of their tractability, will be able to continue to perform — feeding or spreading manure or yarding logs, etc.) there will be idle days, perhaps even weeks, for the horses and they will have to be fed, but there again with good management, those horses can be on pasture and the cost will be small. In the course of the year, repair work may have to be done to the tractor. Tractor parts and mechanic's labor are getting more expensive every day. It is relative to the skills and good fortune of each individual farmer, but often maintenance and repair of the tractor equipment is a major cost item in a farm budget.

Using horses can make a farm less dependent on outside needs such as fuel, oil, grease, mechanical help, tractor parts and such. Horse manure contributes as fertilizer to the farm's soil, reducing outside needs. Horses reproduce, providing their own replacements. Horses, for the most part, are self-repairing. Horses can be an important ingredient in any deliberate program to improve the self-sufficiency of the farm. And horses are good to the soil. They don't compact the soil with a rolling pin effect as tractors do.

All of this seems to suggest that the choice is either tractors or horses. That is most certainly not necessarily so. Many farms enjoy an excellent balanced mixture of tractor and horse-power. These mixed power farms have many advantages to offer. For a variety of reasons many farms may operate most comfortably with a tractor and a team of horses.

There are some hard-to-measure advantages of horses that will be more or less of value to different people. They include the quiet, attractive way of working that horses provide. Anyone who has spent a long, hot, dusty day sitting on a hot, smelly, noisy, vibrating tractor knows how uncomfortable that can be. Horses are quiet and smooth and don't give off 200 degreee heat mixed with diesel fumes. In fact, doing the exact same work, horses can be downright comfortable, even relaxing.

Fig. 3) Horse farming makes money by saving money.

Ferd Mantei with team of Percheron geldings.
Photo by Nancy Roberts

No one can guess what will happen in the near future with our energy systems. Today most farms are connected to survival by a gasoline/diesel hose as an umbilical cord. Cut off that hose and the farm grinds to an absolute standstill. It is worth considering as recent years have proven it is not an altogether impossible situation. Horses and horse equipment do not require gas or diesel fuels and will continue on. In light of what has happened in recent years and what could happen again, the horse farmers have good reason to feel healthy in their relative independence and self-sufficiency.

On the tractor farm, the farmer must be concerned about the age and condition of his equipment relative to the work it must do and its resale value. That depreciation scale for farm machinery is a slick, steep, downhill slide. On the other side, horse values, after maturity, hold up well until the horse is too old to work. Add to this the fact that horses are self-renewing. After an initial investment for good work mares, many farms spend no money on replacements. With foals every year to add to the work string, the farmer will find he has horses to sell. Under good management, after the initial investment in horses and equipment is made, the farmer will find himself in an attractive balance of payments situation. With little or no cash outlay for fuel, repairs and maintenance; and no annual debt service on new equipment, and no depreciation in resale values, the farmer has reason to feel healthy. The reduced total overhead makes for a handsome profit margin potential. Horse farming makes money by saving money.

The choice to use horses for log skidding is certainly affected by much of what has been said. Some considerations peculiar to horse logging have to do with the astronomical difference in initial capital investment required between using horses or using machinery. Horses are much cheaper. Also horses do considerably less damage to the forest floor. Horses are a sound choice for ecological reasons. Horse logging is hazardous business with greater inherent risk to horse and driver than most farm work, so great caution is necessary. A good strong horse or team of horses can yard a substantial quantity of logs and should be considered a practical optional power source for logging.

Most people who have considered the practical applications of real horse-power have little difficulty visualizing many of the ways that work horses would fit into the process of farming and logging. That's not always the case when it comes to the use of horses in harness for the transport of goods and people. But in this area of transportation lies perhaps the most dramatic potential for a whole new (and revisited) world or practical applications.

Fig. 4) Horse drawn conveyances are coming back to the cities.

Photo by Nancy Roberts

In city traffic (be it large or small), stop lights, stop signs and the rhythm of intersecting streets join with the mass of motor vehicles and pedestrians to set a slow and costly (gasoline-wise) pace. That's not to suggest leisurely — with this "jammed" pace comes tension and anxiety. Within the last ten years, from 1970 on, a few businesses have proven to their own satisfaction that they could haul goods, be it garbage, beer or whatever, and people within cities at a tremendous savings in fuel, with no lost time over customary city travel, with no sanitation or undue public risk hazards, and with tremendous public acceptance. Whether it's self-propelled garbage compacting wagons, beer hauling wagons, omnibuses, furniture vans, parcel delivery service, or carriages — the horse-drawn conveyance within the cities and towns of North America may be making as big a comeback soon as has been seen on farms and in the woods.

Those of us under 40 years of age, and some over, may not have had any memory, or even concern, about what almost proved to be the extinction of the draft horse in North America and the death of the teamsters' craft.

Following World War II the decline in draft horse numbers was so rapid that the five major breeds (Belgian, Percheron, Suffolk, Shire and Clydesdale) faced dangerously low breed numbers. Recent years have seen a dramatic popularity turnaround for the big horse.

Certainly the much-publicized beer company Clydesdale hitch has done a great deal to reacquaint the general public with the romance of large draft horse hitches as well as to influence some people to put together show and parade hitches of their own. Many draft horse showmen disavow the beer company hitch and take great independent pride in the origin of their own show traditions. But more important have been the rapidly growing number of farmers, ranchers, loggers and homesteaders who have decided for various reasons that they, once again, needed the work horse in harness.

Over these last short ten years the success stories of the new and/or reborn teamsters have fueled more pilgrims. The upshot of it all is a boom in the draft horse market. There simply does not seem to be enough good draft horses and mules to supply the ever-growing market. That, of course, has its good and bad points.

Ten or twelve years ago, early in this draft horse boom, most of the prospective buyers had very little or no practical experience with the craft of working horses in harness. Whether their aim was to skid logs with one horse, feed cattle in the snow with a team, plow fields with six head, cultivate the garden with one mule, pull a manure spreader, haul kids on hay rides, take the buggy to town, pick corn, mow hay or any of the hundreds of things horses can successfully be used for, too many new teamsters had to learn the hard way that this was a craft which looked much easier than it proved to be. Wrecks were so numerous and some so terrible that the only reasons that the interest in work horses didn't become a forgotten fad were; "It was too solid a notion", and "good old human resolve". These pilgrims stuck to their guns and some were successful in finding old-timers who shared some precious, long-ago-taken-for-granted secrets.

Some nice things happened in that process. Some people were rediscovered, respected, needed and made to feel worthwhile. A beautifully subtle craft based on the cooperative communication between man and horse was spared from extinction by being reborn as once again a living legacy. And the fresh youthful outlook of these new teamsters has already accounted for many exciting, and needed, innovations in horse-drawn technology. All of this is to say that the future looks brighter than ever for the marriage of people and work horses.

Yet for the beginner the question remains, "How do I learn what I need to know?" As I said at the beginning of this chapter, hopefully this text will help you learn what you need to know about working horses in harness. But keep in mind that this book is limited because it is 'just a book', and because the author is 'just one man'. Seek out other sources of information. And be careful to judge the source for what it is.

In this modern, high technology, corporate controlled, "make a fast buck" world there are vultures watching with a keen, well-trained eye for grass roots movements that they can exploit. As soon as the rekindled interest in work horses can be identified by either corporate interests and/or con artists as something marketable, they will do so in droves.

In this digital, out-of-whack world there are so few ventures or involvements that allow us to feel really alive and part of the process of energy at work. The great beauty of the notion of working horses is that it gives the individual that special feeling in large measure. It is such an easy process to feel part of and enjoy. And early in your initiation I sincerely hope that all goes well enough for you to experience a simple question: "Why aren't more people doing this?"

Fig. 5) Percheron geldings hitched to walking plow and
waiting for instructions.   Photo by Nancy Roberts

CHAPTER TWO

ATTITUDE AND APPROACH

The Horse as a Thinking, Feeling Mammal

I've got more faith in horses than in people. You've probably heard that before but not in the same context that I'm referring to.

There are a lot of widely held beliefs about horses which are unfortunate, unkind, unnecessary and stupid. The horse is not "dumb" in any sense of the word. It is not true that the horse is by nature vicious and therefore needing to be overwhelmed. It is not true that horses are incapable of willing cooperation. It is not true that horses must be forced to submit if work is expected.

These myths form the basis for one of the prevalent approaches towards the horse. That approach is based in fear and structured around distrust of the horse and results in an unstable relationship.

Another set of beliefs about horses are unfounded, artificial, sentimental and dangerous. In this vein it is not true that the horse is able to determine good from bad, that the horse is a natural champion and protector of women and children, that the horse is some sort of majestic quivering link with the occult world.

These myths are part of the slick magazine and television exploitive imagery that plays on the hungry vacuum of idle suburban adolescent minds. And these minds too often 'grow up' to join a pseudo-elitist majority of backyard horse owners. These people eventually quit with horses or join the ranks of the first group of "initiated" fearful abusers of the horse.

It is this author's belief that this attitude and approach towards the horse is collectively sustained because most people are with their animals part-time and need quick and easy solutions to the problem of 'using' their horse. Plus the fact that our history on this continent has been one of speedy exploitation made possible because of abundance. So often you hear, "Why, with so many good horses out there, should ya' mess with this outlaw animal? Shoot him!" There is seldom time or concern for what made the animal an outlaw.

CONFUSING RESPECT WITH FEAR

The prevalent attitude and resulting approach towards the horse is based on fear (no matter how well-disguised), even though "respect" is the claim. And that is the core of the problem. People are confusing respect with fear. This is a cultural condition. It is dangerous to respect a horse out of fear. Respect is best found to be a result of understanding which includes a measure of trust. And it is difficult to honestly respect a horse without at least a working desire for some understanding of the animal.

HORSE'S SENSES

In trying to understand the Psychology of the horse, we must look to some of the realities of his world. The horse's senses are different. Exactly to what extent this is true is difficult to say, but science, common sense, and observation will tell us that horses have radar-like acute hearing which serves them in the wild as part of an early warning system. Notice how the horse's ears are directional, aiming at the oncoming sound. They literally turn 180 degrees. Observing the horse's hesitancy or unwillingness to drink water away from home or eat new feed suggests a strong sense of taste and an ability to differentiate. The animal's response to gentle handling and petting suggests that there is something communicated through touch and that the animal is sensitive and undeserving, for response, of beating. The most acute sense of the horse is smell. It, coupled with hearing, works to warn the horse that something's wrong. It is important to understand how sensitive smell is in the horse and to what extent they respond to it. Here is a quote from an important English Horseman's book entitled *Horse in the Furrow*[1] with a story which illustrates the sense of smell in question.

'I heard tell that two carters once called at the Wherry Inn in Halesworth for the usual snack and drink and bait for the horses. They put up the horses in the stable and then went into the pub. After they'd had a couple of drinks one said to the other:

"Shall we have another?"

"No, I reckon we'd better see to the horses."

'But when they went to the stables they couldn't budge the horses from their stalls. They pulled and they cussed and they swore but the horses wouldn't move an inch. After they tried for a quarter of an hour or so, an old man who happened to be in the yard said to 'em: "What's the matter on 'em? Won't they come out? — I can fix that." He may have been the one who done it — mind you, I don't know. But he went inside the pub, and in a minute or two he came out with a jug of milk. He got this jug and put it above the lintel of the stable door and after a minute or two he say: "It's all right: you cin take 'em out now." And sure enough, they led the horses out of the door without any trouble at all.' No explanation was given: no explanation was asked for at this stage: for it had become obvious that the horse's acute sense of smell was involved here without question: because milk has the property of absorbing any obnoxious or strong smell arising anywhere near it.'

In this case a smell prevented the horses from moving. The smell was removed and the horses were willing. This story suggests how it is that in some cultures the manipulation of the understood and perceived mind of the horse served to create 'mystiques'. This exists to this day. More often, it is not a manipulation of horses by man so much as it is of people by people; these tricks commonly being used in the sale of horses.

As marvelous and acute as the first four senses are it is interesting to find how awkward the horse's sight is. The horse's eye is constructed and operates differently from most mammals. Rather than a smooth concave retina, the horse's retina is more concave in some places than others and some portions of the lens are nearer the cornea than others. What this means is that the horse can move its head around to focus in on something. They do have muscles enabling focusing action similar to ours but they are underdeveloped by comparison. So if you witness a horse moving its head around in a peculiar fashion it's probably

---

[1] *The Horse in the Furrow*, by George Ewart Evans. London, Faber & Faber, 1967, 1975

looking for the right combination of lens and light passage to focus on a subject. Because of this strange setup, most horses will shy or bolt away from unexpected unknown sights often as there was not time to focus in on the subject and the perception was confused, perhaps even magnified. That is why a small puddle of water or a wind tossed piece of paper can cause such alarm. Add to this the facts that horses are color blind and have semi-lateral vision (eyes to the side of the head) and you compound the situation. The semi-lateral vision suggests that often frontal views produce double vision. Imagine if the case were the same for you and you came upon not one, but two enormous black holes, slightly fuzzy ones at that, that you were asked to walk into!

Fig. 6) There is a special, unseen, unheard, potential level of communication between horse and man which awaits those who are open to it. Photo by Nancy Roberts

And then there is the sixth sense. There is all sorts of sophisticated technical evidence from equine research pointing to horses having extra-sensory perception. It is not something we can understand yet but it is something to be mindful of. The author's years of working horses have convinced him that there are many times when horses have read his mind. There is a level of communication possible that is limited only by the human propensity for doubt and suspicion.

Now all this is admittedly a very short over-simplified introduction into the horse's sensory world, but it's only meant to suggest that if we could but understand why the horse reacts a certain way perhaps we can earn trust and gain respect.

Maybe a feeling for the limitations of actualities of the horse's sensory world will begin to suggest how it is that the animal looks or thinks about his world and work.

The horse stores experience in the memory bank probably with complex sensory images rather than visual imagery. In other words, a smell might trigger a memory whereas the sight of something might not. And quite simply, if a horse receives signals, be they smell, sound or whatever, that trigger memories of similar safe and even pleasant experiences, he will actually enjoy falling into the routine asked of him. In reverse, if the experience sends signals that remind them of danger, they will naturally want to avoid or escape from the experience. And when a situation is totally new it will often cause uncertainty and suspicion in the horse because there is no memory to fall back on for aid in response. All of this is not too different from how we react to basic physical experiences.

THE APPROACH

Your own perception of the horse's condition and capacity should be your guide in how to work with the animal. But if you feel that force is necessary and that you must scare your animal into obeying you — you've got trouble. Or if, on the other side, you are overly protective of your animal you will not get much done. For example, if a horse is obviously afraid of something, there are three possible courses of action: 1) Take the horse away from that which frightens him; 2) Use force or a greater fear to make the horse confront the object; 3) Allow the horse time to "figure out" the object of his fear with you providing security. If the horse can safely view, smell and otherwise experience the object of fear with your reassurances time will work to either erase or adjust the problem. Obviously the author favors the third approach. The first approach is, perhaps surprisingly, the worst, as it tends to reinforce in the horse's mind that this object of fear is indeed something to avoid. The second approach will, if repeated, break down any bonds of trust between you and the horse and result in an unstable and unreliable relationship.

Horses enjoy repetition and the security that comes of safe habit. In many farming practices horses get noticeably angry when asked to break from a familiar routine and turn the opposite direction at the end of the field. This is an example of those kinds of moments when the teamster's will is softly tested and the horse tries to discover how much control over the developing relationship he can have. This sort of thing coupled with apparent judgments made by horses in working processes indicate that horses are intelligent, thinking mammals.

Horses enjoy company of not only other horses but also people they feel they can trust. Horses demonstrate subtle responses to praise and obvious care and they seem to reward it. There are many cases of horses demonstrating, dramatically, their sorrow at the loss of a companion, be they animal or human. In other words, horses are feeling mammals, capable of the best of what we know to be love.

The best results in working with horses will come from continued efforts to understand the horse's condition and nature of his communication. Always think about the best ways, the most natural ways, to convince the animal that cooperation is good, even special. Work to find subtle, natural ways to convince the animal that being unwilling to cooperate is bad or generally tedious (not painful or ugly). Find ways to get in the horse's way when it doesn't want to cooperate and find ways to help when he wants to cooperate.

Work to develop the horse as your teammate. Think about the horse as your equivalent and see and feel his limitations as your own. The rewards will be fabulous.

CHAPTER THREE

THE DYNAMICS OF DRAFT AND THE MECHANICS OF THE DRAFT HORSE

Fig. 7A) As the horse pushes against the collar, the action is converted to a pull on the traces.

Glen French with his logging team at a pulling match. Photo by Matilda Essig

The title of this chapter might suggest that it is a discussion of harness design. Outside of passing references to how harness is employed in pulling weight, this is primarily a discussion of the shape and structure of the horse relative to the work he is expected to perform.

The moving parts of a horse are a mass of 'links'; bones, joints, muscles, tendons and ligaments working together to accomplish even the simplest of movements. If we are to depend on a horse in harness to perform certain work on a regular basis it becomes simply essential that his total system be in proper working order. First of all, the animal must be put together properly, with no hereditary or injury-related deficiencies which might prove detrimental to getting the work done. In other words, the horse has got to be put together right or else he is going to have trouble doing the work. Second (and to be discussed in depth later), is the impact of diet and general care on the ability of the horse to work. A fat horse or a starved one will have difficulty performing work.

In the working portion of the horse, potential strength can often be measured in direct relationship to the weakest part of the individual system.

Fig. 7) above — The optimum angle of draft from X to the collar as the horse converts pushing into pulling. Notice that the horse moves forward, up and down, with each step.

Fig. 8) below— An exaggeration of an incorrect angle of draft as the tug angle pulls the collar into th the windpipe of the horse. (The belly band assembly would normally prevent this action.)

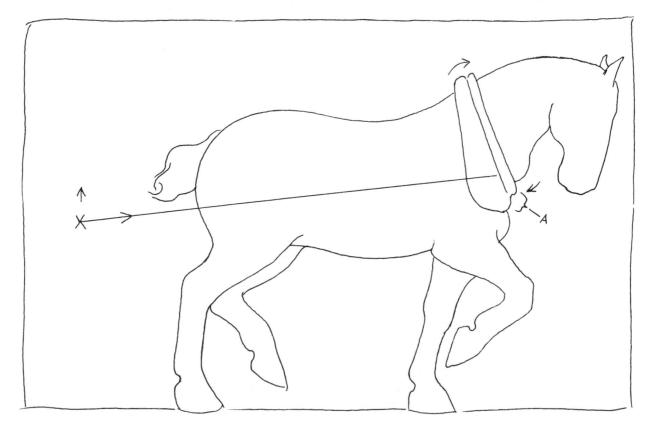

As illustrated (Fig. 7) through the structure of the harness, the horse is able to actually translate a pushing action into a pulling action. Whether it be with a collar or a breast strap harness, the horse's shoulders (or chest) push against an assembly which transfers this into a pulling action with the tugs or traces. Although best communicated through the illustration, perhaps a little additional explanation is in order. Let's limit this to a collar-design harness. The collar, properly fitted around a horse's neck (see HARNESSING chapter), is seated against the shoulder of the horse. Tightly fitted around the collar are steel or wooden 'hames', which function as a kind of bone structure for the otherwise pliable harness. At a point low on each hame, which corresponds with the wide portion of the collar and the point of the horse's shoulder, a tug or trace is secured. The 'tug' (see illustration, Fig. 7) runs back from the 'hame' alongside the horse and is fastened eventually (directly or indirectly) to the load to be pulled.

As the horse moves forward, he pushes, at the point of his shoulder, against the collar. Through the secured 'hame' assembly and the fastened 'tugs', that pushing is converted to a pulling action.

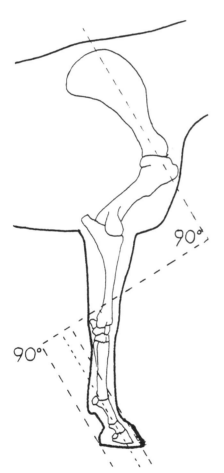

Fig. 9) The natural angle of the shoulder and pastern should be the same. (see ANATOMY chapter)

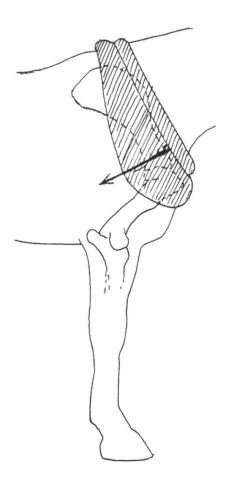

Fig. 10) This is how the collar relates to the skeletal structure of the horse.

If there were no other parts to a harness than the collar, hames, and tugs, and if the load pulled (or the point at which the tugs were fastened) was straight across (or level) this would cause the collar to rock forward (Fig. 8) and press, at the bottom, against the horse's windpipe. Even if this were not the case, as the load or 'point of draft' raises higher the pull becomes less natural and more difficult for the horse. The natural slope of the shoulder and the bone structure of the horse's shoulder and front legs (Fig. 9) lends themselves to a 90 degree (or slightly less) angle of tug to hame (or point of draft — to point of shoulder — to shoulder angle). So there is a natural or optimum angle of draft directly related to the slope of a horse's shoulder, the horse's height and the weight to be pulled. What that suggests is that it is possible for one healthy strong horse to be better shaped to perform work in harness than another equally healthy strong horse. Therefore, it is important to consider the size and shape of any horse expected to work in harness.

All other things being equal, draft or pulling power is in direct proportion to weight, while endurance during work requires the addition of substance (or the size and tone of muscles and bone). Advocates of the Belgian, Percheron and Suffolk breeds are more apt to defend bulk and substance in relatively shorter packages as optimum conformation criteria for work horses, whereas Shire and Clydesdale breeders of the British Isles set their standards by another means, using height and bone as their measurement of draft value. As to which is right it is difficult to say, as both arguments have their advantages and disadvantages. I like to think both are justified and certainly the examples bear me out. The short, compact, thickset Suffolk horses have a well-earned reputation as superior farm work animals. But then, the tall, long, heavy-boned Clydesdale has performed his field work admirably for hundreds of years. So I say that after the dust is settled certain questions of conformation related to work efficiency are actually best said to be related to personal preference.

Two laws of physics suggest that a body in motion tends to remain in motion and that the energy of a moving body is the product of its mass by its velocity. With this the case, the heavy draft horse should have an advantage not only in the ease with which he draws a load when traveling at a rate of speed equal to a lighter rival but also in the ease with which he keeps it going. Gravity overcomes the movement of heavy bodies less rapidly than that of lighter bodies. But don't mistake all of this to suggest that fat is the key to greater efficiency. Fat is soon lost at hard work and is only an incidental assist to pulling. Height and bone as well as muscle tone are the concerns which will guarantee a powerful frame. Of course, there must also be concern for the animals' fuel capacity and conversion efficiency. Just as an internal combustion engine needs to have fuel fed regularly and ignited efficiently so with a working horse. The animals must have the capacity for converting food efficiently into net energy. The ideal animal combines adequate height, strong ample bone, correct muscle tone, capacity for feed, and the best metabolism possible to aid in feed conversion into net energy.

In an adult horse little or nothing can be done to affect height and bone. Care and feeding, as well as controlled exercise, can show dramatic changes in muscle, metabolism and energy conversion. In foals, concern about diet and exercise can have effects on the ability of individual animals in reaching their full inherited potential with regard to bone and height.

The thicker and denser the muscling in a draft horse the better suited that individual will be for heavy work in harness. The longer and thinner the muscling in any individual horse, the greater the potential speed in the animal. A muscle is made up of many cells which join end to end to form a muscle fiber. Muscle fibers are each independent units of strength yet they run parallel to each other and as a mass form a muscle. A muscle's strength is measured proportionately by the size of its cross section or in direct proportion to the number of fibers that are included. Speed, however, is related to contraction rather than size. A muscle cell can contract up to one-fourth of its entire length. After the nerve stimuli have reached the cells (something which occurs almost simultaneously) contraction takes place in about the same length of time, whether the muscle is long or short. A 28 inch muscle will contract its 7 inches in about the same time that a 16 inch muscle will contract its 4 inches. Since the muscular power is applied to the joints at the same place in a draft or large horse as it is in a saddle or light horse, the one with 7 inch muscle contraction cannot help but generate more speed. What we're saying is that long muscles generate greater speed than do compact thickset muscles. Length has no relation to strength except in that the greater number of linearly attached cells offers more opportunity for the presence of a weak cell, thus contributing to overall weakness of the muscle fiber. Compact thickset muscles have greater inherent strength than do long muscles. Race horses will always be long and rangy in type while the best draft horses will exhibit thickness of muscle and stockiness of build.

Fig. 11) Thicker, denser muscling is better suited for heavy work in harness.   Photo by Lynn Miller

Fig. 12) This pulling photo illustrates how the lever principle works: notice that the front legs are used for balance while the back legs are the propulsion.

Author's Belgian geldings
Photo by Matilda Essig

Fig. 13) Each teamster will come to his or her own decision about the best size and conformation for work.

Author's Belgian mares hitched to mower.
Photo by Nancy Roberts

The skeleton of the horse serves two purposes. One is that it functions as the framework for the body. The other is to provide a mechanical advantage to the horse in motion. This second purpose must be properly understood if you are to be able to identify bone structures which are best suited for work in harness. The bony skeleton of the horse provides various combinations of levers which account for the animal's flexible mobility and strength. A lever has three working points: the point where power is applied, the point where weight is applied, and the point over which the lever works as a fulcrum or base. There are three classes of levers. The first has power and weight at the ends and the fulcrum in the middle like a seesaw. In the horse this is illustrated when kicking; the foot and lower limb being weight, the power being in the hips and the hock functioning as fulcrum. The second class of lever is when the fulcrum (or base) is at one end, power at the other end and weight in the middle as with a wheelbarrow. When a horse moves forward you can see this principle demonstrated as the front foot is the fulcrum (or base) the weight comes over and on the joints and the power is in the thighs. This lever is dramatically shown when horses are pulling hard. The strain is in the hocks and the power is in the thighs. The third lever class is where the power is in the middle and the base and weight are at opposite ends, as in a pair of pliers.

The first two lever principles give advantage through increased power. The third lever gives speed at the cost of power. The third class of lever is demonstrated in the horse at the jaw where the weight is at the chewing teeth, the fulcrum at the jaw joint and the power the jaw muscles. Another example would be the limb swinging forward in walking.

The efficiency of the lever depends upon the relative length of the power arm and weight arm. As in a seesaw the longer the power arm the easier it becomes to raise the weight end. So it is necessary to have a longer power arm to gain mechanical advantage. This principle is of great importance to the question of long legged drafters vs. shortset drafters. The weight of the load is a direct force pulling back on, or restraining, the horse. As stated above, the longer the power arm the greater the advantage, hence the theory is that the longer the limb of the horse (which functions as weight arms) the greater the advantage the load will have over the animal. The teamster then requires that his draft horse be lowset in order to gain in pulling efficiency.

Yet there is a second moderating consideration. A horse whose legs are too short may be a disadvantage for in addition to mechanical power the teamster will require a certain speed. A smooth, brisk walk is impossible for a horse after the load drawn has gone beyond a certain point. When that point comes the pace is a drudging walk at best. This point, at which horses are pulled down to a slow pace, comes at the same time to horses of varying height but equal weight. The horse with the longer swing to his stride will make more rapid progress under identical circumstances than the other fellow. Balancing both principles and affecting the lever by adjusting point of draft (see HITCHING diagrams), each individual conscientious teamster will come to their own happy medium at which the height and substance of the draft horse will be most efficient for both propulsion and progression.

The simple length of the limb is not concern enough if you are after maximum efficiency. The lower portion of the leg functions much like a stilt with muscles being above the hocks or knees. Therefore, the shorter the cannons (see ANATOMY diagram) in relation to the upper leg the greater the mechanical advantage and, as a bonus, the greater the stability and surefootedness.

Another, less understood, aspect of the mechanics of a work horse is what we call "nerve power". It is that ingredient which allows a certain extra staying power or ability to overcome stresses. It is the reserve energy that is somehow called upon to take a heavy load up a steep bank or pull a bogged down wagon out of the mud. It is a quality which some refer to as "heart", others as "honesty", and still others as "strength". No motor has this quality. Whatever it is called it is the quality which has made the horse so easy to love. It is a wide open question whether or not all horses begin life with the same inherent potential for a willingness to give nerve power in harness. The argument narrows some when we discuss the effect man's treatment of the horse can have on the animal's "will". I believe that the "nerve" power of a horse is only dependable if the teamster has earned the horse's respect and the horse is secure and willing.

The shape, structure and overall condition of the horse has a direct relationship to the ability and willingness with which the animal meets the tasks of pulling a regular load in harness with room for the variations of different human preferences. There is a margin within which the ideal workhorse conformation, constitution and temperament resides. The good teamster will be able to recognize these ideal qualities and select good horses for work. The better teamster will go one better and be able to use harness fit, hitching and even the subtleties of driving to perfect what they easily recognize as an imperfect animal that nevertheless has some qualities so exceptional as warrant saving. How many seemingly flawless horses have lived long enough to prove they were worthless for anything but the show ring? And how many ugly duckling horses, recognized by able teamsters as special, have lived long and fruitful lives as partners in work?

Fig. 14) "Heart" is that quality which has made the horse so easy to love.   *Photo by Lynn Miller*

CHAPTER FOUR

HORSES, ANATOMY AND THE FUNDAMENTALS OF CARE

Joe Van Dyke's four abreast show hitch of Belgians.
Photo by Matilda Essig.

Climate and diet, varying from country to country, and the uses to which horses were put, have, over the centuries, produced variety in shape, size, color and speed. The earliest civilizations of Europe and Asia began selecting certain superior animals and breeding them with hopes of improving horses for the work in mind. Gradually regions developed families of equine which exhibited consistent characteristics of shape, color, even performance. So in this began the different breeds of horses.

The two predominant forces in the development of breeds of horses were environment and man's expectations. Environment's effect can be seen when we look at the Arabian horse and think of hot, dry, barren expanses of North Africa where the breed was born. Look, in comparison, to the Fjord horse of Scandinavia or the Clydesdale horse of Scotland. Hot and barren, cold with short growing season, or temperate and lush; all have their marked influence on the indigenous breeds of livestock. Add to this the different expectations of man, the domesticator of the horse. In North Africa, the nomadic Moslem tribes expected the horse for transportation of rider/soldier with speed, heat tolerance, and easy keeping qualities. So they selected the best animals to suit their needs. In Scotland and all of the British Isles long ago the great horse had been selected, because of its size and bulk, to carry the knights in armor to battle. After the Crusades of the Middle Ages the farmers of the British Isles continued to breed the great horse for height, bone and substance but for different purposes. These horsemen expected horses to pull plows and haul heavy loads.

Thus there were developed in different regions horses of different breeds. Some desired horses for heavy work, animals of heavy body, stout limbs, and strong muslces. Others desired horses for speed, animals of lighter frame, smaller bone, and sound lungs.

Several classes of equines have resulted and, depending on personal outlook, lines may be drawn and redrawn. This author draws them this way:

Heavy horses   Light horses
Draft ponies   Light ponies
Draft mules   Light mules   Mini mules

I'll mention several breeds of the two major classes, but this represents only a small portion of the many breeds found around the world.

Heavy horses
    Clydesdale from the Valley of Clyde in Scotland
    Percheron of North France
    Suffolk of Suffolk County, England
    Shire of the east-central Shires of England
    Ardennes of Belgium
    Brabant of Belgium
    Belgian (American) originally from Belgium

Light horses
    Cleveland Bay of England
    Standardbred of America
    Morgan of America
    Arabian
    Thoroughbred of England
    Gelderlander — Germany
    Holsteiner — Germany
    Paso Fino
    Appaloosa of America
    Quarterhorse of America
    Hackney of England

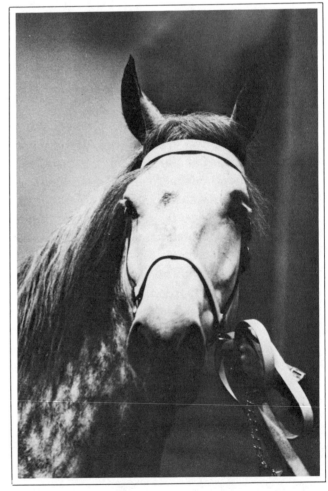

Fig. 16) Draft mule.

Fig. 17) Percheron gelding.   Photo by Nancy Roberts

Fig. 18 An exceptional Clydesdale mare

Fig. 19 A Clydesdale gelding performing in cart class.

CLYDESDALES — This is perhaps the best-known draft horse breed in North America due to heavy beer company advertising. Even so, it is not anywhere near as popular, in terms of numbers, as other breeds. Perhaps this is because this breed is under-rated as a workhorse with many people complaining that height and bone are wrong for heavy work. Such is not the case, and this breed will play a larger part in the near future.

PERCHERONS — In numbers, this is the second most popular draft horse breed with a solid history of contribution to farm and logging work. Certain criteria, used by some breeders who are looking for exaggerated action and artificial characteristics, may lead this stable old breed into genetic trouble in the near future. There simply aren't enough horses of the draft breeds to monkey around with the limited genetic pool and not pay the price.

Photos by Nancy Roberts

Fig. 20 A black Percheron stallion.

Fig. 21 An exceptional sorrel Percheron stud colt.

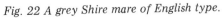

Fig. 22 A grey Shire mare of English type.   *Fig. 23 A black Shire stallion of English type.*

Fig. 24 A team of American-type Shire geldings

SHIRES — *This breed is scarce, with less than 500 registered purebred and percentage animals in 1980. There has been considerable recent importation from England and some constructive hope for increases in the breed in years to come. The genetic pool is small, so there is concern about the strength of the breed in generations to come, but the concern being there is good indication that the future is secure.*

SUFFOLKS — *This breed has fewer numbers than even the Shire and is the least known. As the interest in good, honest hard-working farm and woods horses increases this author belives that the SUFFOLK will gain in popularity. This breed has been selected over generations for work on the farm and has many favored characteristics.*

Fig. 25 A team of Suffolk horses.

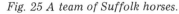

Fig. 26 Mitchell's Contributor Joe, an American Belgian stallion   *Photo by Lynn Miller*

BELGIANS — Of the five major breeds of draft horses the Belgians are the most numerous. The Belgian that has been developed over the years in North America has become unique enough genetically to be considered by some to be a breed of its own, separate from the origins. Certainly, to look today at the American Belgian and Belgian Belgian, is to see a world of difference. There has been some recent importation of the European Belgians. With the introduction of this new/old blood is sure to come some interesting changes. Care must be taken, however, if breed type is to be preserved or else a kind of mongrelization might occur. The genetic characteristics of the Belgian Belgians (of the Brabancan and Ardennes strains) are distinct enough to warrant consideration as a separate breed.

Fig. 27 Belgian horses from Belgium Photo by Matilda Essig

Fig. 28 A draft mule, the sterile hybrid result of cross-breeding a draft horse mare to a mammoth jack.

Fig. 29 Light mules, the result of breeding saddle mares to mammoth jacks, are slightly finer boned and muscled than their draft cousins, but nonetheless are capable of a great deal of work. Photo by Lynn Miller

Fig. 30 Grade draft horses, the result of either cross-breeding draft breeds or saddle and draft breeds, represent the backbone of horse power in the future. As the movement to using horses in harness grows, the demand for good using animals will increase. There is a good future for the horse farmer that raises and trains good grade work horses for sale.
Photo by Nancy Roberts

Fig. 31) Light, or saddle, horses of the many breeds will perform well in harness and are actually preferred by some people.

Photo by Lynn Miller

Fig. 32) A team of Morgan horses at the Upper Canada Village in Ontario. The Morgan horse was originally developed as an all-purpose animal with the conformation for work in harness. The breed has split into two genetic families, one representing the 'old-type' and the other more "modern" show-type. The Morgan is regaining popularity as a family farm all-purpose horse.

Photo by Lynn Miller

Fig. 33) Allan Conder drives ponies on the grain drill. The oft-maligned pony breeds are undeservedly considered to be too small for work. In actuality, ponies are capable of much work and will find a good home on many farms.

ANATOMY

The illustrations best show the position of the various parts of the horse anatomy. (Some discussion of form and function was gone through in Chapter One.) The most important parts of the horse in order of priority (mine) include:

1. Feet (up to and including fetlock joint)
2. Hocks
3. Knees
4. Legs (Note: if these first four are not in order, there is no need to look further. Look at each new horse from the ground up.)
5. Eyes
6. Teeth
7. Shoulder
8. And so forth (from here on all else is equal)

There are volumes written about the anatomy of the horse and this text is not the place to go into the subject in any depth. There are some important things to mention, however.

THE BOTTOM

When a horseman refers to the "Bottom" he is usually speaking of the anatomy of a horse from the knees and hocks down. Whatever the intended use, if it does not have a good sound "bottom" (or feet and legs), a horse is of no value. The drawings in this text illustrate the individual parts of the bottom. If the reader has a particular concern, interest or problem regarding something very specific to this or any part of the horse's anatomy, the author recommends that you seek out specialized sources of information.

The bottom starts with the feet, the first place you should look at any new horse. A close examination of any horse's foot discloses a unique structure and one which has suffered a wide variety of man's theories through the ages. For a horse's hoof to be sound it should demonstrate a strong, yet slightly pliable hoof wall without excessive long vertical cracks. The animal should stand naturally with a hoof wall angle which matches the pastern angle, which in turn should match the shoulder's angle (see Fig. 9). The coronary band should be clean and smooth without obvious wounds or when examined by touch without calcium-like growth under the skin just above the coronary band. Examination of the underside of the foot should find a healthy frog and heel with no sign of black infection alongside the frog in the quarters (thrush). Scraping of the sole should not discover any obvious stone bruises (blood marks). On the whole, the foot should present a balanced look, see Fig. 38.

From the coronary band to the fetlock runs the pastern. This assembly from fetlock through pastern to the foot is the most critical section of the entire horse. Without free and correct motion of these parts a horse cannot be expected to do any work whatsoever. It would not then matter how beautiful the topside of the animal was.

From the fetlock joint up to the knee runs the cannon bone. The proportion of the cannon bone has a direct relationship to the efficiency of the work horse. (See chapter MECHANICS OF DRAFT.) The knees of the front legs serve to balance the animal while the hock joints of the back legs must work under greater strain as the legs move the mass in a digging-like motion. The hock joint is of critical importance to the ability of the horse to pull heavy loads. A good, clean, strong hock joint which exhibits straight-ahead motion is desired. The hock joints should not be set too close together nor too far apart but rather in a symmetrical balance. Fig. 13 illustrates the relationship and proportion of some of the bone structure of the "bottom".

THE TOP

There is a great deal of disagreement in the horse world about what constitutes the ideal "top" for horses of given breeds or types. Long backs vs. short backs; long necks vs. short necks; these are some of the sorts of arguments you might hear. First of all, there is lots of opportunity for optical illusion in the horse's form, which is to say that a long-legged horse might give the illusion of being longer in the back or a long-backed horse might give the illusion of being longer-legged. It takes a skilled eye to see the true form of the horse for what it actually is. And for the person interested in form as it relates to capacity for work, the author's opinion is that personal experience coupled with some sprinkling of personal aesthetic preference is the best guide to making that determination. The next chapter gives some specific information explaining this form and function question regarding the work horse.

The work horse should exhibit ample heart girth which suggests good lung capacity. The horse that is expected to work in collar and harness must have a correct and healthy shoulder both from the inside and outside. Fig.10 illustrates the relationship of the bone structure to how the collar sits and suggests how important it is that there be no abnormalities in bone, muscle or skin.

The horse's head will tell a great deal about the animal and should be regarded carefully when purchasing a new horse. Ears and eyes tell you of the animal's more obvious personality traits such as gentleness, meanness, docility, or nervousness. Look for a calm, quiet, yet alert eye and ears which are comfortably at attention. Teeth can, to the experienced or initiated, determine the age of the horse as there are distinct changes which occur each year. The nose is an early warner of respiratory infection which can be chronic or serious in horses and is most often highly contagious. The general balance or conformation of the head can be an indicator of capacities or character. The most commonly considered relationships are the placement of the eyes, whether too close, too high, too low, etc. Generally look for what appears, to the intelligent eye, to be a balanced head.

As explained in the *Feeding* chapter, the horse has a unique and highly sensitive digestive system. The discussion in the chapter on DISEASES AND DISORDERS touches on the subject of the various causes of disorders of the digestive system.

ANATOMY

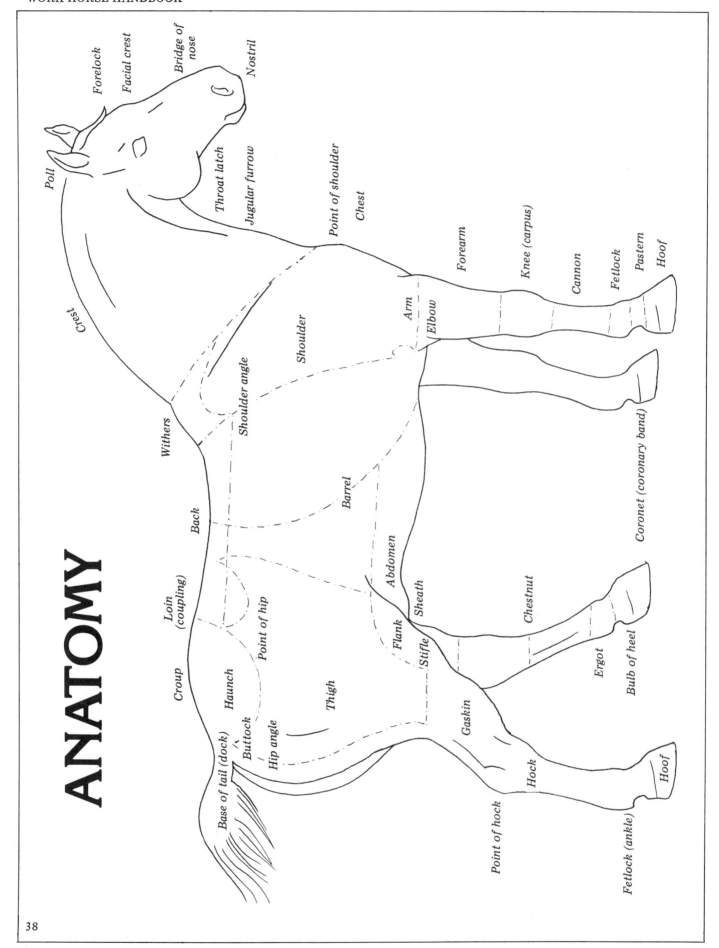

Poll
Forelock
Facial crest
Bridge of nose
Nostril
Throat latch
Jugular furrow
Point of shoulder
Chest
Forearm
Knee (carpus)
Cannon
Fetlock
Pastern
Hoof
Crest
Arm
Elbow
Shoulder
Shoulder angle
Withers
Barrel
Coronet (coronary band)
Back
Abdomen
Loin (coupling)
Point of hip
Sheath
Chestnut
Croup
Haunch
Flank
Stifle
Ergot
Bulb of heel
Buttock
Hip angle
Thigh
Gaskin
Hoof
Base of tail (dock)
Hock
Point of hock
Fetlock (ankle)

HORSE'S SKELETON

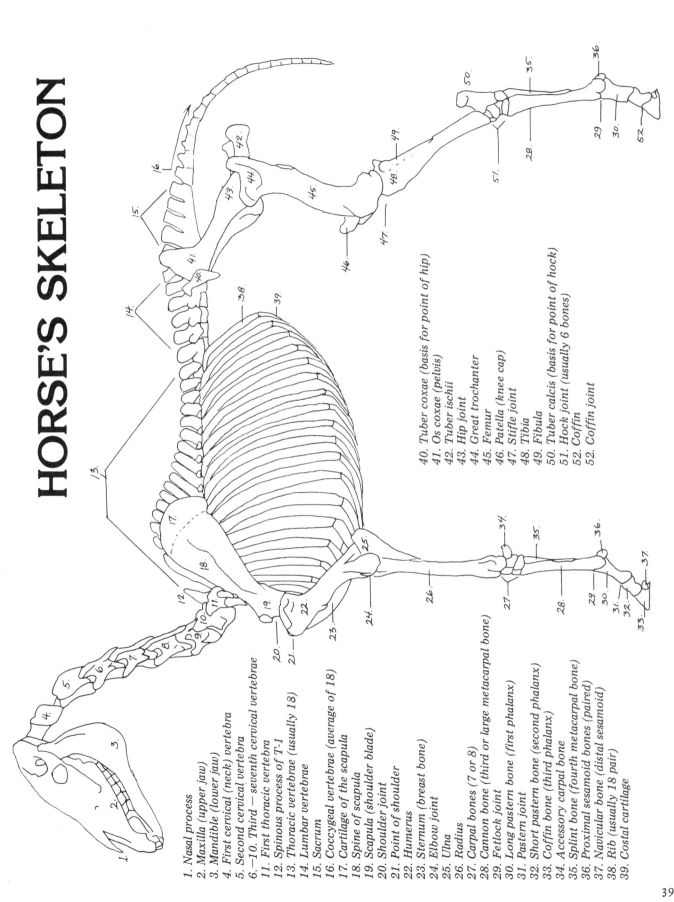

1. Nasal process
2. Maxilla (upper jaw)
3. Mandible (lower jaw)
4. First cervical (neck) vertebra
5. Second cervical vertebra
6.—10. Third — seventh cervical vertebrae
11. First thoracic vertebra
12. Spinous process of T-1
13. Thoracic vertebrae (usually 18)
14. Lumbar vertebrae
15. Sacrum
16. Coccygeal vertebrae (average of 18)
17. Cartilage of the scapula
18. Spine of scapula
19. Scapula (shoulder blade)
20. Shoulder joint
21. Point of shoulder
22. Humerus
23. Sternum (breast bone)
24. Elbow joint
25. Ulna
26. Radius
27. Carpal bones (7 or 8)
28. Cannon bone (third or large metacarpal bone)
29. Fetlock joint
30. Long pastern bone (first phalanx)
31. Pastern joint
32. Short pastern bone (second phalanx)
33. Coffin bone (third phalanx)
34. Accessory carpal bone
35. Splint bone (fourth metacarpal bone)
36. Proximal sesamoid bones (paired)
37. Navicular bone (distal sesamoid)
38. Rib (usually 18 pair)
39. Costal cartilage
40. Tuber coxae (basis for point of hip)
41. Os coxae (pelvis)
42. Tuber ischii
43. Hip joint
44. Great trochanter
45. Femur
46. Patella (knee cap)
47. Stifle joint
48. Tibia
49. Fibula
50. Tuber calcis (basis for point of hock)
51. Hock joint (usually 6 bones)
52. Coffin
52. Coffin joint

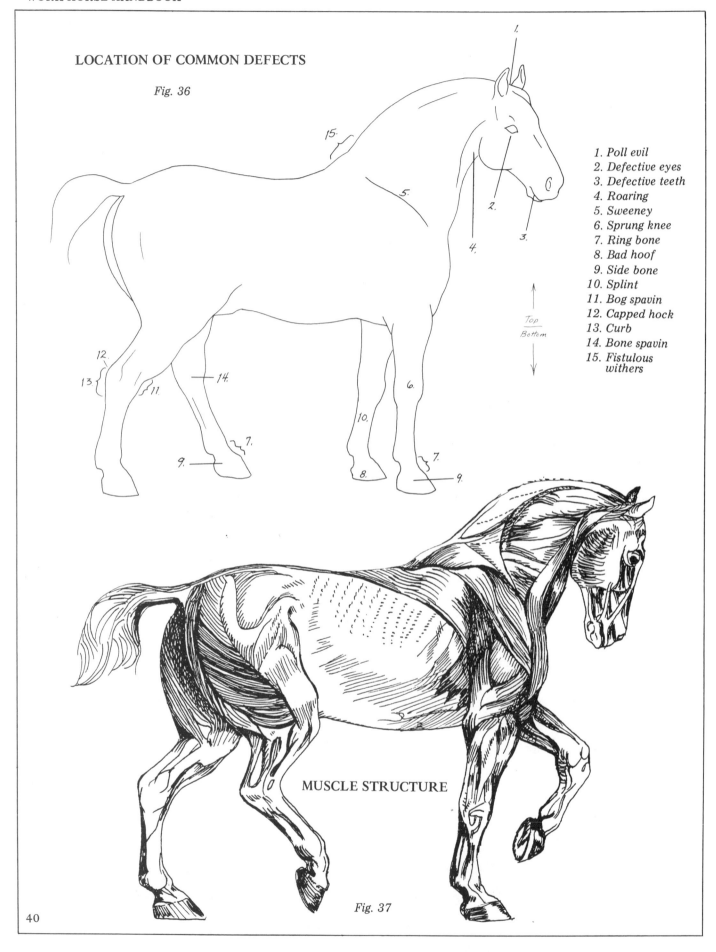

LOCATION OF COMMON DEFECTS

Fig. 36

1. *Poll evil*
2. *Defective eyes*
3. *Defective teeth*
4. *Roaring*
5. *Sweeney*
6. *Sprung knee*
7. *Ring bone*
8. *Bad hoof*
9. *Side bone*
10. *Splint*
11. *Bog spavin*
12. *Capped hock*
13. *Curb*
14. *Bone spavin*
15. *Fistulous withers*

Top
Bottom

MUSCLE STRUCTURE

Fig. 37

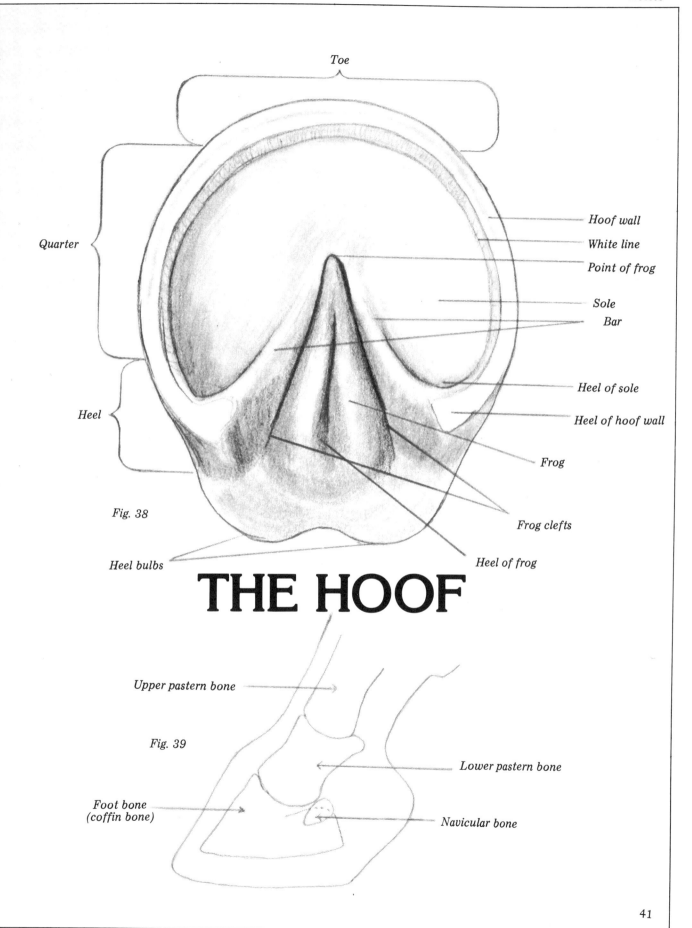

Toe

Hoof wall

White line

Point of frog

Quarter

Sole

Bar

Heel of sole

Heel of hoof wall

Heel

Frog

Fig. 38

Frog clefts

Heel bulbs

Heel of frog

THE HOOF

Upper pastern bone

Fig. 39

Lower pastern bone

Foot bone
(coffin bone)

Navicular bone

ANGLE OF THE PASTERN

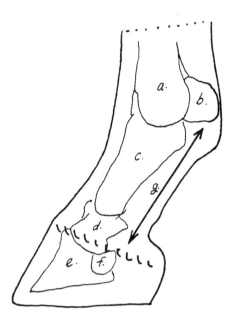

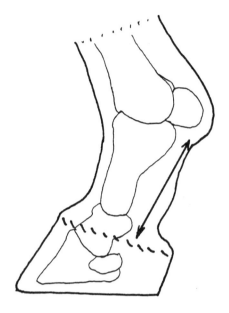

a) Illustrating the correct angle of the pastern and slope of the hoof wall. The line from b. to f. (marked g) corresponds to the position of the navicular tendon which must expand and contract with movement.

b) Showing the horse at the first stage of forward motion with an extended, or stretched, navicular tendon.

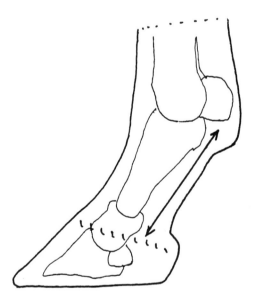

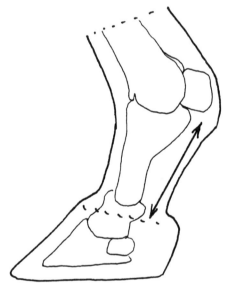

c) Illustrating an incorrect angle caused by too long a toe and too short a heel. This angle causes a flexing of the tendon.

d) Showing the incorrect foot at the first stage of forward motion with added tension on the navicular tendon. This causes pain, resulting in quick 'snappy' action and eventual navicular lameness.

Fig. 40

FUNDAMENTALS OF CARE

UNSOUNDNESS

All of the funny stories you hear relative to horse-trading have one serious implication in common; it is that the selection of a sound and desirable horse is often difficult. The best way to determine soundness is with a careful systematic examination of the horse.

Lameness is not always readily apparent so it is important to have the animal walk and run while you observe. This should be done more than once, having someone turn the animal to the right and left while trotting.

Figure 36 should be used to aid in a careful examination for these possible problems:

Poll-evil. Found at the top of the head, or the poll, and caused from a bruise, indicated from inflammation or a scar. Expect that it will recur and cause problems especially with halters and bridle wear.

Fistula. Found at the withers and caused by a bruise, similar in some repects to poll-evil, but should not be confused with collar sores; indicated by inflammation or scars.

Ring-bone. Bony enlargement found at the front and sides of the pastern, which causes lameness when developed to sufficient size to interfere with the action of the joints and tendons.

Side-bone. Side-bones can best be seen from the front and occur on the sides of the coronary band (top of the hoof); on the forefeet they interfere with action and may cause lameness. When not able to detect them by sight they may be found by slight pressure with the fingers. If the coronary band yields to pressure it is healthy; hardness is an indication of unsoundness.

Splints. Bony prominences found on the inside of the cannon, just below the knee, may cause lameness when first developing, or when close enough to the knee to interfere with movement. They often disappear in young horses.

Bog Spavin. An enlargement of the natural depression on the inner and front part of the hock, which is soft to the touch.

Bone Spavin. Bony enlargement on the inside of the hock where the thick part tapers into the cannon. Pick up the foot, hold flexed, release and start the horse to trot. Lameness indicates bone spavin.

A *blemish* is a defect which detracts from the appearance but not the usefulness of the horse.

DISEASES AND DISORDERS

This does not pretend to be a veterinary text and should not be depended upon as a final aid in diagnosis or treatment. The teamster should look elsewhere for help with diseases and disorders of the horse. The information presented here is done so to hopefully aid the teamster in understanding the reasons for good care of the horse.

The horse is the healthiest of all farm animals when properly managed. Troubles begin when horses are closely confined, overworked, improperly fed or watered, or under-exercised. Under these conditions, the horse is subject to numerous ailments. The ailment may be a discomfort which readily responds to correction of the cause. It may be a disease of nonspecific type, such as colic (acute indigestion), which is caused by a sudden change in ration, feeding frozen or moldy feed and/or other physical intrusions on the digestive system. Or, due to lowered resistance resulting from improper management, the horse may have a specific infectious disease which may be transmitted to the other work stock on the farm if not properly managed.

Recognizing Abnormal Conditions. The importance of recognizing any abnormal condition in the early stages cannot be over-emphasized. Anyone who cares for the stock regularly can recognize the first symptoms of discomfort or disease by the change in the general appearance, behavior, and bearing of an animal. A close checkup should be made at once in regard to the feed the animal has had, the conditions under which it has been kept and whether the animal has been standing idle or possibly is overworked.

Every factor in the immediate history of the case should be considered in order to give the horse proper care. The attendant should put the horse in a box stall where it can be made as comfortable as possible. Notice should be taken regarding respiration, appearance of the coat and skin, presence of fever, and rate of pulse. All secretions and excretions, as well as further behavior, and evidence of pain, swelling, tenderness, and loss of function should be noted.

In many cases good care and correction of the feeding practices are all that are necessary. In other cases a simple laxative, such as a quart of mineral oil, is all that is needed. In still others, rest may be the cure. The first thought, however, should be to look for the cause of the ailment and remove it.

Caring For the Sick Horse. Regardless of the ailment, the care the horse receives will greatly affect the progress of its recovery. Sick horses are usually nervous and should be kept as quiet as possible. They should always be handled with the greatest patience. The stalls should be comfortable, free from drafts, and the bedding kept fresh and clean. The feed should be laxative and easily digested. A little fresh grass or apples may be given if the horse's appetite is poor. Grooming with a soft brush or cloth, and frequent rubbing of the legs, will aid the circulation and help to throw off the body waste. Access to a quiet paddock for free exercise is beneficial but the ill horse should not have to compete with any other animals.

If there is any chance that a disease may be infectious, the animal should be kept isolated from all other susceptible individuals. The well animals may be protected by keeping the sick one in a box stall or paddock that does not connect with any other stalls. The sick horse or mule should be fed and watered from individual buckets. These utensils should be thoroughly sterilized before being used by well animals again.

If there is any evidence that the animal is seriously ill or badly injured, waste no time in securing the advice and services of a licensed veterinarian. Stay away from self-styled horse doctors but in the same vein, do yourself and your animal the service of checking up on the reputation and skill of any vet you might choose. A diploma and a license do not, unfortunately, guarantee that the vet holding them is competent and honest.

Digestive disorders. Digestive ailments, most falling under the catch-all name of "colic" are the most common ailments of work horses and mules. These ailments may occur either in mild or acute form and are caused by indigestible feed, spoiled feed, improper feeding methods, improper watering, or by any other factor that might disturb the digestive system.

During colic attacks the animal refuses to eat his feed, lies down, gets up, paws the ground and shows evidence of distress. The horse will probably make circling motions apparently pointing with its head to the gut. In colic, the pain may be sudden and intermittent, the animal appearing to be relieved between attacks. The respiration and pulse increase decidedly and the animal may perspire profusely.

If the condition is at all severe, fill a quart size soda bottle (with a long neck and narrow opening) with mineral oil and place in the corner of the animal's mouth. Hold the chin up with the head just slightly up from level and pour the oil slowly down the throat. The object is to get most if not all of the oil down the animal to work as a laxative and lubricant. Call a veterinarian immediately! While waiting for the vet, in a severe case, lead the animal around, in a paddock-like area, at a slow steady walk, discouraging the animal from lying down.

Colic can range from a mild upset stomach that corrects itself all the way to a twisted or telescoped intestine which usually results in death. Do not treat any symptom of colic lightly. Make an intelligent, deliberate attempt to determine the exact cause of the colic but realize that in some cases you may not be able to find the cause. The very best insurance against colic is prevention through good care.

Azoturia. Azoturia is caused from over-feeding and under-exercising. It comes on quickly after the horse has been standing idle for a few days on full ration. After going a short distance, the horse appears confused, perspires freely, trembles, and shows difficulty in controlling the hind parts.

If a working horse shows these symptoms, unharness immediately and put him into comfortable quarters, if such are available. Undue exertion must be avoided so don't travel the animal far for rest. Warm blankets should be placed over the loins. After recovery, daily exercise with reduced feed when not working should prevent recurrence.

Influenza is an infection of the mucous membranes in the respiratory tract. The horse seems depressed and stands with its head down. It has a high fever and loses its appetite. It may sneeze and cough, and the mucous membranes of the eyes are often inflamed.

Consult a vet who will advise as to which antibiotics, if any, are to be administered. Keep the animal to itself in quiet, clean, well-ventilated, but draft-free quarters and on a light laxative diet.

Distemper is an infectious disease which may be contracted directly from animals suffering the same or from watering troughs or stabling used by infected animals. Young animals are most susceptible.

The ailment affects the air passages and the glands in the throat. The disease is characterised by loss of appetite, fever, nasal secretions, formation of pus in the air passages, and later by abscesses under the jaw. The abscesses break after a few days and the pain, which has been severe, is relieved.

The attention or recommendations of a competent veterinarian plus rest, comfortable quarters, and good care are the necessary requirements in average cases. Isolation to prevent spread of the disease is important.

Many of the diseases of work horses or mules have symptoms in the early stages that are so much alike that it is impossible for an inexperienced person to distinguish one from another. Any disease of a more serious nature than those mentioned above, as well as severe cases of the same, should be tended to by a competent veterinarian.

Injuries. There are three types of injuries commonly found with work horses: first, lacerations, such as wire cuts; second, bruises, such as kicks from other animals; and third, sores and wounds caused by ill-fitting harness.

Lacerations (Bad Cuts). Excessive bleeding must be stopped. Use of a commercial astringent, or shreds of sterile cotton packed lightly into the wound may hasten clotting of the blood. When the bleeding stops, any foreign matter that has not been washed out by the blood flow should be carefully washed out with a disinfectant solution while washing the entire surrounding area. If the skin is badly torn, stitches may be necessary. If so, a veterinarian should make the determination. Unnecessary stitching could cause unwanted infection. There are a variety of healing powders and ointments available on the market which may help to speed up healing.

Subsequent care of the injured animal is important to prevent complications. If the animal runs through dewy grass or weeds, pollen and other irritating substances may get into the wound causing inflammation, preventing speedy healing. This sort of inflamed, irritated, open wound is a prime target for the development of "proud flesh" or abnormal tumor-like growths. Bandaging may be necessary to prevent foreign matter from getting into the open wound. A clean, dry stall or barn lot would be preferred housing if the wound is in a place that is highly susceptible to dirt or foreign irritants.

Normal healing often causes itching, and in order to relieve this, the animal may lick or bite the wound. In such cases the injury must be protected. Sometimes bandages work, sometimes they don't. Confining the movements of the horse's head by a short halter rope fastened, is one possible course of action.

Bruises are similar to lacerated injuries, but the skin is not broken. If the bruise is sufficient to cause considerable internal bleeding, death may result, or other less final, but nonetheless dangerous, results. If the bruise is not severe, hot compresses applied to the part for two hours, followed by cold compresses for an hour or two, may give relief. A liniment rubbed into the bruised area will help. Absorbine and Bigeloil are two which work very well. The author's experience with bruises have resulted in a preferred course of action. This plan is particularly useful if the bruised part is an active muscle. Through a veterinarian's office secure some "DMSO" and rub this substance on the affected area. Wait one hour and wash or hose down the bruise with cool tap water. Repeat this three times a day until swelling and/or discomfort subsides.

Harness injuries occur frequently. They are most always the result of ill-fitting or poorly constructed harness or because of improper methods of breaking in or toughening the shoulders for work in the collar. The pressure causing the injury should be removed. The injury should be treated as either a lacerated wound or a bruise, whichever the case may be. In mild cases the affected area may be washed with a cold salt water solution and dried. There are several gall cures on the market that are good to use in cases of chronic irritations from ill-fitting harness.

Parasites. Work horses are susceptible to many parasites both external and internal. Parasites reduce the vitality and efficiency of work horses and in some cases can be directly linked to permanent damage and even death.

Internal Parasites. Among the common internal parasites that infest horses are the bots, stomach worms, intestinal round worms, pin worms and tapeworms. These and other internal parasites cause indigestion and colic affecting the walls of the stomach and intestines and indirectly affecting other organs and ultimately the entire condition of the animal.

The manifestation of the presence of parasites in work stock is often so gradual that the owner may not suspect it. The animals which he considers "hard to keep", or requiring more feed and special attention, are usually the ones infested with the parasites. Whenever the condition of the horse indicates unthriftiness without the presence of fever — unless the cause can be attributed to improper feeding or management or abusive attitude — it is very probably due to the presence of internal parasites.

There have been frequent changes, in recent years, in popular programs for the control or eradication of internal parasites. Research continues, as there are many unanswered questions about the real effects of the parasites and of the best methods for control. The most recent research has indicated that complete eradication of internal parasites is now possible with new high-powered chemistry and careful timing. However, further research indicates that to rid the animal of all parasites may be guaranteeing disaster as the presence of small numbers of worms in the system seems to generate natural antibody action that is not only beneficial but possibly essential. For without these antibodies, an animal that is infested with a new crop of parasites would suffer death.

This author believes that the very best system for parasite control must be carefully tailored to the individual animals. By taking fresh stool samples from each animal and having them examined every 6 to 8 weeks by a veterinarian the exact nature and extent of infestation will be known and the correct medicine can be prescribed. This also keeps you in tune with the veterinarian's bank of information from changing research. To simply purchase worming medicine at a local feed store and follow the "company's" recommendations for dosage and frequency is to invite varying degrees of failure. By tailoring the program to the individual animal's actual infestation you guarantee that your efforts and money will be well spent.

Medical treatment of internal parasites should be supplemented by programs for sanitation control. Stables should be cleaned regularly and manure piles should not be available for contact with the horses. Stock that is known to be heavily infested should be kept clear of other animals and care should be taken not to use the same feeding and watering areas and pastures. Rotation of pastures should be an important program for the farm.

External Parasites. There are many external parasites that are a source of worry and trouble to work horses. They irritate the skin, causing various types of skin diseases. Like internal parasites, they cause a general unthriftiness in the animals.

Among the most common external parasites are lice, mites, fleas, ticks, and flies of many kinds. The discomfort of the animal is readily noticed, and usually the source of misery is easily diagnosed. There are two approaches to treatment. One is to keep the pests from the stock. The other is to get rid of the pests altogether. There are a variety of chemical and organic treatments on the market which work in varying degrees to keep the pests off the animals. The author has used a couple of different brands with some success. However, the preferred course of action is to employ a variety of natural and chemical means to control the population of unwanted pests. There are firms that sell natural predators of flies and other insects. In other words, insects which eat the unwanted insects. There are also mechanical means with new traps and electric "bug zappers" gaining in popularity. The best program will be the one which is designed specifically for the farm in question using the best means, after careful consideration of the consequences and the fragile natural balances that exist.

GROOMING

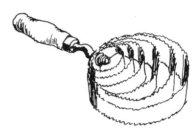

In order that horses may work most effectively, and with the greatest comfort, attention must be given to grooming. Lack of adequate grooming impairs the health and efficiency of work horses. Grooming improves the general appearance of a horse, and, what is more important, removes the loose dirt and internal waste of the body, which has been exuded through the pores of the skin. If this waste is not removed by thorough grooming, the pores of the skin get stopped up, normal bodily functions are impaired and the general health of the horse is hindered. Poor condition is indicated by a dull, harsh skin and a rough, dry appearance of the hair. The skin of a well-groomed, healthy animal is pliable, and soft, with the hair glossy. There are those who do not believe it, but regular grooming has been proven to improve the action of digestive organs and the utilization of feed.

The amount of grooming necessary will vary with whether horses are pastured and out-of-doors or if working and housed. Horses that are pastured do not require much grooming. Under these conditions there is less perspiration, and the waste products are more generally thrown off through the bowels and kidneys. Fast or active work, together with heavy feeding and a degree of confined stabling causes free perspiration, which throws waste through the skin and makes regular grooming necessary.

Care and thoroughness are essential in grooming. It is a good plan to groom the horses at night, for they rest better afterward. A good, brisk brushing will be sufficient the next morning before going to the field. Turning the horses out at night, or allowing them to roll, only partially removes the need of the evening grooming. Only the high spots are touched in rolling, and very little of the body waste material is removed in this way.

Grooming is essential for teams that are at hard work. Special care should be taken to remove all loose dirt and hair from the shoulder and other parts where the harness works. Care must be taken, however, not to use a hard curry comb over the shoulder directly before or after work as it could cause soreness or irritation that would result in a gall. Animals that have been wintered largely on roughage and then changed to a ration with grain will respond quickly to regular grooming. Farm horses are not usually groomed when they are idle. During the winter they grow a heavy coat. Clipping off this coat in the spring can make grooming easier and prevent excessive sweating but great care should be taken not to let the horse get chilled. They will have to be protected from the cold for a time. If the teamster prefers not to clip, sweat scrapers with serated edges are available which if used in the grooming process aid greatly in the removal of shedding hair and speed the animal to their seasonal coat.

CARE OF THE FEET

For an appreciation of the shape of the horse's hoof see Fig. 38. The feet of horses and mules usually remain healthy and the walls tough when at work. The feet should be trimmed and kept square and plumb at all times or else excessive strain on the tendons may result. Unless correcting a temporary or permanent defect, it is not necessary to shoe the farm horse as most work is done on dirt with little concussion. For highway work, winter work or logging it may be necessary to have shoes kept on the animals.

Care of feet is one of the areas of horse management where man through the ages has done his own ego some good and the horse a great deal of harm. The so-called experts do NOT agree to this day what constitutes the best care. When you consider how critical the horse's foot is to movement and work you realize that it is impossible to either cover the subject in adequate depth in this text or to give a beginner the tools necessary to understand, let alone work, on the foot. However, if a person chooses to depend on work horses for a measure of power then he or she will be in line for some schooling in the farrier's art. The cost of having a farrier come regularly and trim and/or shoe your animals will quickly become prohibitive to most working budgets. Add to this the fact that you who work with the animal all the time are better equipped mentally to do the hoof work. But that will come with time and patience. In the beginning you will need to depend on a competent farrier who is not afraid to talk to you about methods and results.

Some things you should know about the care of the feet include: Draft horses that are shod for show purposes have their feet trimmed and forced into artificial shapes which cause the animal to stand and move unnaturally, with excessive false action. The result after a few short years is that these animals are highly prone to forms of navicular lameness as excessive strain has been maintained on those tendons which anchor around the navicular bone near the heel of the foot. There are other forms of lameness which occur as a direct result of these unfortunate shoeing and trimming practices.

The ideal shape and angle of the hoof follows the natural angle of the pastern and the natural spread of the quarters (see Fig. 38). The foot should set flat on the ground and carry a straight line up through the leg. The foot should not toe in or out of the natural line of the leg. The shod foot should not prevent the legs from moving in a natural straight-ahead manner.

Show people will argue until blue in the face against these precepts here included. Unfortunately for many thousands of horses, of any of the animals with "forced" feet, the proponents of those practices cannot find sound horses, without artificial gait and lameness, to prove anything.

These practices are not limited to the draft horse show world. One need only attend any gaited horse show to see the abominable extremes man employs to satisfy his fancy.

Cleaning The Feet. You will, at the very least, have to learn to pick up your horse's feet to be able to clean them occasionally. The feet will have to be cleaned regularly if the animal is walking in gravel and/or mud so as to prevent thrush or stone problems.

With the front feet: stand facing the rear of the horse, but with your legs in a straight line with the horse's front legs. Do not stand ahead of or behind the horse's legs. Lean your shoulder into the horse's shoulder and gently run your hand down the backside of the leg to the fetlock. Making sure that the animal is standing squarely on all four legs, or at least the other three, pick up the foot. Practice keeping your feet and legs out of the natural forward path of that leg you are holding up because if the horse should pull it away from you it will hurt. With a hoof-pick clean out the bottom, watching for bruises, infection and stones. The same procedure is used on the other front leg. The back legs are almost the same. Standing with your legs in line with the horse's legs, run your hand gently down the leg to the fetlock. Pick up the foot, always thinking about where you are in relationship to where the horse could go. Smoothly and quickly, when you have the leg up, step back and under the leg, bracing it with your own. With both the front legs and the back it is important that you do not spoil a horse because of what you do not know. Have your farrier around the first time you try this and ask for his or her help and guidance. That way you will be working towards lessons rather than failure.

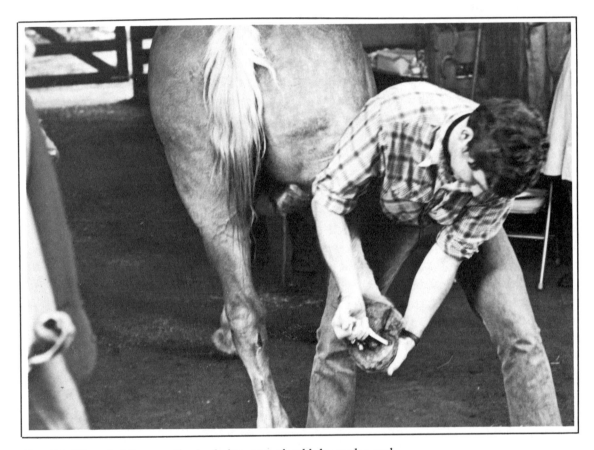

Fig. 41) When holding up the back leg, you should be under and slightly back, bracing the horse's leg with your own.

Conclusion — There is a great deal of material in this chapter. But each of many subjects has only been touched upon to give ideas and understanding, not to give the last word. With most of these subjects the beginner will look on and elsewhere for additional material and that is as it should be.

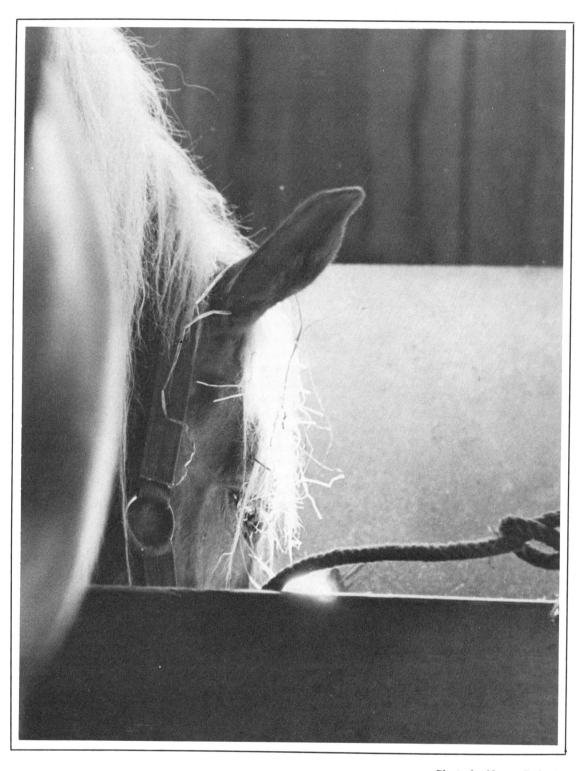

Photo by Nancy Roberts

CHAPTER FIVE
FEEDING THE WORK HORSE

Work horses must have proper feed, properly fed, if they are expected to perform efficiently for a full lifetime. Unfortunately, less care is given the feeding of horses, used or not, than other classes of livestock. Considering the fact that savings of up to 20% in the cost of feeding can be realized by using care and intelligence in providing horses with feed, the person concerned with the viable application of horsepower should put feeding (maintenance) high on the list of priorities. Put another way, careless feed practices can result in greater expense, less work, unhealthy animals and bad feelings. You must be a good feeder if you are to be a good teamster, because it is an essential responsibility that affects performance.

There is a science to good feeding practice. And the comprehensive textbook of that science of feeding livestock has been Morrison's *Feeds and Feeding* since 1898. This book has been revised and re-issued in many editions up to recently. At the time of this writing it is out of print and information could not be secured as to whether or not recent editions contain specialized information on the feeding of work horses. The earlier editions did. Most of the information and many of the charts used in this chapter have been gleaned, paraphrased, and otherwise edited from *Feeds and Feeding, A Handbook for the Student and Stockman* by Frank B. Morrison, 21st edition, published by the Morrison Publishing Company, 1948. Additional information from other sources and from experience have also been used in this chapter.

REQUIRED FEED

Total Digestible Nutrients (TDN) or net energy, in liberal quantities, is the main requirement of a horse or mule doing muscular work. When working, the animal requires just a little more protein than while idle.

The same thing is true with regard to minerals and vitamins. So, surprisingly to many people, feed rations that are relatively low in protein and that have only a moderate supply of minerals and vitamins are entirely satisfactory for adult work horses.

Mature idle horses use two thirds of the consumed feed ration to supply body heat. The other third is all that is required to maintain bodily functions. So, without work, cheap feeds like straw or corn stalks, which are low in net energy and protein, are sufficient because they produce lots of body heat.

Pregnant brood mares require large amounts of protein, vitamins and minerals, and mares nursing foals require even greater amounts. The diet of young growing animals requires adequate amounts of protein, with concern for the intake of calcium, phosphorus and vitamins.

Horses differ greatly from other classes of farm stock, not only in temperament, but most importantly in feed requirements. And individual horses differ from one to another. For this reason, the charts and tables presented here serve only as a guideline. With experience you will find that one horse will need more feed while another requires less. But if an individual horse takes more and more feed and shows poor condition, look to the teeth, to internal parasites and to environment for causes.

A horse at hard work will take up to double the amount of TDN, but preferably close to the same amount of roughage as the idle horse. That means that more of the feed must consist of grains and/or other concentrates in order to achieve the desired balance. The reason that the amount of bulk fed should preferably remain constant is because of the horse's digestive system. The horse is not a ruminant, like a cow, and has a single stomach and a highly sensitive overall digestive system which is prone to irritations which fall under the heading of "colic". As described in Chapter Four, colic is a serious problem and as with any malady that might befall the horse, prevention is the very best insurance. And in the case of feeding, maintaining a consistent program without dramatic changes in quantity, character, or composition of feedstuffs is the best policy. (The exception to this rule is, of course, the reduction of TDN when work is dramatically reduced or else serious conditions like Azoturia might result.)

The horse has a relatively small stomach and requires time to consume and digest adequate amounts of feed. Within this physical reality lies a clue to the best system of and approach towards feeding the work horse. See METHODS OF FEEDING, this chapter.

DIGESTIBILITY

Horses digest their feed less completely than do cattle or sheep, but the difference isn't great except when you look to low-grade roughages such as straw or poor quality hay. Moderate work, even immediately after eating, tends to increase digestion and absorption of nutrients. Severe labor may, however, slow digestion. Reasonable exercise does not waste nutrients by hastening their passage into the small intestine.

Fig. 43) Noon break over, the horses are watered before returning to the field.   *Photo by Lynn Miller*

The digestion of grains and concentrates and their absorption into the system as nutrients can be increased if a degree of roughage is consumed by the horse before eating grain. The author has also found that slowing the process of eating increases digestion and absorption of nutrients (see METHODS OF FEEDING, this chapter).

PROPORTIONS OF ROUGHAGES AND CONCENTRATES

Hay or other roughage may be adequate for the maintenance of mature idle horses. On the other hand, horses at work need concentrates in addition to roughage and the proportions will vary depending on the severity of the work and the age and condition of the animal.

If hay is hard to come by, tests have proven that the amount of roughage can be reduced some. Horses at severe work have been maintained on as little as eight pounds of hay per head daily so long as they had a sufficient allowance of grain. In some cases growing animals have been fed rations which included no hay but substituted such things as beet pulp for roughage (or fiber). These animals made satisfactory gains.

The opposite direction with regard to roughage proportions is a different story. Feeding too much hay or other roughage can be injurious to the animal. If given all the good hay they can eat, horses often eat too much, resulting in labored breathing and quick tiring. As mentioned before, horses have a relatively small sized simple stomach that does not have capacity for great amounts of roughage all at once. Also, if the digestive tract is distended or swollen with too much roughage, the horse will be uncomfortable at hard labor and digestive disturbances could result.

Therefore, instead of the popular practice of keeping mangers full, the allowance of hay should be limited. Not only is this a good way to save feed, but it is also beneficial to the horses. Limiting the amount of hay available at any one time is especially important when feeding rich, palatable hay like alfalfa, clover or early cut timothy.

A probable conclusion from mixed data has 2.5 to 3 lbs. of hay (or more) equalling 1 lb. of corn or oats for the production of work. For maintaining an idle horse in winter, hay will have a higher value and it will probably take only 1.5 to 2 lbs. of hay to equal 1 lb. of grain in value.

PROTEIN REQUIREMENTS

Morrison's feeding standards recommends 0.6 to 0.8 lbs. of digestible protein per day for a 1,000 lb. idle horse. Of course, when the horse is at work, somewhat larger amounts are recommended. There are, however, other standards which frequently call for greater amounts of digestible protein and some tests the results of which indicate that less protein does not harm the animal. There seems to be some correlation between the amount of protein in a ration and its digestibility suggesting that a low protein content reduces digestion. Also, it should be pointed out that young growing horses and pregnant and nursing mares require more protein than do other classes of horses.

MINERAL REQUIREMENTS

The calcium and phosphorus needs of mature work horses are not great. These minerals are essential in adequate supply for brood mares and young developing animals and to a lesser degree even with mature work horses. It is possible to get all the calcium and phosphorus that is required from good to excellent quality hay. But, even though the mineral needs are not high, an unusually low level of calcium and phosphorus in the diet can result in serious bone damage, even for mature horses. It is possible for a low fee to have agricultural stations or private agricultural laboratories do a tissue analysis of hay to determine conclusively the exact mineral and protein content. The expense is well warranted as it may save unnecessary expenditures on either vet bills or for unneeded mineral supplements.

Growing colts require an ample supply of not only calcium and phosphorus but also vitamin D to enable them to slowly develop strong sound bones. It is this author's contention that if the development and growth of the bones are forced too fast it results in substantially weaker and inferior bone.

Some of the effects that may come from a deficiency of calcium and phosphorus include; being run down, emaciated, lame, reducing quality of stallion semen, bone disease.

In areas where there is a deficiency of iodine, brood mares should be fed iodized salt during at least the latter half of their pregnancy to avoid health problems with the newborn foals.

The soils in different parts of this country may have marked deficiencies of certain minerals. Local agricultural authorities will have information about any mineral deficiencies in the soil and that information should be used to guide the individual in amending rations to include necessary trace minerals. On the good mixed farm where the best cropping and fertilizing practices are employed, the roughages and grain will be naturally mineral and vitamin rich and less deficiency-related problems will be seen. The teamster who must purchase all or any significant portion of the horse's ration off the farm should exercise care in acquiring all the needs of the animal. A good plan would be to locate the better farmers in the area and purchase off the farm the roughages and grains needed rather than to rely on mass-produced premix rations.

SALT

Horses must have a regular supply of salt. An allowance of 1.75 to 2.0 ounces per head daily is sufficient and many horses eat less. A good program is to provide free choice salt either loose in a box or in block form. In recent years, block and loose salt has been pre-mixed with trace minerals, iodized and even mixed with a fly repellent which works to repel flies after it is sweated out onto the horse's hide with salt. Horses at hard work need more salt than others as they lose a lot when they sweat.

VITAMINS

Morrison's *Feeds and Feeding* reports that there are commonly no deficiencies of vitamins for mature horses in ordinary rations that contain plenty of good hay, for their vitamin requirements are small. The vitamin needs of brood mares and colts are higher, but they will be amply met if good legume hay or mixed hay is fed when the horses are not on pasture.

The requirements of work horses for vitamin A (or carotene) per unit of body weight are about the same as those for cattle, sheep or hogs. A deficiency of vitamin A could cause night blindness, eye injury, respiratory and reproductive difficulties and eventually death. Colts sometimes develop rickets from a lack of vitamin D or of calcium and phosphorus.

The usual rations fed horses, containing plenty of good hay will ordinarily provide all of the B-complex vitamins they require. But because of the nature of the horse's digestive system, it is important that they be provided adequate amounts. Without this complex, normal growth cannot be expected.

Moonblindness, or periodic opthalmia, can be prevented, but not cured, by adding 40 milligrams of riboflavin per head to the daily ration.

VITAMIN AND MINERAL SUPPLEMENTS

There are many commercially prepared vitamin/mineral/enzyme/micronutrient/trace mineral type premixes on the market. Some are even advertised to be of specific value to horses and three or four actually claim to be formulated with the work horse in mind. The advertising claims of effectiveness are aimed at two sensitive areas of justified concern throughout the entire horse industry. Those concerns are for the rehabilitation of horses in poor condition (there are many — mainly the backyard inmate) and for improving the increasingly poor fertility of not only mares but stallions as well. Vitamins and minerals in adequate supply are important to the health of the work horse but they will not correct problems such as internal parasite infestation or inadequate feed. As for the reproduction system, stallions should not be kept as such and used for breeding unless they are superior representatives of their breed and/or type and unless they are found to be free of genetic defects or characteristics which will be detrimental to the future. Unfortunately, horses will continue to be abused and misunderstood by man. Economics seems the one area where we should make inroads towards changing management habits; but people continue to purchase expensive "cures" and "wonder tonics & potions" for problems that can be prevented with adequate feed, common sense and much less money.

This author has used very expensive vitamin/mineral premixes on Belgian work horses including a stallion in service, open and bred mares, young stock and working geldings, for a period of one year. For six years, this author has used no mineral mix, just home-grown hay and grain plus iodized salt and occasionally molasses or apples as treats mixed with the oats. The result for this author is NO DIFFERENCE. There was absolutely no recognizable difference in physical condition or performance.

Certainly there may be specific instances where the expensive premix mineral rations are of constructive value to a particular individual animal.

All the necessary nutrients, minerals, vitamins and even micronutrients can be provided in a well-balanced ration of good quality hay and grain. And if there is a specific soil deficiency (of, say, boron or some other mineral), that can be remedied by purchasing just the missing or deficient mineral (or vitamin) and including it in the feed ration. In this manner, you will be saving money over the cost of premixed minerals. Four years ago, the author spent $300 in one year for the mineral supplement referred to above, for 10 horses.

The intelligent procedure to follow would be to first inquire of your local government soils office to find if there is any mineral deficiency in your specific soil type. Then have your soil, or the soil where your feed will be grown, tested. And finally have the forage and even the grain tested at your local agricultural college laboratory to determine what it contains and lacks. From the tables contained in this chapter and from other reference sources you should be able to compute your animal's requirements for specific vitamins and minerals. You should be surprised to find that most, if not all, will be supplied amply by the natural ration. If there is a discovered deficiency check with the feed store, the veterinarian and the ag college about sources for the ingredient and compare the price and information. Now compare the cost of providing this missing ingredient with the cost of feeding a "special" premix. A mix will probably provide quite a few unnecessary, unneeded and/or expensive vitamins and minerals.

WATERING HORSES

Horses must have plenty of good quality water. It could take 10 to 12 gallons or more of water per horse per day. In warm weather and when at hard work, horses will drink more water than at other times: that is simply because of the evaporation of water from their bodies. Curiously, horses will drink more water when on a diet of rich legume hay rather than straight grass hay.

When horses drink water doesn't appear to have any bearing on digestion. It is, however, important to keep the animals on a regular schedule of access to water if it is not free choice. A horse that has been worked hard should be watered before being fed, especially grains, but HE SHOULD NOT BE ALLOWED MUCH WATER WHEN VERY WARM. The best practice is to give the animal a short drink and allow him to cool a little while eating roughage than allow another drink before the grain ration.

A HOT HORSE GIVEN FREE CHOICE COOL WATER COULD DEVELOP A COLIC CONDITION.

A HOT HORSE GIVEN FULL GRAIN AND HAY RATION FIRST AND THEN ALLOWED FREE CHOICE TO WATER WILL GET COLIC!

During exceedingly hot weather horses should be watered every hour or two while at hard work. They feel like you do when working in the heat and a short drink will help to refresh them. Taking a can or barrel of water to the field, if farming, might save you, in 100 degree heat, from having animals overheat and get sick.

FEEDS

Commonly, across the U. S., horse rations usually consist of one or two grains and one or maybe two roughages. Oats are by far the most common, and most well thought of, grain for horses. They are certainly the safest grain as they have a good balance of nutrients and the bulk and fiber necessary for correct digestion. But even though many horsemen consider oats to be indepensable, satisfactory results are had with grain mixtures that contain no oats, but are properly balanced and have adequate bulkiness.

A primary consideration in making up or deciding on the grain or concentrate ration for the working horse should be cost plus availability.

It is critically important for horses that their feeds not be moldy, spoiled or extremely dusty. Damaged feeds will cause problems with the digestive tract and system and dusty feeds will cause serious problems with the respiratory works.

HAY — When horses were the power mainstay in this country, timothy hay was the standard by which all other roughages were measured. The major reasons for the popularity of timothy hay were that it is a safe feed, being free of dust and less likely to spoil and that it provided, if of good quality, adequate protein, mineral and vitamins. As horses fell from popularity so did timothy and farmers turned to grasses and grass-legume mixtures which were suitable for a variety of livestock. Well-cured legume-grass or straight legume hay is entirely satisfactory if fed properly. You do have to be careful that the hay is properly cured and that horses are not given free choice because they will eat themselves sick. Legume hay is higher in total digestible nutrients and so less should be fed than straight grass hay.

SILAGE — This author is wary of feeding silage to work horses due to the sensitivity of the digestive system and the nature of silage. Morrison's *Feeds and Feeding* says that poor quality silage should never be fed horses but that good quality silage, free of mold or decay, can be 1/3 to 1/2 of the roughage ration. They also say that horses should be gradually accustomed to silage and that horses at hard work should not be fed much silage.

GRAINS — Oats are unexcelled in feeding horses but corn, wheat, barley, and the grain sorghums can all be used successfully in place of oats when fed carefully as either an appropriate mixture or grind. Corn is best fed in the form of ear corn or shelled corn. The other grains mentioned should be crushed or ground and should be mixed with some bulky feed to avoid danger of colic. Ground or crushed rye should not be more than one-third of the concentrate mixture. Hominy feed is a satisfactory substitute for oats and molasses is sometimes fed to horse as an appetizer or conditioner.

Wheat bran is an excellent grain supplement because of its bulky nature and laxative effect on horses. Linseed meal also has a laxative effect with the added feature of being a good conditioner.

PASTURE — Availability of good pasture for work horses can save a great deal of feed costs and has a rejuvenating effect on the animals as well. Pasture is especially important for colts and brood mares.

When horses are worked regularly, if pasture is available, the animals should be turned out after they have eaten a little roughage and all of their evening grain ration. The pasture will help keep the animals fresh and spry.

Fig. 44) Pasture will keep your horses fresh.   *Photo by Lynn Miller*

Be careful with early spring grass as it can cause problems with diarrhea and even colic. It is best to get the animal slowly onto the spring grass, feeding plenty of hay and allowing short but regular visits to pasture for a few days increasing the amount of time spent on the lush grass until the animal can be left out. Even then it is a good idea to provide some dry hay to slow the laxative effect of the new grass. If horses are being worked and have access to spring pasture NO other laxative type feed should be used, as the effect of the grass will be more than ample in this respect.

In the fall, after the farm work is completed, if the teamster has access to crop land with residues such as corn stalks, the horses can be turned out to clean up the waste as long as some hay is available. Care should be taken to make sure that growing colts and brood mares are receiving adequate nutrients in any season. Horses used extensively on the highway should be turned out on pastures for spells to allow their feet to recover from the concussive effect of the pavement.

Mixed pastures which contain a considerable measure of white clovers or other legumes are the very best for horses. The use of pastures grown in a regular crop rotation, instead of parasite-infested permanent pasture, will greatly help in reducing worm problems in the work horse. Since horses are less susceptible to bloat than cattle or sheep, alfalfa or other legume pastures are excellent for them. The best and safest results will always be had from pastures which combine grasses and legumes.

METHODS OF FEEDING

This author's experience and observations have led to the conviction that good quality feed in adequate portions is only half the battle in maintaining work horses in good condition. How the animal is fed can have the determining factor in efficiency. In this regard it is up to the care and intelligence of the individual teamster whether success will be a regular visitor or a casual passerby. But it should be said that good feeding practices need not be complex or difficult, in truth better feeding will ultimately be easier and save time and money.

The teamster, of course, will have to make the decisions of how much to feed to which class of animal. As stated, the amount of feed necessary for a work horse will depend on the size of the animal, on the severity of the work and also on whether he is an easy keeper or a hard one. As a rule of thumb to guide you: allow a total of 2 to 2.5 lbs. daily of concentrates and roughage combined per 100 lbs. of live wieght. The charts and tables contained in this chapter break that down further. You will have to learn to recognize the "easy keepers" from the "hard keepers" and adjust individual rations so that the fat horse is not getting fatter and the other is up in full shape. The only way to learn that is by looking, paying attention and using common sense.

Usually the daily amount of grain or other concentrates is divided equally into three feeds and given at morning, noon and night. It is best to feed only a small amount of hay in the morning, so the horse's digestive tract will not become distended too much when he is at work. With hay the common plan is to feed one-fourth the ration in the morning, one-fourth at noon and the balance (½) in the evening. This author prefers to do the same sort of split with the grain ration as well because the horses have more time to eat in the evening and because the absorption of nutrients will be more complete than if the animal's metabolism and digestive process is being affected by strenuous labor.

The slower a horse eats, or the longer it takes for the animal to digest its feed, the more value will be derived. If you allow your horse to bolt his grain you are doing him and yourself a disservice. You can make the animal eat the grain slower by placing round flat stones three inches or wider in the grain box. The same thing might be accomplished with corn cobs. A popular plan in England is to mix the grain with chaff or chopped roughage.

To follow suit, it is a good practice not to allow horses access to both hay and grain the minute they arrive at the manger. Their natural inclination will be to consume the grain quickly first and then take their time eating the hay. The best practice is to have them come to the manger with only hay in front of them. Allow them to eat a little hay then place the grain in their feed boxes. The roughage in the digestive tract will slow the digestion of the grain and make for better utilization.

To avoid digestive problems and possible deaths from azoturia (see Chapter 4), the allowance of grain for horses at hard work MUST BE REDUCED on idle days to 50 to 70 percent of the amount usually fed. It is best to feed on such days, in place of the grain, a mixture of two-thirds grain and one-third bran. Some feed a small allowance of grain at noon on idle days, with only a bran mash both morning and night.

If the animals are working full days, an hour should be allowed for the noon meal. This author prefers to allow two hours and work a little later than usual as it helps the horses to finish the days work in better condition. If working during extreme heat it may prove valuable to work very early and take several hours off midday, finishing the days work in the cool of the evening.

When the horses come in at the end of the work day they should be given a short drink of water, be unharnessed, allowed access to hay, allowed another drink of water, given hay and grain ration, and when sweat has dried, be brushed well. If the animals are to be stabled all night they should, well after finishing the main ration, be allowed to drink all the water they wish.

WINTERING FARM HORSES — If horses are to be idle in the winter they can and should be maintained on the cheaper roughages available. If the horses are expected to get by on just corn stover or straw, five pounds of good quality hay should be provided to each horse three times a week. Light grain feeding should begin before the heavy work season is anticipated, such as the spring. Idle horses should be able to exercise freely and in the winter, if running on pasture, should be provided some sort of shelter break to protect them from the worst weather. Be sure to provide free choice salt and water.

FEEDING THE BREEDING UNIT

BROODMARES — It can be profitable to keep a good team of brood mares to do part or all of the work required and also raise a pair of colts each year. A brood mare does not require very much more feed than a gelding doing equal work.

Mares are less fertile than other farm animals and the conception rate is rarely over 60 to 70% (often lower). Unless the mare is properly fed and cared for a good reproductive success cannot be expected.

Brood mares must have plenty of exercise to keep their muscle tone and attitude right. For this reason working the brood mare is an excellent practice and it contributes to their general health. But care must be taken not to cause the mare to pull too hard, especially where the going is slippery. Stay away from deep mud or snow and be careful in backing heavy loads. Take every precaution to prevent the mare from slipping and/or falling, especially when pulling. Mares can work in harness up to three days before foaling without hardship. How soon they are put back to work will depend on their condition after foaling.

The feed rations of brood mares should contain liberal amounts of protein, calcium, phosphorus and vitamins. Young growing mares and those suckling colts will require the most as the charts illustrate. Good quality grass-legume hay should provide adequate amounts of the required nutrients. Less than ideal roughage can be offset by feeding grain or concentrates. Care should be taken not to allow the broodmare, settled or open, to get too fat.

The average gestation period for work mares is 11 months or 335 days, but that can vary considerably. Shortly before foaling, the grain allowance should be decreased and enough bran or other laxative feeds used to prevent constipation. Unless the mare can safely and comfortably foal in an empty small pasture, the best foaling setup is a roomy, disinfected, well-bedded box stall (10' x 10' is too small, 14' x 14' is better). Before foaling, the horse owner should know where a competent veterinarian can be reached and what signs to look for as indications of difficulty for the mare.

The mare should be given a half bucket of lukewarm water before foaling, if she will readily drink it. After foaling and back on her feet she will need another drink. A light bran feeding after foaling is best and this may be followed by oats or oats and bran.

Beginning two or three days after foaling, the mare and foals should be given some exercise each day, but be careful not to put them with other horses, as fighting and injury will probably result. If the mare has no trouble foaling she can do light work in harness within a week. If she has had trouble, allow a longer rest.

Farm mares should not usually be bred until they are three years old. Breeding a well-grown and cared for two year old filly will not set her back but care should be taken to provide all of her nutritional needs.

Fig. 45) A young Belgian mare carrying her first foal.   *Photo by Lynn Miller*

Fig. 46) Good pasture is the best feed for mares that are nursing.
Photo by Lynn Miller

THE FOAL — To reach good size at maturity, a foal should make about half its entire growth during the first year. This means that it will have to be fed liberally. Soon after birth the foal should receive the mare's colostrum (or first milk), because this increases the resistance to disease and infection and furnishes critical vitamin A. The foal's navel should be carefully disinfected with tincture of iodine.

Care should be taken to provide the kinds and quantity of feeds that will stimulate and maintain good milk production in the mare. Good pasture is best. If it is not available, good quality legume-grass hay with an allowance of grains will suffice. It is possible for the milk flow of the mare to be too great and the result may be indigestion of the foal. Cutting back on the feed of the mare will regulate this infrequent problem.

THE STALLION — The most important thing to the well-being of a stallion is ample exercise and the best exercise is work. Also the best advertisement of a stallion is the sight of him at work. It is a bad plan to restrict a stallion to a box stall. He should at least have free access to a paddock area.

The stallion should be fed good quality roughages and grain, and his ration, during the breeding season, should equal that of a horse at hard work.

FEEDING FOALS — Foals should learn to eat grain as early as possible. By the time they are weaned, foals should be eating two to three pounds of concentrates per day. This should go along with good quality hay and free choice water.

If the mares and foals are on pasture, a small fenced-off area, set up as a "creep feeder" can be provided with a gate just big enough for the foals to enter and help themselves to grain, but small enough to keep the mares out. One way to get the foals used to this arrangement is to let the mares in for the first few days with the youngsters. After the mares are locked out make sure to provide a salt lick to keep them nearby while the foals are eating.

At between five and six months, the foal should be weaned from the mare. To wean, the foal should be removed from the mare and not allowed back with her until they have both forgotten each other. The grain allowance of the mare should be slowly slacked off.

After weaning, the foals should be kept growing thriftily with liberal feed rations carefully calculated to provide calcium, phosphorus and vitamin needs. Unfortunately, the current boom in draft horse prices and the fetish for "big" horses at any cost has many farmers feeding heavy protein-rich rations, forcing colts to excessive gains without concern for adequate exercise and mineral/vitamin needs. The result is a great many big beautiful two and three year old draft horses with poor bone and muscle tone. These animals do poorly when put to the test of long days at hard work. Some of the better modern day horse feeders feel that it is more important to grow bone, height and proper muscle structure before any concern for "fat".

FEED AMOUNTS

Work horses and mules should be fed approximately the following amounts of grain and hay per 100 lbs. of animal live weight:

At hard work — 1 to 1.4 lbs. of grain, 1 lb. of hay
At medium work — .75 to 1 lb. of grain, 1 to 1.25 lbs. of hay
At light work — .4 to .75 lb. of grain and 1.25 to 1.5 lbs. of hay
Idle — Chiefly on roughage with grain if roughage is poor quality

The standards for horses at hard work are actually working for 7 to 8 hours per day.

VITAMIN CONTENT OF FEEDING STUFFS

Feeding stuff	Caro-tene	Vita-min A-activity	Thia-min	Ribo-flavin	Nia-cin	Panto-thenic acid
	mg. per lb.	I. U. per lb.	mg. per lb.	mg. per lb.	mg. per lb.	mg. per lb.
Alfalfa hay, all analyses	11.4	19,000	1.3	6.2	17.4	8.1
Clover-and-grass mixed hay, mostly clover, U. S. grade no. 3	3.2	5,333				
Corn, dent, yellow	2.2	3,667	1.9	0.5	9.0	2.3
Oats, grain	0.05	83	2.8	0.5	6.3	6.0
Wheat bran	0.08	133	3.9	1.4	63.5	13.6

AVERAGE COMPOSITION AND DIGESTIBLE NUTRIENTS
in percentages

Feeding stuff	Total dry matter	Dig. protein	Total dig. nutri- ents	Average total composition			
				Protein	Fat	Fiber	Mineral matter
Dry Roughages							
Alfalfa hay, good (28-31% fiber)	90.5	10.3	50.4	14.3	1.8	29.7	8.2
Alfalfa and timothy hay	89.8	6.6	49.1	11.1	2.2	29.5	6.7
Bluegrass hay, native western	91.9	6.7	52.6	11.2	3.0	29.8	8.0
Clover, Lodino, and grass hay	88.0	11.1	53.3	16.3	2.2	20.7	7.1
Clover and mixed grass hay, high in clover	89.7	5.5	52.2	9.6	2.7	28.8	6.2
Corn stalks, dried	82.8	0.8	40.7	4.7	1.5	28.0	5.3
Mixed hay, good, more than 30% legumes	88.0	5.2	50.9	9.2	1.9	28.1	6.0
Oat hay	88.1	4.9	47.3	8.2	2.7	28.1	6.9
Prairie hay, western, good	90.7	2.1	49.6	5.7	2.3	30.4	7.4
Timothy hay, before bloom	89.0	5.4	56.8	9.7	2.7	27.4	6.5
Vetch and oat hay, over ½ vetch	87.6	8.4	52.7	11.9	2.7	27.3	8.2
Silages							
Corn, dent, well-matured, well-eared	28.4	1.3	20.0	2.3	0.9	6.3	1.6
Concentrates							
Barley feed, high grade	90.3	10.8	73.2	13.5	3.5	8.7	4.1
Beet pulp, dried	90.1	4.3	67.8	9.2	0.5	19.8	3.4
Buckwheat, ordinary varieties	88.0	7.4	62.2	10.3	2.3	10.7	1.9
Corn, dent, grade no. 1	87.0	6.8	82.0	8.8	4.0	2.1	1.2
Corn ears, including kernels and cobs (corn and cob meal)	86.1	5.3	73.2	7.3	3.2	8.0	1.3
Linseed meal, o.p. 37% protein or more	90.9	33.1	77.4	38.0	5.9	7.7	5.6
Molasses, cane, or blackstrap	74.0	0	54.0	2.9	0	0	9.0
Oats, Pacific coast states	91.2	7.0	72.2	9.0	5.4	11.0	3.7
Wheat, average of all types	89.5	11.1	80.0	13.2	1.9	2.6	1.9
Wheat bran, all analyses	90.1	13.7	67.2	16.9	4.6	9.6	6.1

AVERAGE COMPOSITION AND DIGESTIBLE NUTRIENTS
in percentages

Feeding stuff	Mineral and fertilizing constituents				Digestion coefficients		
	Calcium	Phos-phorus	Nitro-gen	Potas-sium	Protein	Fat	Fiber
Dry Roughages							
Alfalfa hay, good (28-31% fiber)	1.27	0.22	2.29	2.01	72	34	43
Alfalfa and timothy hay	0.81	0.21	1.78	1.78			
Bluegrass hay, native western			1.79				
Clover, Lodino, and grass hay	1.05	0.26	2.61	1.97			
Clover and mixed grass hay, high in clover	0.90	0.19	1.54	1.46	57	47	61
Corn stalks, dried	0.25	0.09	0.75	0.50			
Mixed hay, good, more than 30% legumes	0.90	0.19	1.47	1.46			
Oat hay	0.21	0.19	1.31	0.83	60	65	51
Prairie hay, western, good	0.36	0.18	0.91		37	38	64
Timothy hay, before bloom			1.55		56	36	75
Vetch and oat hay, over ½ vetch	0.76	0.27	1.90	1.51	71	52	51
Silages							
Corn, dent, well-matured, well-eared	0.08	0.06	0.37	0.27	55	80	65
Concentrates							
Barley feed, high grade	0.03	0.40	2.16	0.60			
Beet pulp, dried	0.67	0.08	1.47	0.18	47	0	75
Buckwheat, ordinary varieties	0.09	0.31	1.64	0.45	72	80	45
Corn, dent, grade no. 1	0.02	0.28	1.41	0.28	77	90	57
Corn ears, including kernels and cobs (corn and cob meal)		0.22	1.17	0.29			
Linseed meal, o.p. 37% protein or more	0.39	0.86	6.08	1.10			
Molasses, cane, or blackstrap	0.74	0.08	0.46	3.67	0		
Oats, Pacific coast states			1.44				
Wheat, average of all types	0.04	0.39	2.11	0.42	84	81	70
Wheat bran, all analyses	0.14	1.29	2.70	1.23	81	83	49

MORRISON FEEDING STANDARDS

	Requirements per head daily								
	Dry matter	Diges- tible protein	Total digestible nutrients	Calcium		Phosphorus		Caro- tene	Net energy
weight	lbs.	lbs.	lbs.	grams	lb.	grams	lb.	mg.	therms
Horses or mules, idle									
1,000 lbs.	13.0-18.0	.6- .8	7.0- 9.0	15.0	.033	15.0	.033	55	(5.6- 7.2)
1,100 lbs.	13.9-19.3	.7- .9	7.5- 9.7	16.5	.036	16.5	.036	61	(6.0- 7.7)
1,200 lbs	14.8-20.6	.7- .9	8.0-10.3	18.0	.040	18.0	.040	66	(6.4- 8.2)
1,300 lbs.	15.7-21.8	.7-1.0	8.5-10.9	19.5	.043	19.5	0.43	72	(6.8- 8.7)
1,400 lbs.	16.6-23.0	.8-1.0	8.9-11.5	21.0	.046	21.0	.046	77	(7.2- 9.2)
1,500 lbs.	17.5-24.2	.8-1.1	9.4-12.1	22.5	.050	22.5	.050	83	(7.5- 9.7)
1,600 lbs.	18.3-25.4	.8-1.1	9.9-12.7	24.0	.053	24.0	.053	88	(7.9-10.1)
1,700 lbs.	19.1-26.5	.9-1.2	10.3-13.3	25.5	.056	25.5	.056	94	(8.2-10.6)
1,800 lbs.	20.0-27.6	.9-1.2	10.8-13.8	27.0	.060	27.0	.060	99	(8.6-11.1)
Horses or mules at light work									
1,000 lbs.	15.0-20.0	.8-1.0	9.0-11.0	15.0	.033	15.0	.033	55	7.5- 9.1
1,100 lbs.	16.2-21.6	.9-1.1	9.7-11.9	16.5	.036	16.5	.036	61	8.1- 9.8
1,200 lbs.	17.4-23.1	.9-1.2	10.4-12.7	18.0	.040	18.0	.040	66	8.7-10.5
1,300 lbs.	18.5-24.7	1.0-1.2	11.1-13.6	19.5	.043	19.5	.043	72	9.3-11.2
1,400 lbs.	19.6-26.3	1.0-1.3	11.8-14.4	21.0	.046	21.0	.046	77	9.8-11.9
1,500 lbs.	20.8-27.7	1.1-1.4	12.5-15.2	22.5	.050	22.5	.050	83	10.4-12.6
1,600 lbs.	21.9-29.2	1.2-1.5	13.1-16.0	24.0	.053	24.0	.053	88	10.9-13.3
1,700 lbs.	23.0-30.6	1.2-1.5	13.8-16.8	25.5	.056	25.5	.056	94	11.5-13.9
1,800 lbs.	24.0-32.0	1.3-1.6	14.4-17.6	27.0	.060	27.0	.060	99	12.0-14.6
Horses or mules at medium work									
1,000 lbs.	16.0-21.0	1.0-1.2	11.0-13.0	15.0	.033	15.0	.033	55	9.4-11.1
1,100 lbs.	17.4-22.8	1.1-1.3	11.9-14.1	16.5	.036	16.5	.036	61	10.2-12.1
1,200 lbs.	18.8-24.6	1.2-1.4	12.9-15.2	18.0	.040	18.0	.040	66	11.0-13.0
1,300 lbs.	20.1-26.4	1.3-1.5	13.8-16.3	19.5	.043	19.5	.043	72	11.8-14.0
1,400 lbs.	21.5-28.2	1.3-1.6	14.8-17.4	21.0	.046	21.0	.046	77	12.6-14.9
1,500 lbs.	22.8-29.9	1.4-1.7	15.7-18.5	22.5	.050	22.5	.050	83	13.4-15.8
1,600 lbs.	24.1-31.6	1.5-1.8	16.6-19.6	24.0	.053	24.0	.053	88	14.2-16.7
1,700 lbs.	25.4-33.3	1.6-1.9	17.5-20.6	25.5	.056	25.5	.056	94	14.9-17.6
1,800 lbs.	26.7-35.0	1.7-2.0	18.3-21.7	27.0	.060	27.0	.060	99	15.7-18.5
Horses or mules at hard work									
1,000 lbs.	18.0-22.0	1.2-1.4	13.0-16.0	15.0	.033	15.0	.033	55	11.3-13.9
1,100 lbs.	19.7-24.0	1.3-1.5	14.2-17.5	16.5	.036	16.5	.036	61	12.4-15.2
1,200 lbs.	21.3-26.1	1.4-1.7	15.4-19.0	18.0	.040	18.0	.040	66	13.4-16.5
1,300 lbs.	23.0-28.1	1.5-1.8	16.6-20.5	19.5	.043	19.5	.043	72	14.5-17.8
1,400 lbs.	24.7-30.2	1.6-1.9	17.8-21.9	21.0	.046	21.0	.046	77	15.5-19.1
1,500 lbs.	26.3-32.2	1.8-2.0	19.0-23.4	22.5	.050	22.5	.050	83	16.5-20.3
1,600 lbs.	28.0-34.2	1.9-2.2	20.2-24.8	24.0	.053	24.0	.052	88	17.5-21.6
1,700 lbs.	29.6-36.2	2.0-2.3	21.4-26.3	25.5	.056	25.5	.056	94	18.6-22.9
1,800 lbs.	31.2-38.1	2.1-2.4	22.5-27.7	27.0	.060	27.0	.060	99	19.6-24.1

Brood mares nursing foals, but not hard at work									
1,000 lbs.	15.0-22.0	1.2-1.5	9.0-12.0	35.0	.077	29.0	.064	70	7.6-10.0
1,100 lbs.	16.2-23.8	1.3-1.6	9.7-13.0	36.0	.079	30.0	.066	77	8.2-10.8
1,200 lbs.	17.4-25.5	1.4-1.7	10.4-13.9	37.0	.081	31.0	.068	84	8.8-11.6
1,300 lbs.	18.5-27.1	1.5-1.9	11.1-14.8	38.0	.084	32.0	.071	91	9.4-12.3
1,400 lbs.	19.6-28.8	1.6-2.0	11.8-15.7	39.0	.086	33.0	.073	98	10.0-13.1
1,500 lbs.	20.8-30.4	1.7-2.1	12.5-16.6	40.0	.088	34.0	.075	105	10.5-13.8
1,600 lbs.	21.9-32.1	1.7-2.2	13.1-17.5	41.0	.090	35.0	.077	112	11.1-14.6
1,700 lbs.	23.0-33.7	1.8-2.3	13.8-18.4	42.0	.093	36.0	.079	119	11.6-15.3
1,800 lbs.	24.0-35.2	1.9-2.4	14.4-19.2	43.0	.095	37.0	.081	126	12.2-16.0
Growing colts, after weaning									
400 lbs.	9.2-11.3	.8- .9	5.6- 7.2	40.0	.088	30.0	.066	24	4.9- 6.3
500 lbs.	10.9-13.3	.9-1.0	6.6- 8.4	40.0	.088	30.0	.066	30	5.7- 7.3
600 lbs.	12.4-15.2	1.0-1.2	7.6- 9.6	40.0	.088	30.0	.066	36	6.5- 8.3
700 lbs.	13.9-17.0	1.1-1.3	8.5-10.8	40.0	.088	30.0	.066	42	7.3- 9.3
800 lbs.	15.3-18.7	1.2-1.4	9.4-11.9	40.0	.088	30.0	.066	48	8.0-10.1
900 lbs.	16.7-20.4	1.3-1.5	10.2-13.0	40.0	.088	30.0	.066	54	8.7-11.0
1,000 lbs.	18.0-22.0	1.4-1.6	11.0-14.0	35.0	.077	26.0	.057	60	9.2-11.8
1,100 lbs.	19.3-23.6	1.5-1.6	11.8-15.0	30.0	.066	23.0	.051	66	9.9-12.6
1,200 lbs.	20.6-25.1	1.5-1.7	12.6-16.0	30.0	.066	23.0	.051	72	10.6-13.4

MINERAL MATTER CONTENT

Feeding stuff	Calcium	Phosphorus	Potassium	Sodium	Chlorine	Sulfur	Magnesuim	Iron	Manganese	Copper
	%	%	%	%	%	%	%	%	mg. per lb.	mg. per lb
Alfalfa hay, all analyses	1.47	0.24	2.05	0.13	0.37	0.32	0.29	0.025	20.5	3.7
Clover and mixed grass hay, high in clover	0.90	0.19	1.46	0.17	0.64	0.13	0.25	0.022	42.1	3.2
Oat hay	0.21	0.19	0.83	0.15	0.46		0.16	0.049	36.6	
Prairie hay, western, good	0.36	0.18					0.25			
Timothy and clover hay, ¼ clover	0.51	0.20	1.48	0.17	0.59	0.13	0.17	0.017	36.6	2.5
Barley, common	0.06	0.37	0.49	0.06	0.15	0.15	0.13	0.008	8.0	5.8
Corn, dent, grade no. 1	0.02	0.28	0.28	0.01	0.06	0.12	0.10	0.003	2.6	1.8
Linseed meal, 37% protein or more	0.39	0.86	1.10	0.06	0.04	0.42	0.60			
Oats, grain	0.09	0.34	0.43	0.09	0.12	0.21	0.14	0.007	19.9	3.8
Wheat grain, average of all types	0.04	0.39	0.42	0.06	0.08	0.20	0.14	0.006	19.9	3.7

HORSES AND MULES

Horses and mules at hard work, weight 1,200 lbs.

1. Grass hay, 12 lbs.; oats, 16 lbs.
2. Grass hay, 12 lbs.; corn, 13 lbs.; linseed meal or other high-protein supplement, 1 lb.
3. Legume hay, 12 lbs.; corn, 13.5 lbs.
4. Legume hay, 6 lbs.; grass hay, 6 lbs.; corn, 14 lbs.
5. Shredded corn fodder, 6 lbs.; legume hay, 6 lbs.; oats, 15 lbs.
6. Oats or barley straw, chopped, 4 lbs.; legume hay, 8 lbs.; oats, 16 lbs.

Horses and mules at medium work, weight 1,200 lbs.

1. Grass hay, 14 lbs.; oats, 11 lbs.
2. Grass hay, 14 lbs.; corn, 9 lbs.; linseed meal or other high-proteien supplement, 0.75 lbs.
3. Legume hay, 14 lbs.; corn, 9 lbs.
4. Legume hay, 7 lbs.; grass hay, 7 lbs.; corn, 9.5 lbs.
5. Shredded corn fodder, 7 lbs.; legume hay, 7 lbs.; oats, 10 lbs.
6. Oat or barley straw, chopped, 5 lbs.; legume hay, 9 lbs.; oats, 11 lbs.

Horses and mules at light work, weight 1,200 lbs.

1. Grass hay, 16 lbs.; oats, 6 lbs.
2. Grass hay, 16 lbs.; corn, 4.5 lbs.; linseed meal or other high-protein supplement, 0.5 lbs.
3. Legume hay, 16 lbs.; corn, 4 lbs.
4. Legume hay, 8 lbs.; grass hay, 8 lbs.; corn, 4.5 lbs.
5. Shredded corn fodder, 8 lbs.; legume hay, 8 lbs.; oats, 5 lbs.
6. Oat or barley straw, chopped, 6 lbs.; legume hay, 10 lbs.; oats, 6 lbs.

Idle horses and mules, weight 1,200 lbs.

1. Grass hay, 17.5 lbs.; linseed meal or other high-protein supplement, 0.75 lbs.
2. Legume hay, 17 lbs.
3. Legume hay, 9 lbs.; grass hay, 9 lbs.
4. Corn or sorghum stover, 11 lbs.; legume hay, 8 lbs.
5. Corn or sorghum silage, 15 lbs.; oat or barley straw, 6 lbs.; legume hay, 7 lbs.
6. Oat or barley straw, 6 lbs.; legume hay, 12 lbs.

Brood mares nursing foals, but not at work, weight 1,200 lbs.

1. Alfalfa, soybean, or cowpea hay, 16 lbs.; corn or other grain, 6 lbs.
2. Red clover hay, 16 lbs.; oats or ground barley, 3 lbs.; corn, 3 lbs.
3. Mixed clover-and-timothy hay (containing 30% or more clover), 16 lbs.; oats, 6 lbs.
4. Timothy or other grass hay, 16 lbs.; oats, 3 lbs.; bran, 3 lbs.; linseed meal or other high-protein supplement, 1 lb.

CHAPTER SIX

THE STABLE

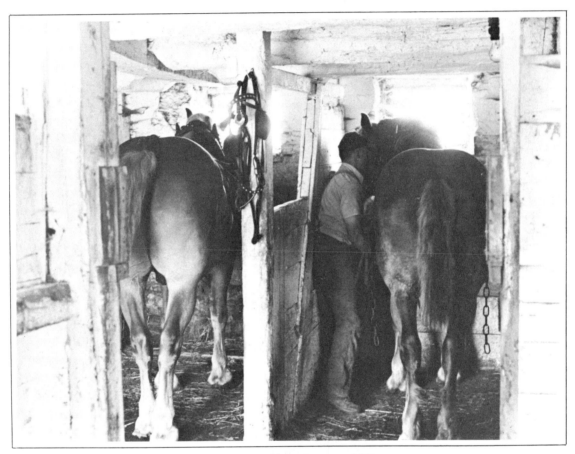

Fig. 47) The stable.   *Photo by Lynn Miller*

Comfortable quarters, conveniently arranged, are a help in keeping work horses healthy, in thrifty shape, and efficient as a power source. The barn or stable need not be expensive or fancy but it should provide ample room for the number of horses and mules kept, plus storage for plenty of feed and a separate room for harness. You may want to include in the same structure covered space for miscellaneous hitch gear or possibly even some wagons. It is a good idea not to include storage space for any flammable or combustible materials either in or near the stable. Blacksmiths, welding or mechanics shops should not be included in or near the stable nor should petroleum fuel tanks.

If you are building or rebuilding a structure to serve as a work horse stable, it is a good idea to consider certain working dynamics. For instance, with each stall filled with an animal and one or two animals harnessed, how difficult will it be for those working horses to be taken in and out of the barn? How are the passageways arranged? Are you expecting to have to lead a harnessed gelding close behind a tie stall that contains a pregnant mare or a stallion? Are the stalls set up so that some might be used, free access, from an outside paddock area by a convalescing animal or a stallion?

Another regular dynamic that needs to be considered in stable design is cleaning. Will you be able to clean the barn easily or will it require some special time-consuming maneuvers? It is difficult for the beginner to have any concept of convenience or inconvenience in stable design without some working experience with using horses daily. Some understanding might come from visiting a working farm that uses horses and paying attention to the time and physical requirements of stabling during the beginning of the day, at noon, and in the evening. One thing is certain: if the stable design, location and/or condition causes the teamster to take more time than is absolutely necessary in getting his animals to work and then getting them settled after work, then the building is contributing to the inefficiency of horses as power. If the building works smoothly, it is adding to the efficiency of the horses as power.

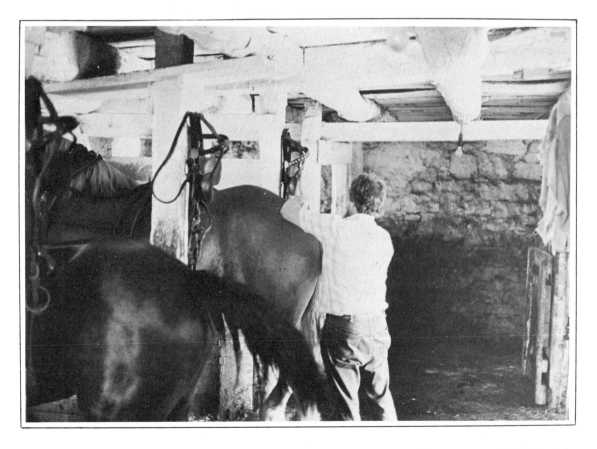

Fig. 48) Before building your horse barn, visit practicing horse-farmers and get a first-hand "feeling" for how the stalls "work".
Photo by Lynn Miller

Fig. 49) Some people prefer box stalls and if properly constructed, they do work well, but they require more time getting to the animals for regular work.   *Photo by Lynn Miller*

There are many types of horse barns or stables varying widely in material and structure. In warmer southern climates barn buildings need not be so weather-tight and substantial as is the case in harsher northern climates. The two-story gambrel-roofed building with hay storage overhead is an excellent structure for both its inherent insulating features and the ease of feeding.

The horse barn should be located on a comparatively high piece of ground so that the drainage will be good. A poorly drained, muddy yard is hard to keep clean, and the mud is likely to contribute to thrush and other ailments. And, of course, the barn and yard should be located so as not to pollute water supplies.

Some farmers use large open sheds, feeding horses together at a free choice trough or manger. This setup may work for fattening idle animals, but it is not recommended for work horses. When horses or mules are at work the time available for eating, especially at noon, is limited, and the timid animals may be crowded away from the trough so that they do not receive their share of the feed. This is why separate stalls with individual mangers are essential arrangements for the work horse.

Some say that box stalls are more comfortable than tie stalls. The author prefers tie stalls because they take up less barn space and because the horse that uses a tie stall MUST develop better barn manners than the animal that is shut in a box stall. It is possible to set up the barn with convertible stall space so that a box stall is easily used as two tie stalls when necessary. This is the best plan when time, money and available space is a concern.

TIE STALLS

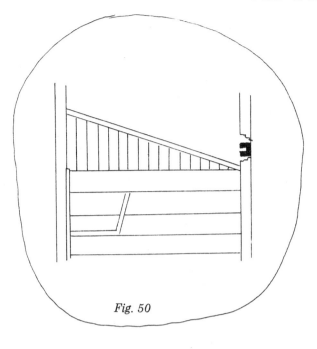

Fig. 50

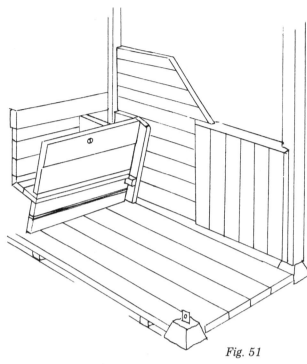

Fig. 51

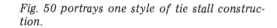

Fig. 50 portrays one style of tie stall construction.

Fig. 51 is a view of another and Fig. 52 gives dimensions of the same one. Fig. 53 is a cross-section of a type of gambrel-roof barn showing a possible position (left bottom) for tie stalls.

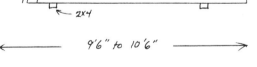

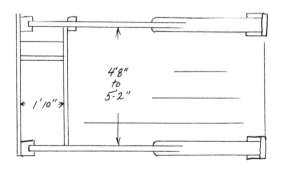

Fig. 52

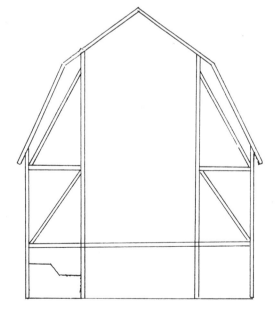

Fig. 53

Fig. 54) An ample tie stall, well bedded.   Photo by Lynn Miller

Fig. 55) Horses standing in another design of tie stall. The horse in the
second stall stands waiting, with collar on, to be harnessed.

Whether or not you decide to use convertible stalls, your stable should include a bare minimum of one large box stall for use in the case of sick animals, foaling and some special instances that requires free confinement. The size of box stalls vary with minimum requirements of a work horse being at least ten feet wide either way and up to fourteen feet wide either way. Tie stalls should be an absolute minimum of four feet wide with five feet being a better width. Six feet wide is a waste and may allow the spoiled youngster to turn himself halfway around. The tie stall should be six to eight feet long (or deep) to the manger. Fig. 50 illustrates some stall variations with dimensions. A well-tamped clay floor is considered to be the best for horse stalls (never use concrete or asphalt), and wood is a second choice.

Windows should be placed so that at no time during the day must an animal look directly into the sunlight. If a horse or mule must look for hours into direct sunlight, it can cause permanent damage to the eyes. The easiest thing to do is put the windows high above the eyes of the horse. Horses rarely suffer from cold if kept dry and protected from drafts but they do require adequate ventilation. Make sure there is plenty of fresh air in the barn.

Feed (grain) boxes and mangers must be built of strong materials, just like the rest of the stall, as idle horses will tear them apart if otherwise. With tie or box stalls the manger should run the entire length of the front (or one side) as this allows, in the case of box stalls, for the division into tie stalls and, in the case of tie stalls, is necessary to hold enough feed for the animal. Fig. 56 illustrates design and dimension of mangers and feed boxes. This author prefers a manger with a false bottom up off the floor for two reasons. First, it will make for a shallower manger, reducing the amount of space in which a horse's nostrils might be trapped with dust. (If the bottom boards are spaced a sixteenth of an inch apart, the dust will fall through.) And second, it allows the manger to be higher so that anxious young stock or bored adults do not step into the manger.

When designing your barn, set up grain storage space so that it is impossible for a loose horse to get in to it, for if an animal should get into free choice grain it will eat until it gets colic and dies.

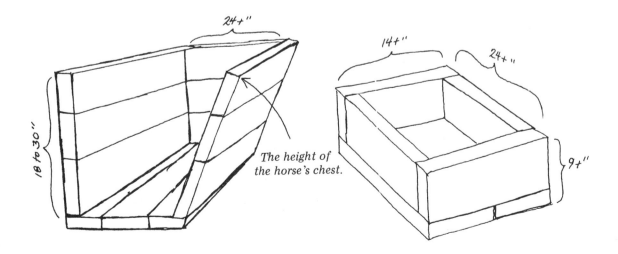

Fig. 56) Suggested dimensions for individual mangers and grain boxes.

The harness room should be located very near the stalls of your working stock so that the harnessing chore is made easier. It is not a wise practice to keep harness hanging behind the horse because the manure and urine give off fumes that will contribute to the leathers breaking down. (For an example of this, set an old, unwanted leather boot near or on a fresh manure pile for a couple of weeks and then test the leather.) In high moisture areas the teamster may want to protect his or her harness investment with a double-walled (maybe even insulated) tack room that can be kept shut. In the winter a light bulb left on will have a drying effect on the air in a small room. See the *HARNESSING* chapter for information about proper hanging and storage of harness.

Keep in mind that the barn is advertisement to the public of what using horses means. A dirty, ill-kept barn with junk and debris everywhere is, of course, a hazard to the work horse, but it is also telling the public that a "teamster" is not taking care. Advertisement can go the other way as well. The author's favorite horse barn is on the Bear Paw ranch of Gary Eagle where on the big swinging doors there is painted "EVERY FARM NEEDS A TEAM".

Fig. 57) A style of double tie stall.

Fig. 58) The horse barn on the Bear Paw Ranch.

CHAPTER SEVEN

HARNESS

In order to take maximum advantage of the horse's inherent capacity for pulling (or draft), man, through the ages, has designed rigging, the specific purposes of which were: first to hang, fasten or balance (otherwise anchor) ropes, chains or leather straps, that would be used to pull with, to a point on the shoulder of the animal. Second, to outfit the head and mouth in such a manner that a person could control and guide the animal. And third, if using a wheeled vehicle, provide some manner in which the vehicle could be backed.

The history of the development of harness is fascinating and includes a rich variety of different designs and solutions. There is not room in this text to cover the history of harness. Instead we are limited to a discussion of modern-day western-type harness. Hopefully this examination will provide some basic understanding of how and why harness works.

STYLES OF HARNESS

Fig. 56 is a diagram of a standard design farm team harness referred to in this text as a *western brichen* harness. The important parts are identified. Figure 60 illustrates another design of farm team harness referred to in this text as a *market tug* harness. The notable differences between the western brichen harness and the market tug design are the absence of the back pad (or saddle) and the two piece tug. Figure 61 is a diagram of a brichen-less harness referred to in this text as a *plow* harness. Figs. 63 & 64 are examples of light buggy harness. An understanding of how and why these styles differ may come from a discussion of the individual parts.

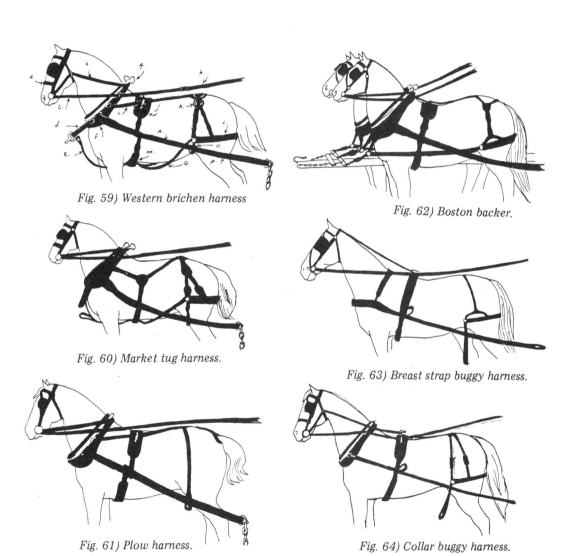

Fig. 59) *Western brichen harness*

Fig. 62) *Boston backer.*

Fig. 60) *Market tug harness.*

Fig. 63) *Breast strap buggy harness.*

Fig. 61) *Plow harness.*

Fig. 64) *Collar buggy harness.*

Parts of Western Brichen Harness
a. bridle, b. check rein, c. line, d. breast strap, e. pole strap, f. collar,
g. hame, h. line, i. back strap, j. back pad, k. hip drop assembly, l. brich-
en, m. belly band, n. tug, o. tug carrier, p. tug, q. quarter strap.

PARTS OF THE HARNESS

The Collar

Figure 67 illustrates the different popular shapes of collars. Some of the reasons for the different shapes include: horses and mules have different shaped necks with mules commonly being more flat-sided. Stallions have thick necks with big crests and require larger-wider collars in order that they set back against the shoulder in the required manner. Some animals, because of the shape of the neck, will require additional room at the bottom of the collar to free the windpipe. The shape, both in terms of condition and position, of the shoulder can affect how well a collar works, so the width of the draft (or widest part of the collar) could make a difference. Personal preferences of different teamsters have an effect on some of the aspects of collar design.

> NOTE: When storing collars in a hanging position, always turn upside down. Hanging right side up (with the collar-cap) will result in a slow distortion of the collar's shape that will be difficult if not impossible to correct. If a warped or twisted collar is fitted to a green horse it could possibly result in some damage to the horse's shoulder and/or the horse's attitude towards work.

Figure 66 shows the place of the collar around the horse's neck. (See HARNESSING chapter for correct way to put the collar on.) The collar provides a place from which to fasten the hames and tugs and on which to attach the remainder of the harness. Proper fit and condition of the collar is critical to the horse's well-being and capacity for work. A well-crafted collar has no value if it does not fit. Vice versa, a poorly constructed or dilapitated collar may fit perfectly and not work properly. If a collar is TOO SHORT, TOO LONG, TOO WIDE or TOO NARROW it will cause both the horse and the teamster misery. Fig. 66 and Figs. e & f illustrate the proper fit of the collar which requires enough room between the horse's windpipe and the bottom of the collar to allow a flat hand to pass freely when the collar is seated against the shoulder. Also, the sides of the collar should fit cleanly, not tight, with perhaps a finger's width clearance at best. The collar should seat flatly against the shoulder and not rock on a wide spot in the neck. To this end, the full face collar is for a flat-sided neck, the half sweeny collar for a slightly full neck and a full sweeny collar is for a thick, full neck.

> NOTE: When fitting an overweight horse to a collar, keep in mind that the neck will lose size as the horse is worked. Excessive weight (with resultant crest) will be reduced and probably disappear when the horse is toughened-in or conditioned. Even the well-fed horse in show-type condition (or flesh), if in good working muscle tone, will not have an excessively heavy neck.

Equally important to the prevention of sore shoulders on the horse is the correct position of the hames so that the point of draft (or point at which the tug attaches to the hame), is where it should be (Fig. 9). The hames must be the proper length so that the curvature conforms to the groove (or hame seat) of the collar. The hames are measured, as illustrated in Fig.70 , from the bottom to the uppermost hame strap fastening point. Even with hames of proper length it is impossible to have them incorrectly adjusted on the collar. Common error is to either have them too high on the collar or offset with one side high and one side low. This causes problems for the animal. The hames should center near the widest point of the collar (the draft) and the collar draft should be on the point of the horse's shoulder.

MEASURING & FITTING THE COLLAR

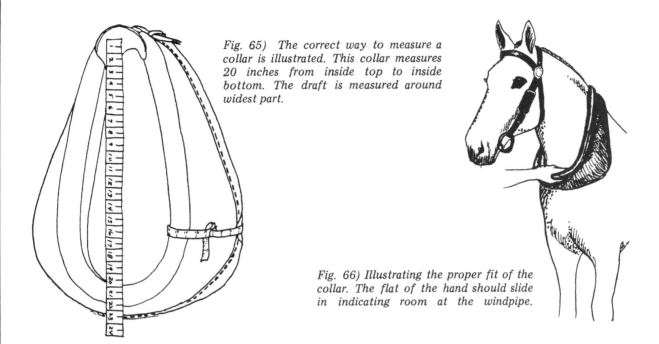

Fig. 65) The correct way to measure a collar is illustrated. This collar measures 20 inches from inside top to inside bottom. The draft is measured around widest part.

Fig. 66) Illustrating the proper fit of the collar. The flat of the hand should slide in indicating room at the windpipe.

Fig.65 illustrates the procedure for measuring a collar. This measures 20 inches on the ruler. For the size of draft draw a tape measure around the collar at its widest point as illustrated.

It is difficult to accurately measure a horse's neck for a collar without fitting. In other words, there are so many variables involved in the size and shape of a horse's neck that the only accurate and easy way to size the neck is to use several collars and put them on one at a time until fitting is found. In the heyday of the harness horse, collar makers had sliding shape-conforming measuring devices which were used.

Hames

The hame, see Fig.68 , is usually of steel or steel reinforced wood construction. It is rib-like in design and two are used with each harness. They are strapped top and bottom, tightly, into the outside groove of the collar. The tugs attach to the bolt assembly (at point of draft), the breast strap to the bottom ring, the back strap to the second ring and the driving line passes through the top ring. The brass or nickel-plated balls found atop the hames are purely ornamental. On some hames small rings may be found just below the hame ball. These rings are used to snap spreaders into.

It is customary to leave all the working straps of the harness attached to the hames when stored. See HARNESSING chapter.

It is normal to have three or at least two adjustable top hame strap positions and for a pair of hames to be so adjustable up to 3 inches in length.

The length of hames, of course, corresponds to the size of the collar. In other words, when referring to 22" hames we are talking about the size of the hame and not its overall length. To determine the size of a hame, measure (as in Fig. 70) from the bottom of the

COLLARS

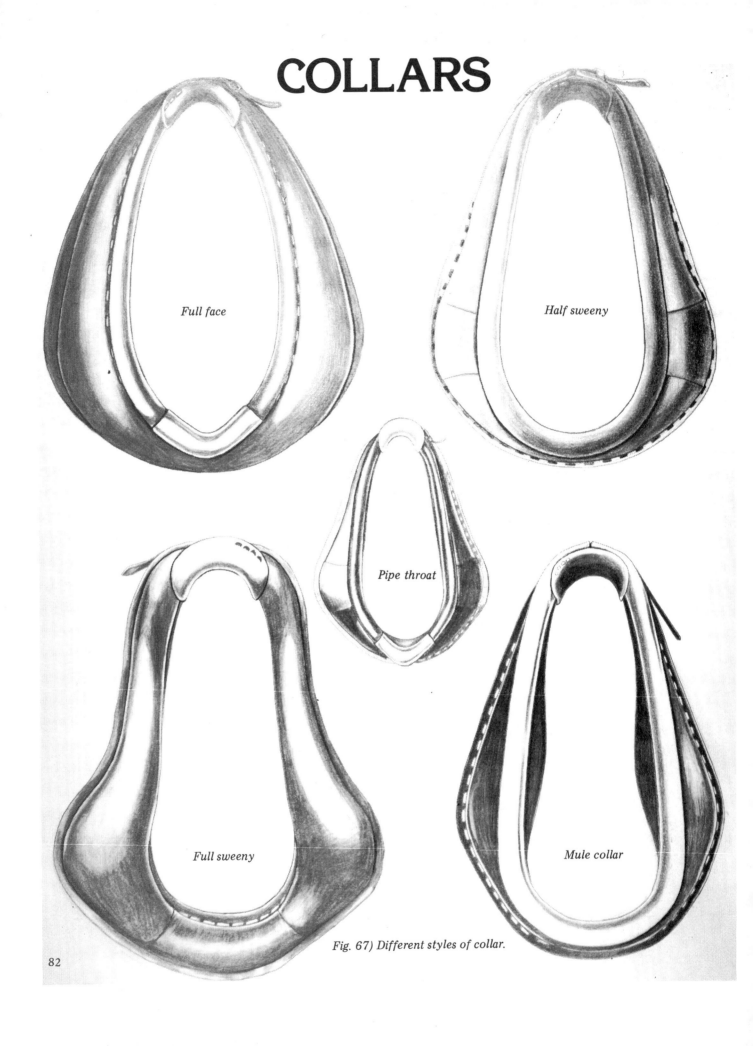

Full face

Half sweeny

Pipe throat

Full sweeny

Mule collar

Fig. 67) Different styles of collar.

82

hame straight to the point at which the top hame strap fastens. Since this point on the hame is adjustable, you'll find that it will commonly measure to within a two inch range, for example 20"-22" or 26"-28". It is necessary to match the size of hames to the size of the collar. See the section, this chapter, under COLLARS which refers to the placement and adjustment of hames.

Hame Straps

The hames are secured top and bottom into the groove of the collar by the use of hame straps, see Fig. 68. These short stout straps are commonly made of leather, sometimes nylon and less frequently bindered chain. In the case of leather and nylon, the strap normally passes through the right side hame (one strap top and one strap bottom) first and then the left side so that cinching up the straps can be done easily from the left side of the animal.

The strength and proper adjustment of hame straps are critical to proper performance and safety. If a strap should break while pulling, dangerous injury may well result. If a too loose strap should cause the hames to pull forward out of the collar groove, the animal might choke severely. A strong, properly and tightly adjusted hame strap is important. In pulling contests or heavy logging it is not uncommon to see hame straps that are stitched two-ply thick. Also, second hame straps will be used top and bottom. On top a strap will pass around the hame and twist around the other hame. From the top this would look like a figure eight. On the bottom a longer strap will pass through the breast strap ring (below the tug) and on top of the hame strap over to the same ring on the other side. Then a regular length hame strap (or shorter) would pass completely around the collar at the windpipe, and, of course, over both hame straps. Cinched down, this strap serves to hold the hame strap assembly from slipping up to the windpipe. To appreciate how critical the hame strap is to pulling performance and all work in harness, one need only inspect the care that professional pullers take with this part of their harness.

The hame strap, because of its handy size, is the perfect extra part to keep on hand for alterations or quick replacements or repair. The author recommends that the teamster keep one extra hame strap for each harness regularly used.

Tugs or Traces

Tugs, or traces, as they are frequently called, attach by a steel pin, bolt or hook, to the hames. They are attached directly or indirectly, at the opposite end to whatever is to be pulled. It is critical that they be of strong, pliable leather. In some cases tugs of rope or chains will be found. There are many different designs of tugs, sometimes varying in strength, length and hookup, depending on the job they are to perform. The leather farm tug is commonly fixed with a chain at the end by which it is attached to the single trees. In some cases, more common with logging or pulling contest harness, the tugs have metal hooks on the ends and an adjustable butt chain with large rings on both ends (one for each tug), fastened to the singletree. (See chapter RIGGING THE HITCH.)

HAMES & HAME STRAPS

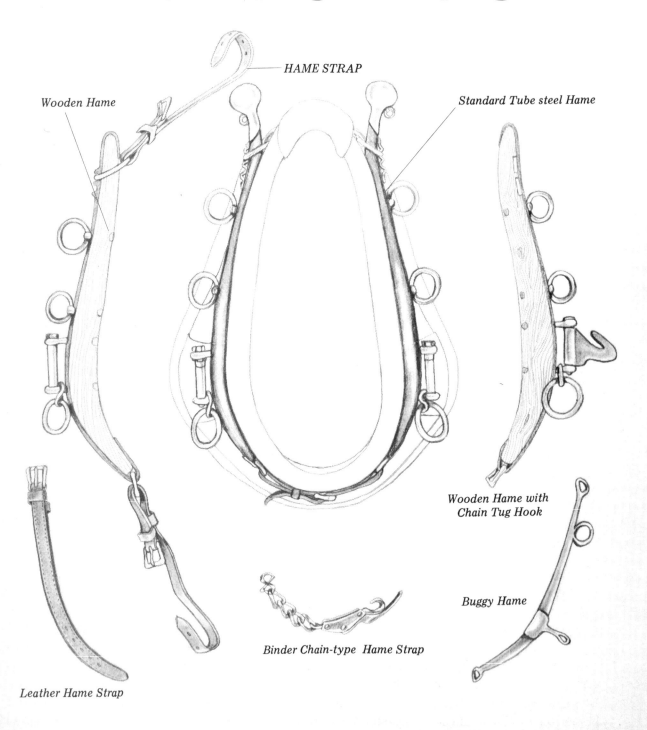

HAME STRAP

Wooden Hame

Standard Tube steel Hame

Wooden Hame with
Chain Tug Hook

Buggy Hame

Binder Chain-type Hame Strap

Leather Hame Strap

Fig. 68) Illustrating different hames and hame straps.

TUGS & BELLY BANDS

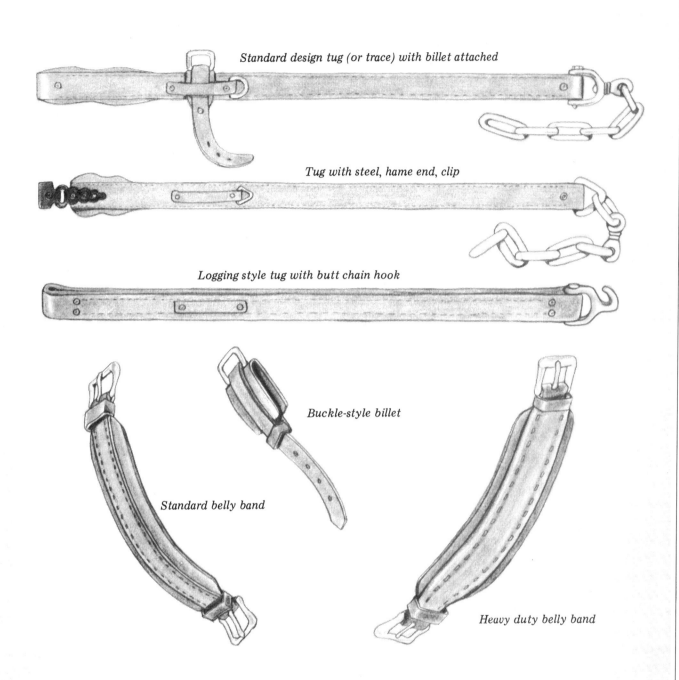

Standard design tug (or trace) with billet attached

Tug with steel, hame end, clip

Logging style tug with butt chain hook

Buckle-style billet

Standard belly band

Heavy duty belly band

Fig. 69) Illustrating tugs, belly bands and billets.

When the horse is pulling he is actually pushing against the collar. That pushing action is transferred through the tugs into a draft or pull. If a tug should break while the animal is pulling, a fall would result that could cause damage. Since the animal has two tugs, one on each side, it is important that there be no mechanical reason preventing the horse from moving cleanly and freely between the tugs, especially if they are chain or rope.

Back Pads

The back pad, or saddle as sometimes called (see Fig.71), seats just back of the horse's withers as far forward as the animal's conformation comfortably allows. It properly carries and evenly displaces any downward pressure or weight that might come from either tugs (on the draft angle) or shaves (such as with a single horse hitched to a cart). In most team harness the back pad serves primarily to organize the girth position of the belly band and to support the traces through the billets. Since it does not, in common western use, carry much weight, its size is lighter than European harness where horses are commonly used single and a greater weight is transferred through the shaves to the horse's back. Indeed, in some styles of western harness, such as the market tug harness (see Fig.60), the back pad is done away with altogether.

Some styles of back pad will have billet straps sewn into either end for fastening around the tugs. More commonly the back pad will have "D" rings in either end through which back pad billets may be fastened.

Belly Band

This harness part is named to be almost self-explanatory, see Fig. 69. Fastened on either end to the belly band billets which in turn are fastened around the tugs or traces, this assembly serves an important, and on occasion, vital purpose. Without the stabilizing restriction that the belly band serves to upward movement of the tug, a horse might, when hitched to a high hitch point of draft, be choked as the collar were pulled up against the windpipe (see Fig. 8). In a very heavy pull, a horse will tend to lower itself in the back as it digs in, and the front end of the animal will usually remain up. This will cause the same dynamic as a high hitch point and the belly band serves to correct that problem. The animals appears to lay down into the belly band. This is why in pulling contests the wider heavy belly band is preferred (see Fig.69). It is customary to leave the belly band fastened to the right-side billet, undoing it on the left side when unharnessing. The belly band is usually constructed with a buckle on each end. In some instances some will be found with a "D" ring in one or both ends. The billet then has a snap to go into the "D" ring. This arrangement is not recommended because it can rub the hair off the horse's underside and cause sores.

Billets

Billets are short heavy straps which go around the tug or fasten into the back pad and have a free end to enter a buckle (see Fig. 69).

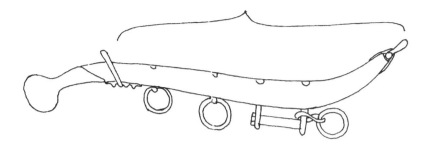

Fig. 70) The correct way to measure a hame's length.

Breast Straps

The breast strap is a wide, long, strong strap which fastens from the lower hame rings on both sides of the hames, see Fig. 72 . There are a wide variety of different setups for the breast strap as it works with or without the pole strap in its function with the neck yoke. The author prefers the all-in-one assembly where the pole strap is joined to the breast strap by a bolt and roller assembly snap. Fig. 72 shows this and three other variations which include: no neck yoke snap on either pole strap or breast strap; snaps on both; a snap on just the breast strap.

The breast strap functions in an important capacity as part of the backing and braking system of the harness. In some regions, such as eastern Canada, the breast strap works alone as the braking and backing system. The author cannot recommend such a practice where there are heavy loads to draw over steep terrain.

Another related function of the breast strap is on rare occasion to adjust the height of the end of the tongue, such as with a mower.

The breast strap is commonly looped through the right side bottom hame ring. It is then fastened by heavy snap to the left side bottom hame ring. Sometimes you will find a breast strap with snaps on both sides, usually in an all-in-one assembly. The breast strap must be strong because if it should break at a critical moment the load behind the team could come up on their back legs and cause trouble.

Pole Strap

The pole strap works with the breast strap and quarter straps to tie the collar and brichen together to function as the complete braking and backing system for the harness. This heavy strap usually has a heavy "D" ring in the back end and either a snap or loop in the front end (see BREAST STRAP description). There are variations in design of the pole strap and those differences often need to match the design of the breast strap, see Fig. 72. On the front end the pole strap fastens in some manner to the neck yoke. On the back end, the pole strap is snapped into by the two quarter straps. In western style harness it is most common for the pole strap to pass over the belly band loosely. In some regions the pole strap will have a sewn loop in the back end that allows the belly band to pass through.

Care should be taken that the harness is properly adjusted so that the pole strap does not pull the belly band forward into the back of the horse's front legs when either backing or braking a load. Adjusting the length of the quarter straps would be the most direct way to prevent this.

The pole strap needs to be strong. Should it break at the wrong time, the load behind the horses could come up on them.

Back Straps

The back straps on a western style brichen harness run from the hip drop assembly forward on both sides of the animal and fasten into the hame ring just above the tug. In most cases these straps pass through loops on the back pad and are buckled or conwayed into the hame rings. In some instances, the back straps have snaps in the front ends for fastening to the hame rings (usually in a detachable brichen setup). In eastern Canada, turrets are used on the back pads for line guides so there is no room or place for the back straps to pass through back pad loops. What is commonly done in this case is to just allow the straps to run free over the back pad to the hame ring fastening point. It seems to work just fine.

The adjustment of the length of the back straps will affect the position of the hip drop assembly on the animal. The back straps are normally adjusted by a sliding conway buckle (see HARDWARE illustrations).

Hip Drop Assembly

The hip drop assembly (see Fig.71) is a set of connecting straps which serve to hold the brichen in its proper place. From center, top of the hip, hip drop straps, usually two to a side, sometimes three, run down to fixed positions along the brichen. The straps are adjustable in length to allow for correct height and position of the brichen. The entire assembly must be properly adjusted to seat and hang from the center of the top of the hips (adjust back straps) before the brichen can be properly adjusted for height and angle. The harness must be pulled back with the animal well into the collar before an accurate adjustment can be made. If the hip drop assembly is too long in the back strap adjustment the brichen will hang low and not work in braking and backing. If it is low enough it could cause the animal to refuse to back.

Brichen

The brichen is a heavy multi-ply leather strap which wraps around the horse's backside under the tail. This strap is held in position by the hip drops. The brichen must be in the proper position if it is to function right. The strap should naturally hang level and work with the quarter straps as they pass under the belly, see Fig. 71. The brichen should be loose when the animal is pulling a load. It should be tight when backing or when restraining or braking a load. The brichen works through the quarter straps, pole strap and breast strap to the neck yoke, as a backing and braking system.

BACK PADS, BRICHENS, HIP DROPS & CRUPERS

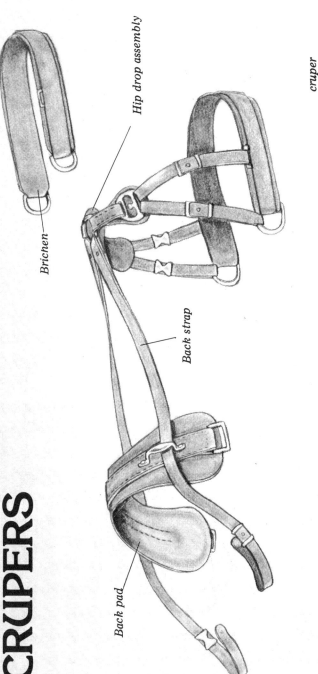

Brichen

Hip drop assembly

Back strap

Back pad

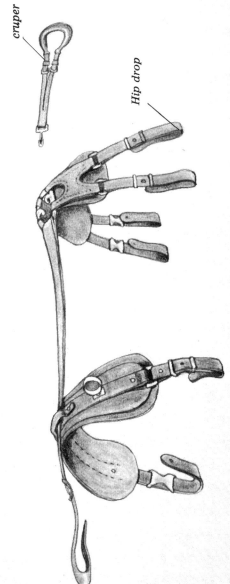

cruper

Hip drop

Fig. 71) Back pads, brichens, hip drops, and crupers.

Fig. 72) Breast straps, pole straps and quarter straps.

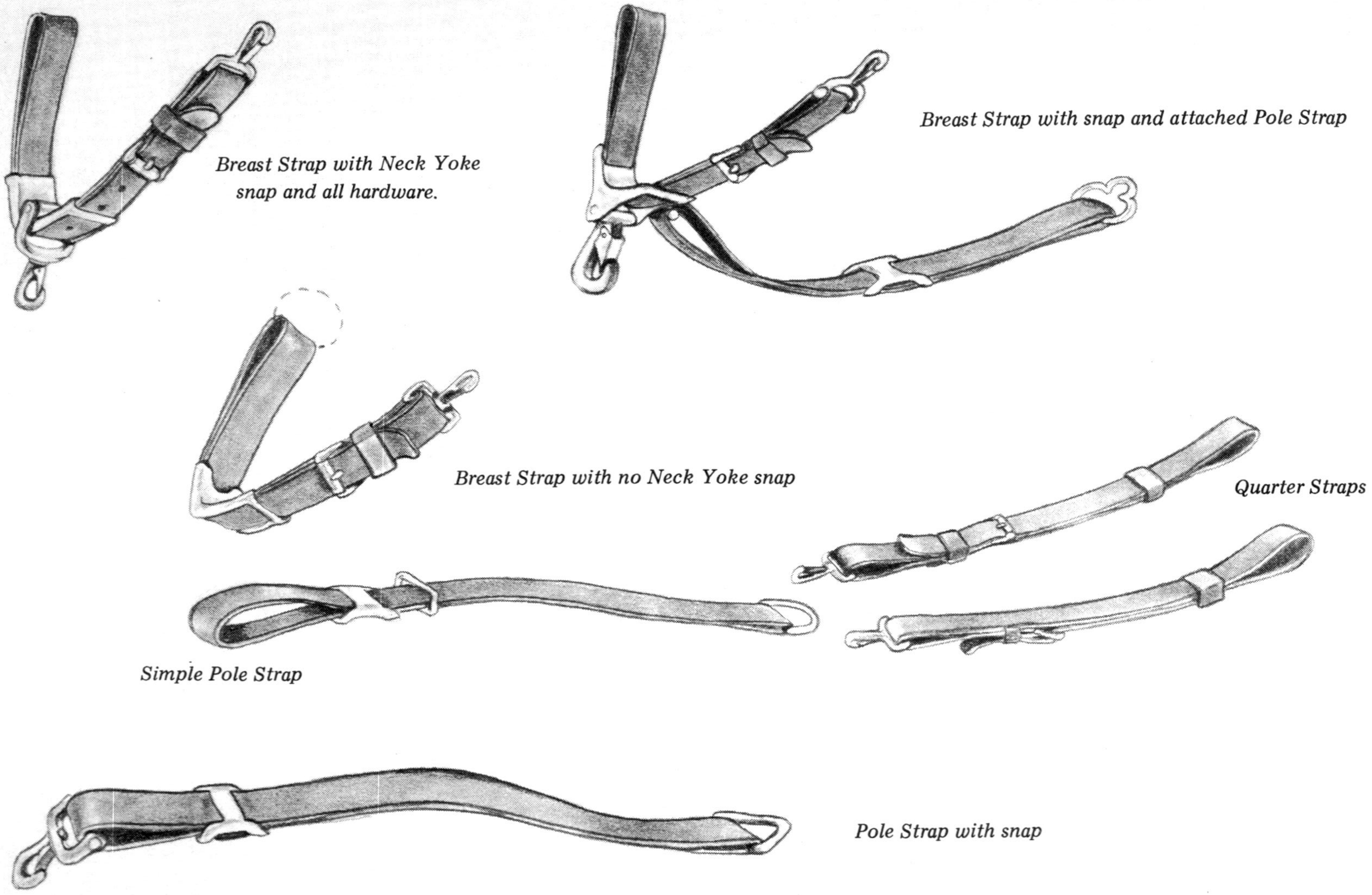

Breast Strap with snap and attached Pole Strap

Quarter Straps

Breast Strap with Neck Yoke snap and all hardware.

Breast Strap with no Neck Yoke snap

Simple Pole Strap

Pole Strap with snap

BREAST STRAPS, POLE STRAPS & QUARTER STRAPS

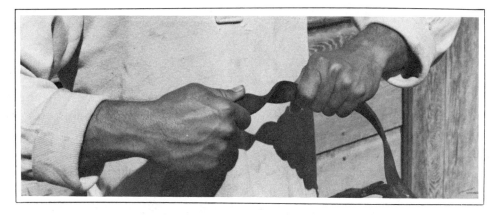

Fig. 73) To test the strength of old leather, twist and pull hard. If it breaks or looks suspicious, THROW IT AWAY!

Quarter Straps

There are two quarter straps to each harness. These straps loop and buckle through the "D" rings on the ends of the brichen. The front end of each quarter strap has a heavy duty snap which fastens to the back end of the pole strap. If the quarter straps are adjusted too tight they will cause the horse some discomfort by rubbing when the team is hitched to a tongue setup. If the straps are too long they make the use of the brichen in braking and backing ineffective and a horse might easily step over the quarter strap and break the harness. Even when hitched and pulling there should be some slack in the quarter straps (about the width of two hands flat), but not too much. Only when there is a backing and braking action should the quarter straps come tight against the belly. The quarter straps should be good strong leather.

Crupers

The cruper is a strap which fastens, not too tight, around the animals's tail. In a brichenless plow harness, a cruper is used to hold the harness in place on the animal, so that the rear portion of the rigging doesn't slide off to one side or the other. Even in some brichen harness the cruper might be used for the same purpose. If there is an excessive pull against the cruper it may well cause the animal discomfort and account for some unusual reactions. Care should be taken when putting the cruper on any animal for the first time. (Fig. 71 illustrates the cruper.)

Trace Carriers

The trace carriers are self-explanatory. They fasten to the "D" rings on the ends of the brichen (below the quarter straps) and serve to keep the traces, or tugs, up and out of the way. In a cruper harness it is not uncommon to see trace carriers on longer straps fastening on the top center of the hip to the back straps. Certainly in many instances they are not used at all. In the southern U. S. where heat and economics dictate thrift, it is most common to see cultivating harness without trace carriers.

Bridles

Fig.80 illustrates common variations in work bridles. There are, of course, many more designs. The bridle is a vital key in the teamsters ability to communicate with the animal. This apparatus fits, comfortably, over the horse's ears and down the sides of the head to hold a bit in the mouth, preferably with slight or no tension. A throat latch passes under and is fastened, usually on the left side, with just enough room for a finger or two to pass between the throat and the strap. The bit is held in place by two bit straps, one on each side, which allow for some adjustment of position in the mouth. These bits straps are critical as should one break or come undone you will have NO control over the animal. In a used harness the bit straps are one item that the author recommends be replaced with new parts. Usually the bridle can also be adjusted for overall length at the top sides over the blinders or top center. In a bridle with blinders on it is important that length be adjusted so that the animal's eyes come on center of the blinders. If the animal can see over or under the blinder, it will prove worse than ineffective. As for the arguments for and against blinders, this author chooses to simply refer to the recognized purpose of the blinder. By restricting the horse's vision to the path it must follow, the teamster limits the chance that an unexpected sight might spook the animal. The animal that works comfortably without blinders may react suspiciously to having to wear them. The same is true in reverse. Personal preference will play a big part in the experienced teamster's decision about blinders.

Most bridles are set up with check reins. The check rein serves to hold the horse's head up in its natural standing position. It restricts the animal from putting its head down for grazing or rubbing. The check rein fastens into the bit, passes up and through a hardware ring (called a combination swivel), fastens to the throat latch, and then back along the neck, over the withers and forward again in the other side through the same pattern to the opposite bit ring. There are a variety of methods for fastening the check rein back. Some of the most common include hooking into some part of the back pad, snapping into a strap that comes forward from the hip drop assembly or simply adjusting the length of the check rein to allow it to work properly if hung over one or both of the hames. In any event, the important thing here is not to overdo the check rein, and force the animal to hold its head in an unnatural position. To do so will cause you problems later, not the least of which will be the loss of confidence from your animal.

It is not uncommon to see animals being worked with no check rein. A skilled teamster will be able to identify how one animal, or one job, performs better with or without the check rein.

After a bridle has been fitted to a particular animal, it would be a good idea to keep it for that horse. In other words, each horse should have its own bridle, if not harness, as it will stretch and bend to shape like a shoe to your foot.

Lines

Driving lines differ substantially depending on how many animals are being driven, in what configuration, and at what job. One horse is normally driven with two single lines with either snaps or buckles on the ends. A team of horses is driven with two checked team

LINES

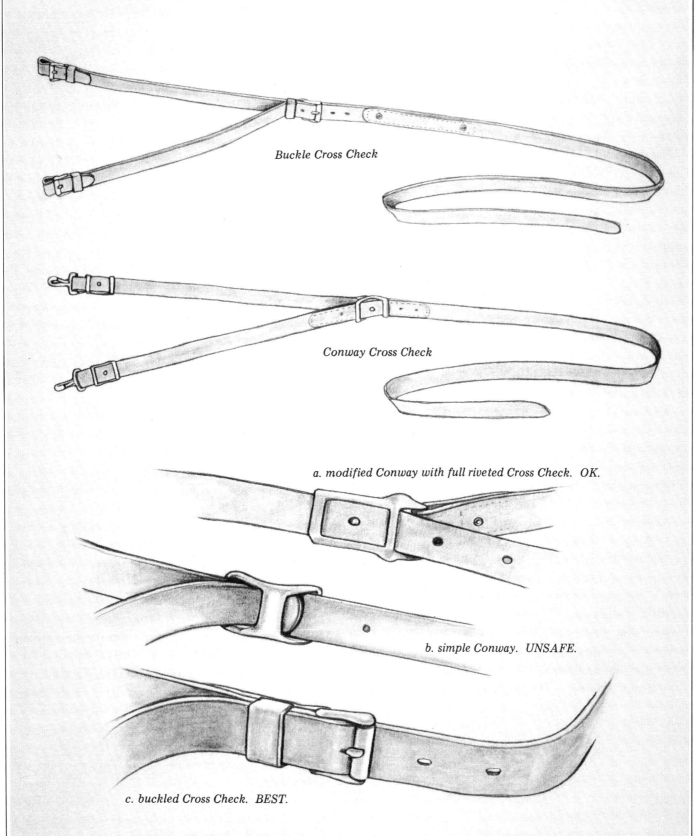

Buckle Cross Check

Conway Cross Check

a. modified Conway with full riveted Cross Check. OK.

b. simple Conway. UNSAFE.

c. buckled Cross Check. BEST.

Fig. 73 LINES

93

lines, see Fig. 73. For the various differences, see the chapter, this text, entitled RIGGING THE HITCH and the illustrations of driving lines.

If you are working with used harness, make doubly sure that your lines are strong and pliable and adequately stitched or riveted. One way to check the tensile strength of the line leather (or any old leather), is to twist a short section of the line severely and pull on it. The leather should not tear or even look suspicious. Also check the leather closely under any hardware, especially near the bit snap or buckle. And finally, check the splices to see if the stitching is beginning to rot or the splice is coming apart or any rivets are badly corroded. There might be "a lot of good leather" in a used line but these other points may be bad enough to guarantee disaster. A used line can be repaired and strengthened but until you know what you're doing, it is best done by a competent harness shop.

Unfortunate experience, namely a needless runaway, has caused this author to have strong and definite preferences in the construction design of team lines. Fig. 73 illustrates the differences and preferences.

A friend of the author and a true master teamster, Ray Drongesen, prefers not to use lines with snaps for the bits. Instead, Ray uses buckles in the end giving him just a little extra security. A horse, when standing at rest in harness, might play with the line, mouthing the snap and unsnapping the line. Then when the unsuspecting teamster gives the command to go, there is a surprise. This doesn't happen with buckled lines.

As illustrated in various places throughout this text, the basic setup for team lines is as follows: The main line length passes along the outside of the horse (and team) through the top hame ring and fastens below any other strap, to the bit ring or shank (snaps face out). The cross check passes over the same horse's back through the top hame ring and across to the teammate's bit ring. The same procedure is followed in reverse for the other line. There are some variations of setup which might include spreaders and/or center line drops, but the basic principle and the functioning dynamic remain the same.

The length of the lines will vary considerably with the job to be done or how far away from the horses the teamster must stand, or if using ponies. Customarily, the length is between 18 and 20 feet with some cases calling for lengths from 15 to 25 feet.

Bits

There are thousands of designs of bits invented through the ages reflecting the human's ever-changing attitude about the best relationship and performance to be expected from (or with) the horse. Some bits are incredibly cruel to the horse's mouth and/or jaw. Others are so benign as to be almost ineffectual as they do not allow for a range of various sensitive pressures to the horse's mouth. Thank goodness there are some bits that combine gentleness and flex so as to provide the teamster with the fullest range of communication through the hands to the animal's head and mouth.

If you think of the bit as simply an iron tool in the horse's mouth which will stop the animal if pressure is applied, please read the chapter in this text entitled ATTITUDE AND APPROACH. The author's preference in bits is for the common snaffle and a few variations. The illustrations included here will give some idea of the range of designs and the captions will help to explain the effects of these different bits.

BITS

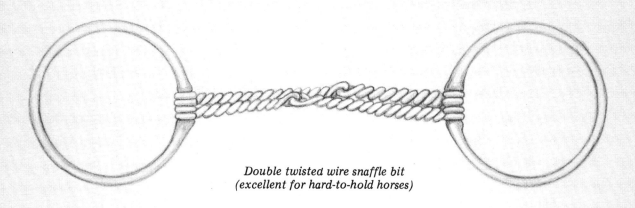

*Double twisted wire snaffle bit
(excellent for hard-to-hold horses)*

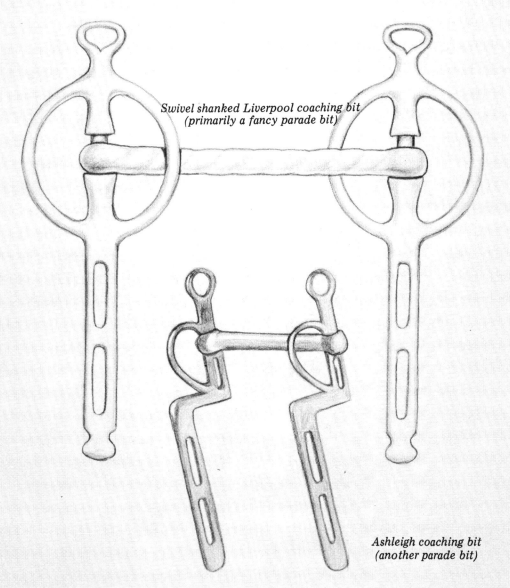

*Swivel shanked Liverpool coaching bit
(primarily a fancy parade bit)*

*Ashleigh coaching bit
(another parade bit)*

Fig. 74

BITS

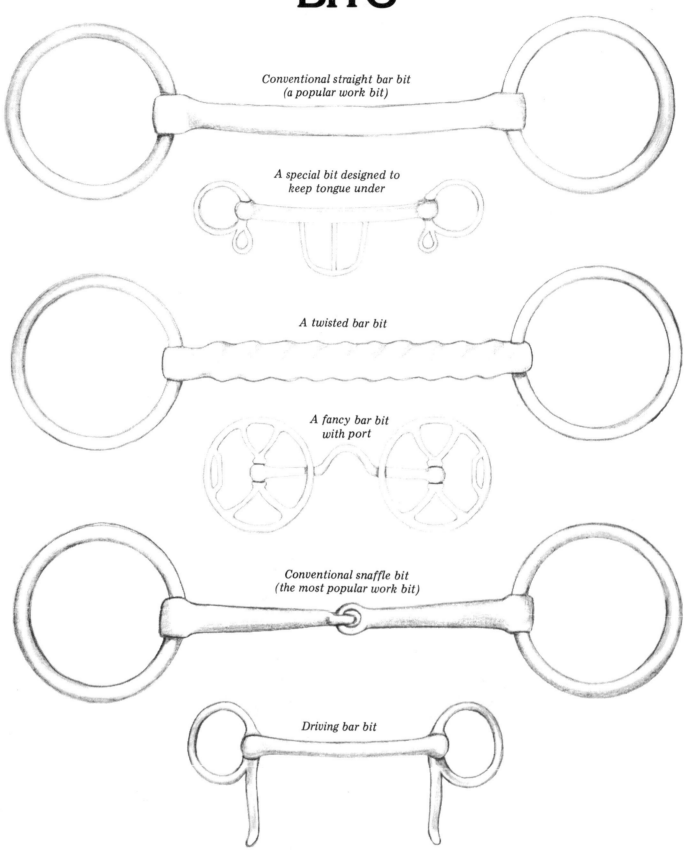

Conventional straight bar bit
(a popular work bit)

A special bit designed to
keep tongue under

A twisted bar bit

A fancy bar bit
with port

Conventional snaffle bit
(the most popular work bit)

Driving bar bit

Fig. 75

BITS

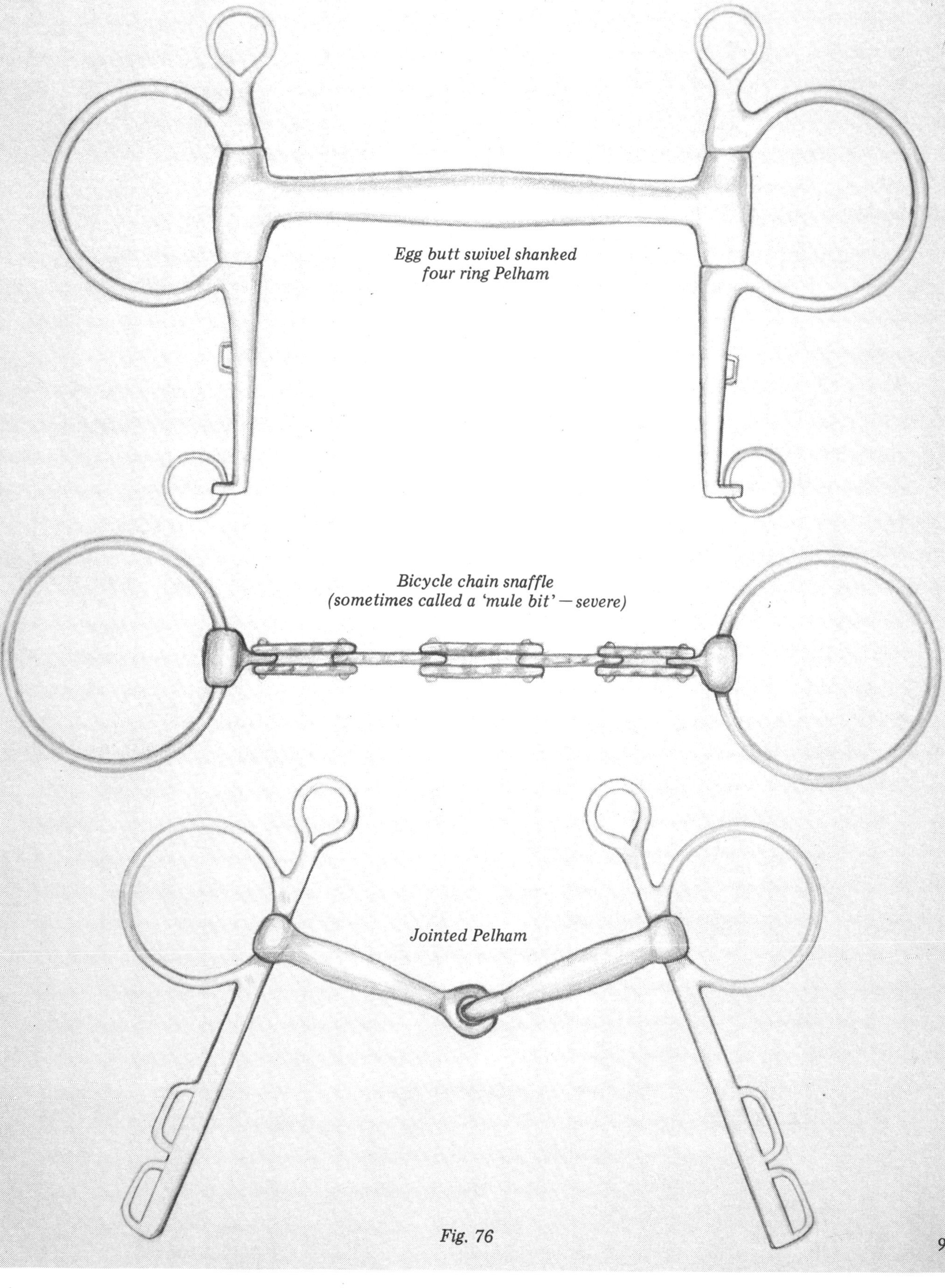

*Egg butt swivel shanked
four ring Pelham*

*Bicycle chain snaffle
(sometimes called a 'mule bit' — severe)*

Jointed Pelham

Fig. 76

Spreaders

It may be desired to have a team of horses walk further apart from each other. This can be accomplished by using line spreaders (see Fig. 77). No adjustment is made in the actual lines. The cross checks are passed through the end of the spreader rather than the inside top hame ring. The spreader itself is fastened near the top of the inside hame of each horse, there being two spreaders commonly used with one team. At times teamsters will get fancy and use four spreaders, with two per horse, but this serves no purpose other than decoration. You may have to use a longer neck yoke and double tree if you move your horses further apart, see RIGGING THE HITCH. Spreaders and spreader rings lend themselves readily to fancy design and are used frequently in western harness to dress up the horses.

Center Line Drops

The center line drop is just a large ring, sometimes with a fancy bit of leather design fastened to it, through which both center (cross check) lines pass on their way to the horse's bits, see fig. 148. This is used primarily for fun but it does serve also to keep the lines organized and it is felt by some that it prevents the lines from getting tangled so easily.

Shaft Loops and Hold Back Straps

These are harness part found only on single horse harness that is to be used between shaves. For more information and illustrations see the section on single horses in the RIGGING THE HITCH chapter.

Hardware

References have been made to "D" rings, snaps and conway buckles. These are just a few of the different hardware parts found in harness construction. Included here are some drawings of these parts to help you identify them.

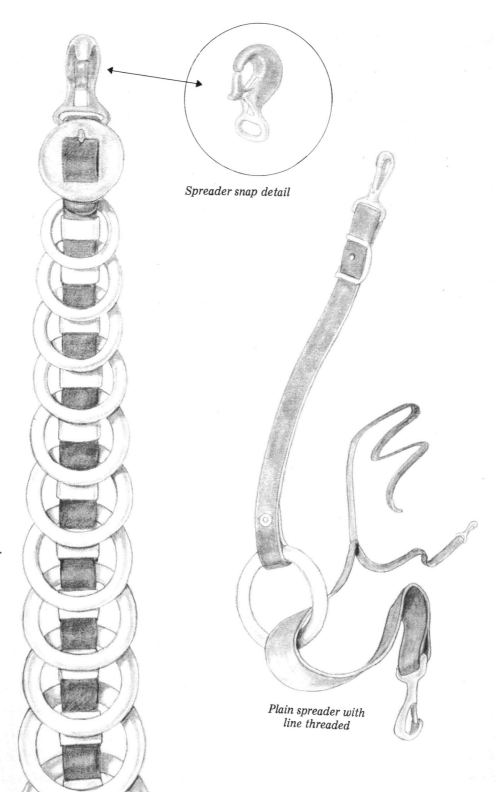

Spreader snap detail

Fancy spreader

Plain spreader with
line threaded

SPREADERS

Fig. 77

HARNESS HARDWARE

Special D ring

Check rein guide

Hip drop ring

Trace carrier

Square D

Hame ring with stud

Line snap

Hame stud

Hame clip rivet-type

Hame clip bolt-type

Hame stud

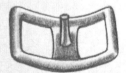
Conway buckle

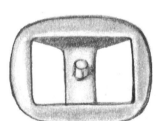
Conway broad-face

Tug chain D

Line-end conway

*Bolt & roller assembly
Breast strap snap*

Breast strap iron

Fig. 78 HARDWARE

HARDWARE & MISC.

Breast strap snap

Tug iron

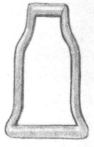

Hame strap guide

Breast strap hame ring

Sweat pad fastener

Fancy hame ball

Plain hame ball

Rivet

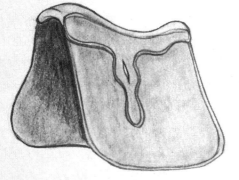

Hame housing

D ring

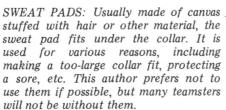

Sweat pad

HAME HOUSING: Usually made of heavy grade leather, these fit over the top of the collar with the hame tops fitting through slits. The housings protect the horses in rain.

SWEAT PADS: Usually made of canvas stuffed with hair or other material, the sweat pad fits under the collar. It is used for various reasons, including making a too-large collar fit, protecting a sore, etc. This author prefers not to use them if possible, but many teamsters will not be without them.

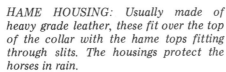

Halter

Fig. 79

BRIDLES

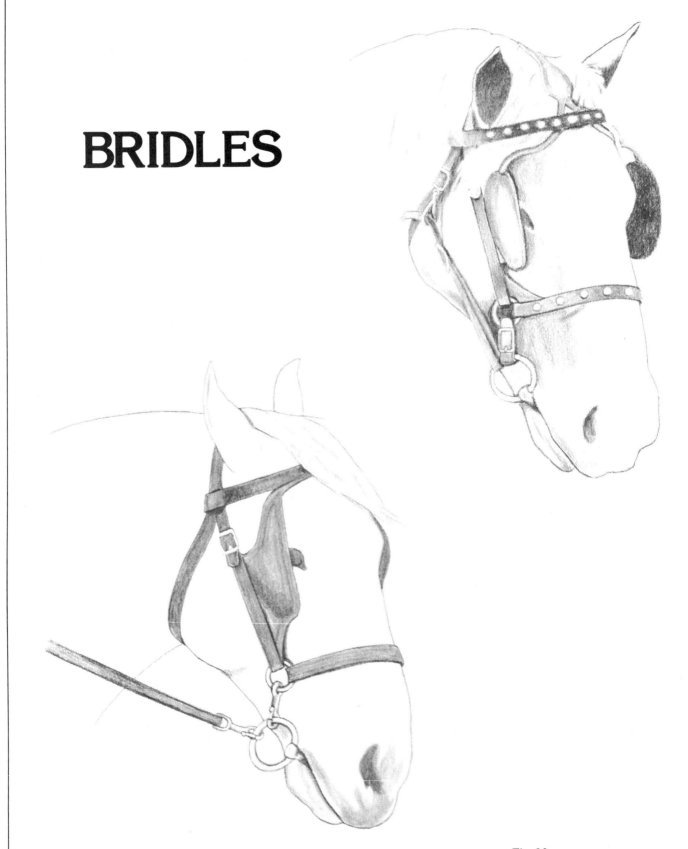

Fig. 80

CHAPTER EIGHT

HARNESSING

The series of illustrations contained in this chapter portray one proper way to harness a horse. There will be individual, cultural and design differences in harnessing procedure. What you have here is a good safe way to begin. There are some practices contained here that would make good habits. It is too easy with a quiet, gentle horse to get used to bad harnessing habits that can cause you trouble when applied to colts or frightened animals.

Something to keep in mind: if you're new to this business, don't try to harness a horse in a tie stall or confined space. If the animal should do anything unexpected you may find yourself in danger.

Fig. a. The first thing to put on the horse is the collar. Most collars open at the top.

Fig. b. The common way to put the collar on the horse is to open the top, being careful to support it from both sides, and put it around the neck. (NOTE: Some teamsters will put the collar on over the head of the horse without opening.)

Fig. c. Approach the horse from the left side. Supporting both sides of the open collar, slip it up and around the neck. Do not let the outside go, as it could drop and crack or break the collar at the windpipe.

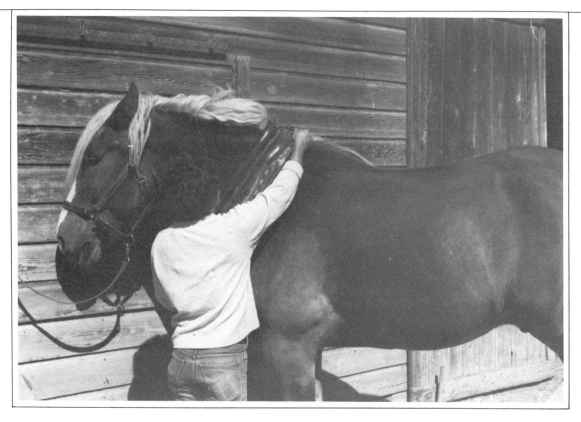

Fig. d. Fasten the top of the collar and pull any mane hair out from under it.

Fig. e. To determine whether or not a collar fits, slide the flat of your hand between the collar and the animal's windpipe. If it is tight for your hand the collar is too small. If there is room for two or three hands it is too big.

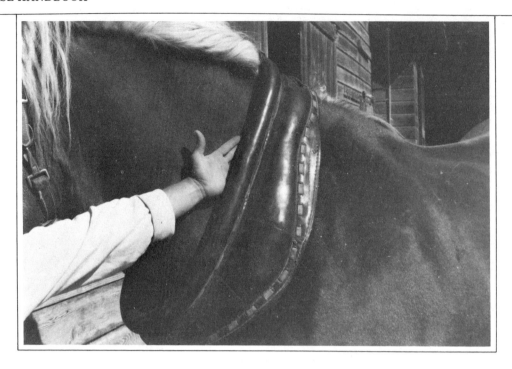

Fig. f. Also check the side of the collar. There should be just barely enough room for a couple of fingers to slide in between the neck and the collar.

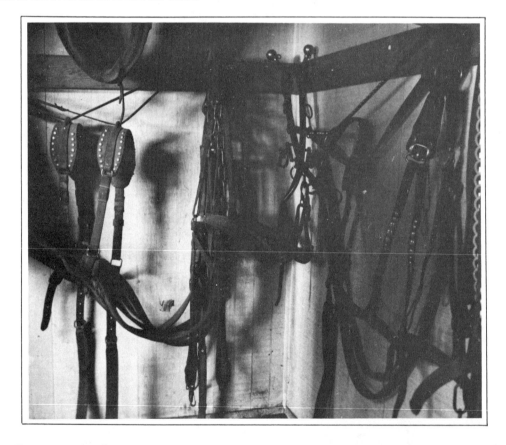

Fig. g. The harness in storage should hang with the hames on the left side as you face it. To pick up the harness, pass your right arm under the top center of the hip-drop assembly and on forward under the back pad. With your left hand, put the hip-drop assembly up on your right shoulder. Do the same, if possible, with the back pad. Now pass your right arm on a little farther and take hold of the right hame. With your left hand, grab the left hame and lift the harness.

Fig. h. Carry the harness. By lifting the right hame high, you should be separating the harness' left and right sides.

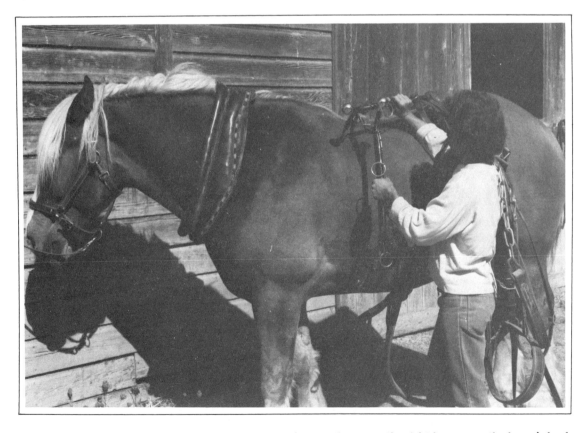

Fig. i. With the right hame high, and with the horse's attention, pass the right hame over the horse's back.

Fig. j. Pass the hames on over the collar while still carrying the bulk of the harness on the right shoulder.

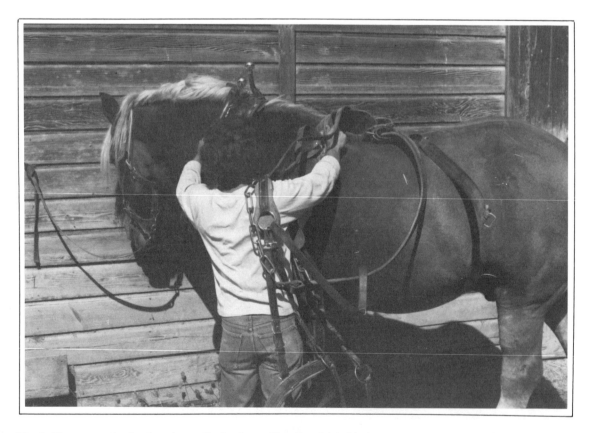

Fig. k. Now, pass the back pad over the back working the right side tug over . . . .

Fig. l. . . . and finally, the hip-drop assembly and brichen. Leave the harness on top of the back until positioning and securing the hames.

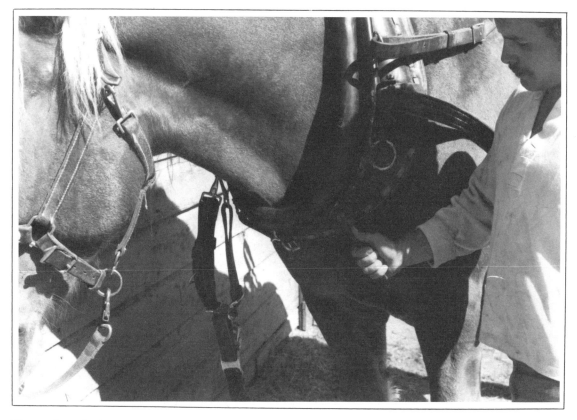

Fig. m. Seat the hames in the collar groove. (The top hame strap should remain fastened and the bottom strap is used in harnessing and unharnessing.) Make sure the hames are centered on the collar so that the point of draft (where the tug fastens) is correct and equal on both sides. Then fasten the hame strap . . . .

Fig. n. . . . and make sure it is tight.

Fig. o. After the hames are secured, pull the harness back and in the right position with the brichen down over the tail.

Fig. p. Pull the tail out of the brichen.

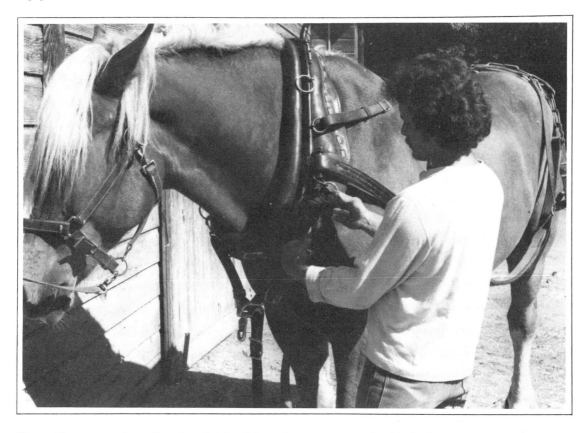

Fig. q. If you are using a "western brichen" team harness, snap or buckle the breast strap into the bottom hame ring of the left side.

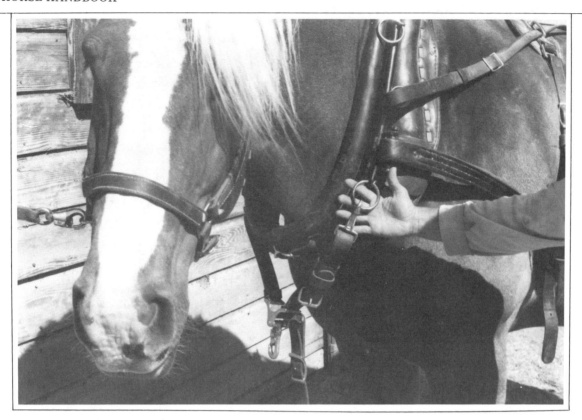

Fig. r. (Showing the breast strap snapped.)

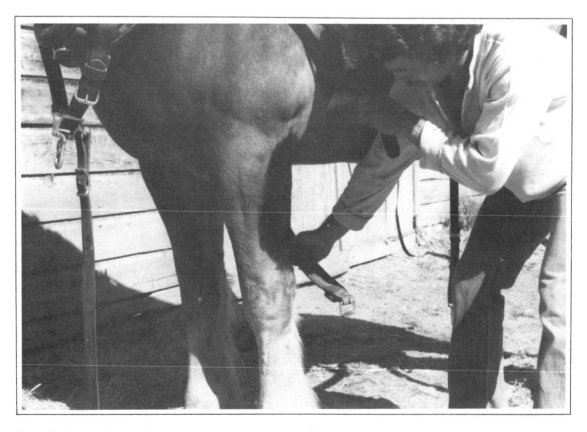

Fig. s. Pull the belly band across . . . .

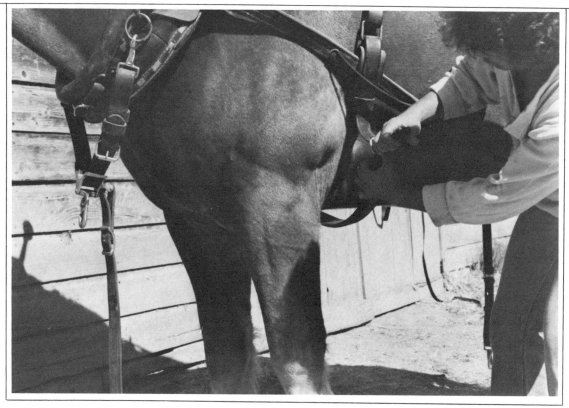

Fig. t. . . . and buckle it into the billet with slack.

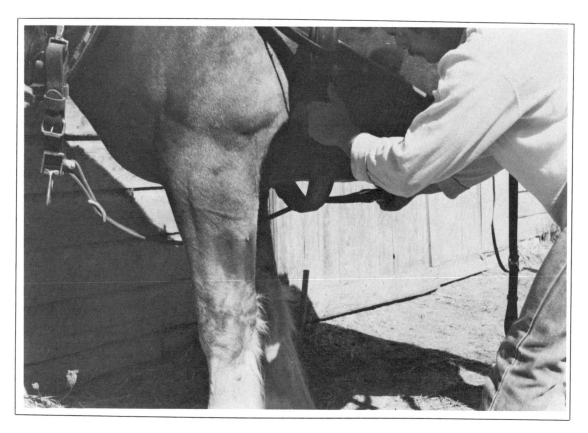

Fig. u. Then pull the pole strap over the belly band. (NOTE: In some harnesses the belly band passes through a loop in the pole strap, see HARNESS chapter.)

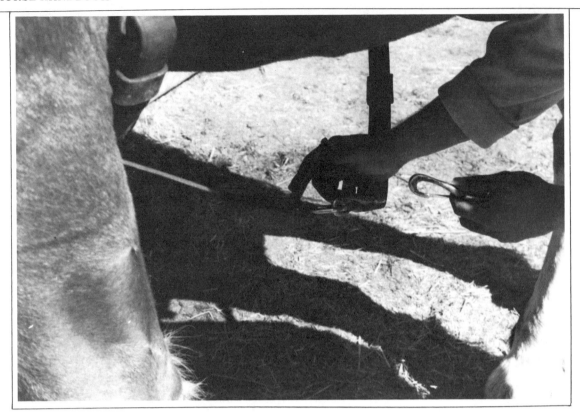

Fig. v. Snap the quarter straps (one from each side) into the end of the pole strap.

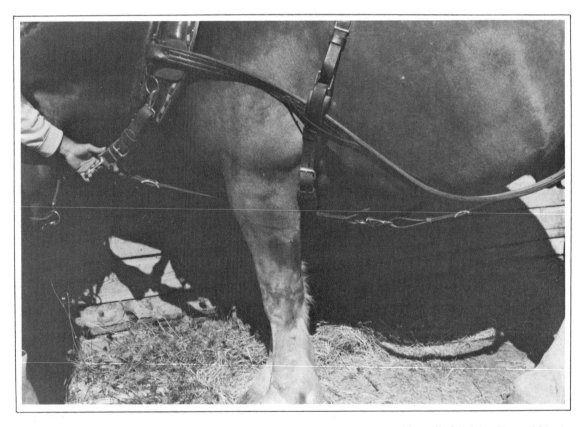

Fig. w. This illustrates the breast strap, pole strap and quarter strap assembly pulled tight as it would be in backing.

Fig. x. Hold the top of the bridle with your right hand spreading it to fit the width of the horse's head. With the thumb and forefinger of the left hand, hold the bit wide and position it to go into the horse's mouth.

Fig. y. Pulling up the bridle with the right hand, put the bit into the horse's mouth. If the animal hesitates to take the bit, place thumb and forefinger in opposite corners of the mouth and gently press. The mouth should open for the bit. (NOTE: Be careful not to put a frozen or extremely cold bit into the animal's mouth.)

To unharness: Remove the bridle and put a halter on the horse, tying him up. Unsnap the quarter straps, unbuckle the belly band, unsnap the breast strap left side and unbuckle the bottom hame strap. The harness should be free. Be careful not to let the harness fall off, backwards, as it could spook, especially a green horse. If you're in a tight tie stall be slow, calm and cautious in taking off the harness. The collar is the last thing to come off and once again care must be taken to support both sides. It is a good practice to buckle the collar back together as soon as it is taken off the horse. Also, when storing always hang upside down. The best time to clean a collar is immediately after being taken from the horse; wipe with a rag and neats-foot oil.

HARNESSING CHECKLIST

1. Always speak to the horse before approaching from the rear.

2. Check horse's shoulder for lumps or galls. Check inside collar surfaces. Make sure surface is clean. Put on collar, being careful to support both sides. Make sure collar fits properly.

3. Put on harness. Attach hame strap first. Make sure hame strap is tight. Buckle belly band. If brichen harness, attach pole strap, quarter straps and breast strap.

4. Put on bridle. Make sure bit fits properly and both ears are through.

5. Attach driving lines with snaps facing out.

6. Double-check all straps and lines.

>   *If hitching two or more horses, make sure lines are properly set and snapped to bit rings.*

>   *With used harness, all parts MUST be strong. These are expected results if certain parts should break:*

>>   *One bit strap breaks — bit falls from mouth, loss of control, unable to stop or turn horse.*
>>   *Any part of lines break — same results as above. May be able to turn horse(s) in one direction.*
>>   *Hame strap breaks — harness is pulled back off horse, likely to result in wreck.*
>>   *Pole strap, quarter strap or breast strap breaks — unable to back up vehicle, unable to prevent vehicle from rolling up on horse's heels.*
>>   *Belly band breaks — may cause horse to balk on heavy pull.*
>>   *Tug breaks during pull — horse falls forward and down, might cause injury to horse.*

>   *All of the above parts should be carefully checked when considering the purchase of used harness.*

CHAPTER NINE

HITCH GEAR

In this photo, taken at a Plowing Demonstration on the Thomas Ranch in Waitsburg, Washington, you see (top left) eight mules, (top right) six horses, (and center) four horses.
Photo by Lynn Miller

So you've got some willing horses or mules or ponies or donkeys in harness and you want to go to work. The next thing or in between things, you need are the *Hitch Gear*. This chapter features illustrations of all manner of hitch equipment with basic descriptions of function. Some of them won't make sense to you until you get into the next chapters and see how they fit together to get the job done.

There are cultural differences and individual inventions which aren't illustrated here. However, these illustrations coupled with the information in the next (and previous) chapters should give you a sound understanding of the principles (and possibilities).

NECK YOKES

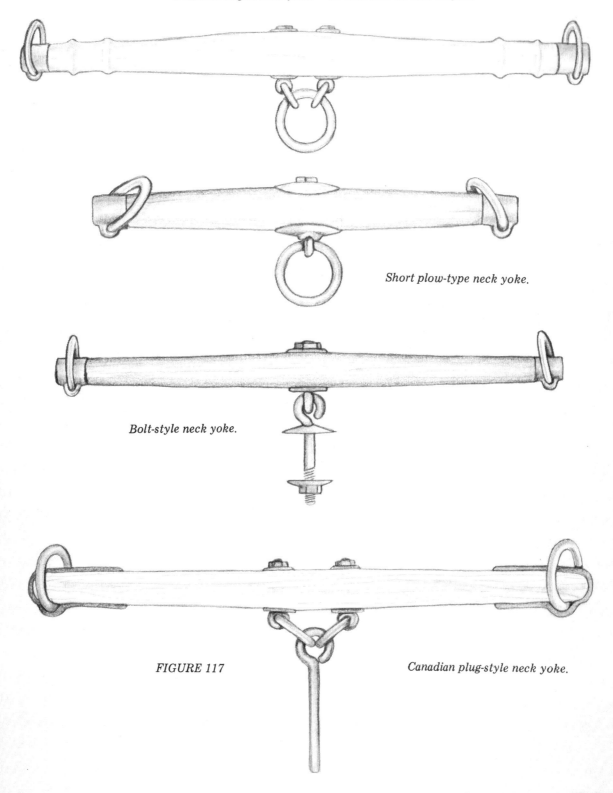

Standard wagon neck yoke — 38 inch and 42 inch lengths.

Short plow-type neck yoke.

Bolt-style neck yoke.

FIGURE 117

Canadian plug-style neck yoke.

HITCH GEAR

Singletree standard dimensions are 26, 28, 30, 36 and 38 inches with the longer dimensions being for wagon use.

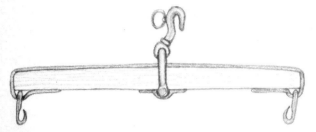 

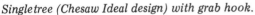

Singletree (Chesaw Ideal design) with grab hook.   *End-iron style singletree.*

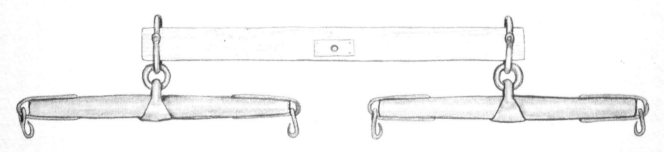

Wagon doubletree set with stay chain clevises. Standard wagon doubletree lengths are 42, 46 and 48 inches.

Narrow plow-type doubletrees are 36 to 40 inches in length.

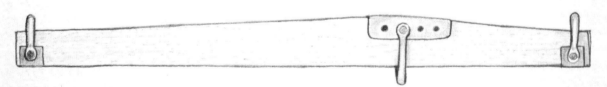

Three horse evener is 50 to 54 inches in length depending on the length of doubletree used. Hitch point is 1/3 over.

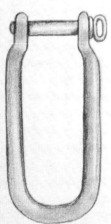 

Standard clevis.   *Swivel (plow-hitch) clevis.*

FIGURE 118

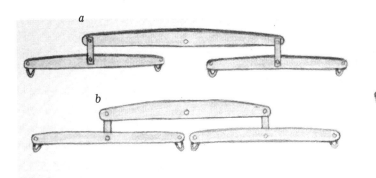

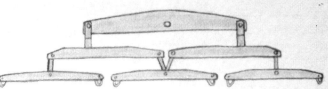

f & g) *Three abreast eveners steel-type.*

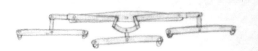

a & b) *Steel doubletrees, wagon (above), mower/plow-type (below).*

c) *Steel tripletree for a wheel evener in multiple hitch.*

h) *Wooden three abreast evener.*

FIGURE 119

i) *Three abreast evener for wagon hitch.*

d) *Four abreast evener steel-type.*

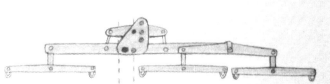

j) *Four abreast evener steel-type.*

e) *Five abreast evener steel-type.*

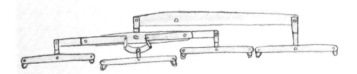

k) *Six abreast evener steel-type.*

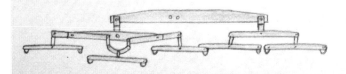

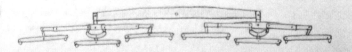

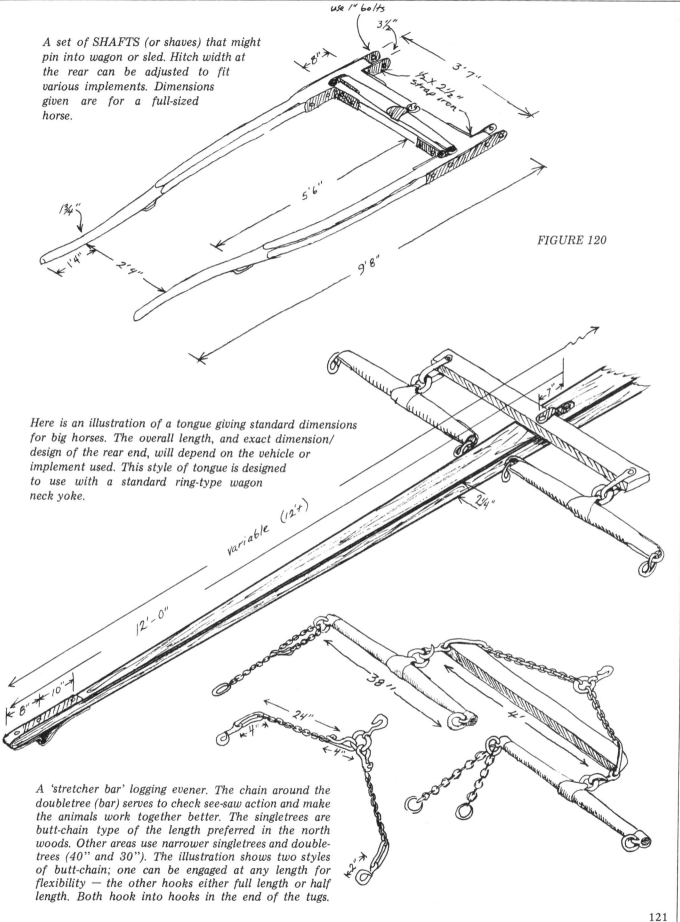

A set of SHAFTS (or shaves) that might pin into wagon or sled. Hitch width at the rear can be adjusted to fit various implements. Dimensions given are for a full-sized horse.

use 1" bolts

3½"

8"

3'7"

½ X 2½" strap iron

5'6"

1¾"

1'4"

2'4"

9'8"

FIGURE 120

Here is an illustration of a tongue giving standard dimensions for big horses. The overall length, and exact dimension/design of the rear end, will depend on the vehicle or implement used. This style of tongue is designed to use with a standard ring-type wagon neck yoke.

7"

variable (12'+)

2¼"

12'-0"

8" 10"

38"

24"

4"

4"

4'

2"

A 'stretcher bar' logging evener. The chain around the doubletree (bar) serves to check see-saw action and make the animals work together better. The singletrees are butt-chain type of the length preferred in the north woods. Other areas use narrower singletrees and doubletrees (40" and 30"). The illustration shows two styles of butt-chain; one can be engaged at any length for flexibility — the other hooks either full length or half length. Both hook into hooks in the end of the tugs.

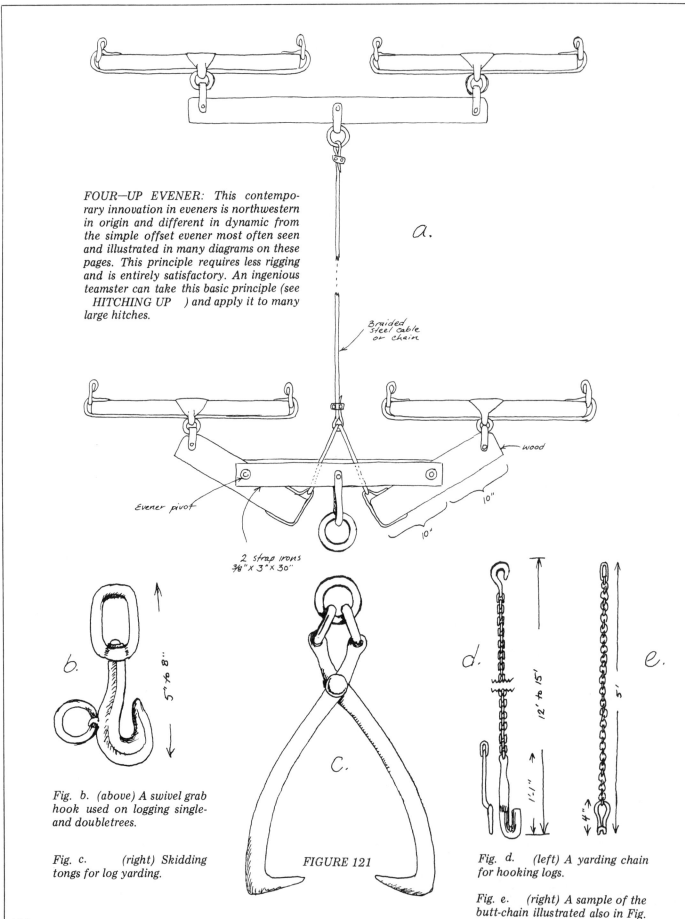

FOUR—UP EVENER: This contemporary innovation in eveners is northwestern in origin and different in dynamic from the simple offset evener most often seen and illustrated in many diagrams on these pages. This principle requires less rigging and is entirely satisfactory. An ingenious teamster can take this basic principle (see HITCHING UP) and apply it to many large hitches.

a.

Braided steel cable or chain

wood

Evener pivot

10"

10"

2 strap irons ⅜" x 3" x 30"

b.

5' to 8'

c.

FIGURE 121

d.

12' to 15'

1'-1"

e.

5'

4"

Fig. b. (above) A swivel grab hook used on logging single- and doubletrees.

Fig. c. (right) Skidding tongs for log yarding.

Fig. d. (left) A yarding chain for hooking logs.

Fig. e. (right) A sample of the butt-chain illustrated also in Fig.

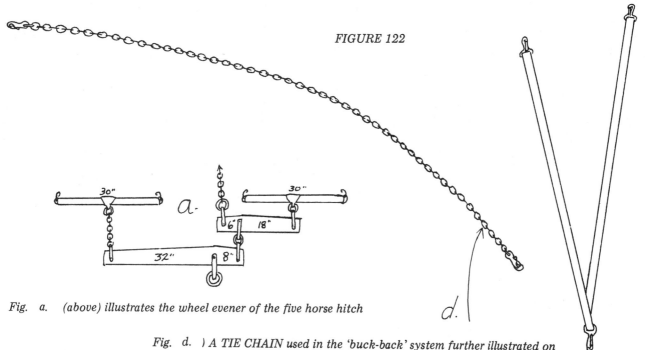

FIGURE 122

Fig. a.   (above) illustrates the wheel evener of the five horse hitch

Fig. d.   ) A TIE CHAIN used in the 'buck-back' system further illustrated on these pages. This chain snaps into the halter of a wheel or swing horse and goes forward and hooks into the trace or evener ahead. In this manner the animal is "led" where the leaders are driven.

Fig. b.   (below) shows the wheel evener of a 3 x 3 six-up

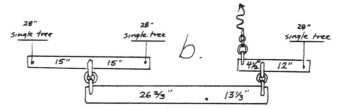

These evener illustrations are given to explain the "offset" principle which works like a common see-saw that is moved to allow a light person to equal the weight of a heavier person. These eveners equalize the load so that all animals must pull equal.

Fig. c.   (below) illustrates the wheel hitch of a basic four-up plow hitch.

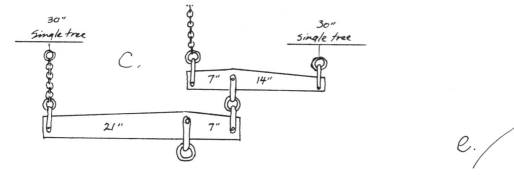

Fig. e.   ) A BUCK-BACK STRAP. This item is best illustrated in the next chapter in the multiple hitch illustrations. It snaps into both sides of the bit on the same animal and then runs back to snap into the adjoining animals' trace or to the lead chain. In this manner, the "bucked-back" horse is prevented from moving ahead unless the hitch does.

This is a steel fabricated singletree.

This is a wooden standard style singletree.

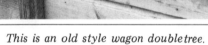

This is an old style wagon doubletree.

This is a Chesaw Ideal (new) pulling doubletree.

This is a steel (center hitch) tripletree.

FIGURE 123

CHAPTER TEN
PRINCIPLES OF DRIVING FOR WORK

Photo by Scott Duff

Driving the horse is, in its finest sense, the true reward of understanding, trust and communication between the animal(s) and the teamster. Driving the horse, in its worst sense, is tricking and/or forcing a caged or bound, sometimes terrified, animal into unwanted activity. That represents a world of difference and there is, of course, a whole range of variations in between. For the beginner must come the realization and understanding that he or she is fully half (if not more) responsible for this potential relationship with the draft

Photo by Nancy Roberts

animal. The difficult aspect for most people to accept is that the animal is also half (if not more) responsible for this potential relationship. It is for this reason that the author makes this strong recommendation:

> The beginnner should place a premium on those qualities in a work horse which will make a safe and trusting introduction into driving for work. Experience, training, quiet docile temperament are all qualities to look for. These qualities should be looked for in the previous handler/owner of the animals as much as in the animal because this is good indication that the apparent character of the horse runs deep or shallow.

> If the animal seems quiet to a fault with no spunk and if the teamster brags loudly of his skill and the tricks and abuse he has used — be suspicious. If you but know how to translate, most anyone selling a horse will tell you all you need to know even without wanting to.

No matter how quiet, willing and well-trained a horse might be (whether old or young), an inexperienced teamster, with the best of intentions, can ruin the animal in a very short time. Consider this: if you were deep-sea diving for years without mishap and one day almost drown because a newcomer on the boat fouled up the rigging — how would you feel about going right back down again, leaving your life in those same hands again? The same feelings are true for the horse in harness. This is the reason that the beginner cannot afford to jump into driving horses without having an experienced teamster around at first. No amount of information from magazines or books will ever convey to the unitiated the incredible subtlety and fine balance required of a good teamster. That will only come, slowly, of experience tempered by careful observation. If a beginner or interested person has the opportunity to attend a draft horse driving clinic, school or workshop it is in their best interests to do so. It is in such a setting that they should get guidance during those critical first moments.

Hopefully your first experiences will be positive (without unnecessary accidents), and you will quickly begin to absorb a reserve of natural responses and reflexes that will serve you in your work with horses.

Remembering back to this author's first times with driving lines in hand: the first thought is of the awkwardness of the process. That is oversimplifying the experience because so many feelings pass through simultaneously, such as: the evasive simplicity of the process, clumsiness, power, maybe a hint of terror, a frustrating feeling of being totally lost — so many feelings and they all serve to confuse the learning process.

The only way to successfully communicate how to drive horses is to try to convey what the animal goes through, feels, sees, is asked to respond to.

Try to put yourself in the animal's position. First of all, realize that you do not speak the same language as this stranger you must deal with. You are in a leather suit of straps with a piece of cold steel in your mouth, and probably, leather flaps restricting your vision. The steel in your mouth seems to have differing pressure, a pressure which apparently corresponds to the two leather straps connected to either end of the steel (bit). You get an array of signals; confusing voice commands, maybe a slap of the leather straps (lines), maybe some pressure on both ends of the bit — maybe one side, maybe none. From all of this you somehow figure out that a forward motion is expected. Now, back up a minute . . . .

If you, as a so-called thinking human, actually had to go through such a process would you:

1. Be "willing" to cooperate;
2. Be able to "figure out" (reason) what is expected of you?

This author will forever be amazed at the depth of the horse's inherent willingness and ability. (And equally amazed at humanity's inability and shortsightedness when it comes to the relationship with horses.)

BE SENSITIVE — THINK — DESIRE COOPERATION

PERFECT TENSION

Imagine (before doing) that the horse has a bit in its mouth and you have two leather ribbons (lines), one in each hand which attach directly to the sides of the bit. Obviously, if you pull back with both hands you apply equal pressure by way of the bit to the horse's mouth. If you pull back with the right line you will be pulling on the right side of the bit and vice versa for the left side. If you slack up on the lines the bit should ride loose in the horse's mouth. So the horse's mouth is working as a signal point, relaying to the animal, from your hands — through the lines — by way of the bit, a signal that should result in a desired maneuver.

Fig. 126) Dave McCoy carefully guides his horses through a log skid competition course.

Fig. 127) Dale Greenough speaks to his horses with the lines.   Photos by Nancy Roberts

Fig. 128) Ray Drongesen driving his team on a mower. Ray is an example of that group of master teamsters that the novice should try to get to know. Careful observation of such artists with horses will do no less than convince you that this is either easier or harder than it looks. It is indeed a subtle craft and the most successful craftsmen are those who are sensitive to the animals and the process.   Photo by Christene George

The horse's mouth is sensitive, just like yours. If the animal's mouth is required to take a great deal of abusive, hard, jerking pressure from the teamster it will result initially in sores and cuts and ultimately in callouses and desensitized tissue. So, in time, a horse will be incapable of reaction to subtle pressures. The horse will become "hardmouthed".

If there is no pressure from the lines, the horse will be confused about desired maneuvers and a mess will result. Loose lines also make it difficult for the teamster to respond quickly, if necessary, to problems. And third, loose lines stand a good chance of getting tangled in some other part of the harness. The teamster, then, must find a delicate balance of just enough line pressure if optimum performance is the goal. And to achieve that "perfect tension" when actually driving is a difficult task as each change in motion and direction requires a sensitive give and take with the lines. As the animal moves, to maintain an always even tension, without abusing the horse's mouth, requires that the teamster use the arms like soft shock absorbers or springs or hydraulic cylinders always moving to find balance.

To illustrate what is meant we'll go through the steps of ground driving a single horse and then ground driving a team of horses.

GROUND DRIVING THE SINGLE HORSE

Use a well-schooled and experienced horse and have a teamster handy to help. Since this is an exercise and no vehicles or load will be pulled or drawn, the type of harness involved does not matter much. With a bridle and bit in place and with collar and hames set up properly (see *Harnessing* chapter), snap or buckle one single line to the right side bit ring and pass the line through the top right side hame ring and on back. Do the same with the left side. With the right line in the right hand and the left line in the left hand, stand well back of the horse and take up the lines so that there is only a little slack (NEVER allow a belly in the lines). Give a verbal command to go. (Do not slap the horse with the lines unless as a last resort to prevent balking.)[1] As the horse steps ahead, find an even tension for both lines and maintain it. Be careful, however, not to hold the lines too short or pull back too soon as the horse first steps ahead because you could stop him before he gets started and further confuse signals later. So, as the horse walks, practice pulling in a little with one line while letting the other line out an equal amount. Watch how the horse turns to follow its head. Now pull back both lines steadily and say "whoa" in a clear, firm voice (no need to shout). The horse should stop. When the horse stops let up on the pressure to both lines. To make the horse back, pull on both lines evenly and say "back". Hopefully, you will understand why to slack up on the lines after the animal has stopped. The novice will often end up stopping a horse only to find the animal backing up. If you want to stop, just remember to slack up on the lines after the animal quits its forward motion (at the whoa command).

Now back to the driving. Try this exercise. With an even tension (no slack) give the command to go and stay behind the animal but moving slightly to the right. Do not "steer", just walk, maintaining an even firm tension on the lines and passing, while behind the animal, to the right side. The horse should be making a slow, steady left turn as you stay behind the animal (moving right). This exercise should give you the physical sense of how subtle the turning process actually is. It should not be necessary to yank an animal over to make a turn.

Another exercise is to pull the left line slightly and let out an equal amount of right line — the animal should turn left. Then try a right turn. Now all this may seem too basic. The real test is to draw two lines 30 inches apart and 20 feet long. Then in another area set 4 pylons 4 feet apart. Now ground drive the single horse "straight" down between the two lines and then weave the pylons (as illustrated), driving the animal exactly where you want to go. It will sound simple. It will BE difficult the first time. You will probably hold one or

---

[1] The TV western notion of slapping standing horses with the lines and hollering to get them to go is an insensitive and exaggerated myth. It is a bad habit for beginning teamsters and should be avoided with a fervor. For an explanation of why it is bad: imagine what you are doing by conditioning the animal to go whenever it feels a slap on the back and/or a holler. There are any number of possible situations where an unwanted "signal" to go will fall on them, whether it is a branch in the woods or a neighbor's pat of the hand. It is infinitely better to develop a full vocabulary of easily understood words and to trust the animal's great ability to understand them and respond to them. Also remember that the horse has an acute sense of hearing, so you need not yell all the while. As you develop your vocabulary with the horse you will also be developing a unique set of "keys" to your power system.

Fig. 129) A simple single horse driving exercise.

both of the lines too tight or too loose and the horse won't go where you want to go. Don't blame the horse; he's only following your instruction (or making his judgment of a mass of confusing signals). If things don't work right, stop and try to understand what you're doing wrong. Practice ground driving until you at least have some measure of respect for what you don't know and an appreciation for how much understanding the horse is capable of.

GROUND DRIVING THE TEAM

With an experienced teamster plus two well-schooled harnessed horses accustomed to working together, set up the driving lines as explained and illustrated in *Rigging the Hitch* (this text). Take up the lines, left in left hand — right in right hand, and step well back of the team. Take up any slack in the lines and give a verbal command to go, allowing the lines to come to a perfect tension in your hands. As the horses move ahead just try to maintain perfect tension and keep the team moving straight as an arrow. Then pull both lines back steady and say "whoa". The team should stop and you should slack off on the lines. With even tension on the lines ask the team to "back". Then ask the team to go ahead again, this time carefully navigating a right turn. Pull in on the right line and slack up the same amount on the left line. Notice that the right lines go to the right side of the bits on both horses (and vice versa left). Now try a left turn. As you drive, practice keeping your arms out ahead of you in a comfortable position. This allows room for you to stop or turn the horses quickly if necessary. IF YOUR ARMS ARE AGAINST YOUR BODY AND THERE IS SLACK IN THE LINES YOU ARE COMPLETELY OUT OF CONTROL, NO MATTER HOW THE HORSES ARE PERFORMING!

The novice will experience a hesitation about allowing the lines to pass through the hands or in taking in line. Fig.130 illustrates a simple maneuver for taking in slack while making a turn. It may seem unnecessary to explain such a simple thing, but when the novice, no matter how high the IQ, is lost in a panic of a new moment, the most basic of instructions is vital.

It takes only a moment for the beginner to feel the difference between the single horse and the team. Hopefully, the beginner will acquire a special respect for those reasons why first experiences should be had in the company of a skilled teamster.

Fig. 130) These photographs demonstrate a simple cross-over maneuver for gathering in lines. When one line is slack . . . .

Fig. 131) . . . reach across, with other line in hand, and take hold of both lines.

Fig. 132) Now pull up the slack, with the one hand holding both lines . . . .

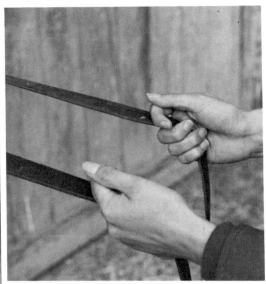

Fig. 133) . . . and take hold of the lines, one to each hand.

Fig. 134) Or you can simply cross over and pull the slack through your hand.

Ground driving, photos of the author and his Belgians by Nancy Roberts.

Dan Kintz "speaks" to his pulling team without talking, using "perfect tension" for a winning combination. Dan is one of the best northwestern teamsters.   *Both photos by Nancy Roberts*

Willard Wilder skillfully guides six Percherons in a Draft Horse Festival show entry with Bill Dean, draft horse auctioneer, riding.

COMMANDS

We've spoken of giving the command to go. You will develop a habit for that sound or word or phrase which is most comfortable. Suggestions include a short whistle, a kissing noise exaggerated, a clicking or clucking noise (and "giddeeup" seldom works unless the individual animal has been used to it).

It is a good habit to say "Whoa -BACK" to standing animals for a backing command as they may not hear the simple "back" and feel the tension on the lines and get a crossed signal. For this reason make sure that the animals are listening: LOOK AT THE EARS!

"GEE" (as in gee whiz) is the universal English-American command for right turn. "HAW" is the command for left turn.

It is always a good idea to speak to the animals by name often. Before giving any command, WATCH THE HORSE'S EARS and MAKE CERTAIN ALL ANIMALS ARE LISTENING and EARS ARE FACING BACK.

After you work horses for a few years you will be surprised to find that they can understand and follow a variety of simple verbal commands.

HANDS HOLDING LINES

We spoke early in this chapter about the need to be sensitive about the bit in the animal's mouth and how you apply pressure. If you listen to teamsters and read what literature is available you will find passing (and reverent) reference to old so-and-so's "hands". It is a high compliment to say a teamster has good hands. The best teamsters control hitches of any size with the slightest of pressure and a soft, sure voice. It is a finesse. But to say a teamster has "good hands" is misleading. What is meant ultimately is that the good teamster is a sensitive human who is always culturing that sensitivity and never taking certain procedures for granted.

When driving with two lines, whether it be a single horse, two or whatever, there are three natural positions for holding lines (see Fig.139); over the hand, under the hand and between the first two fingers. The latter will more closely approximate, in the teamster's hand, what the bit feels like in the horse's mouth. And it is just such an "earned" empathy which serves to build that particular sensitivity of which we speak.

As was said at the beginning of this chapter, driving can and should be the reward of a special kind of teamwork between teamster and animal(s). But that's up to you. If you find you must force your way in this craft you will tire of it quickly and never appreciate the possibilities and the beauty.

Fig. 139) Holding lines over the fingers and under the thumb. This position is a second choice as it is moderately sensitive.

Fig. 140) Holding lines between first two fingers. This is the first choice position as the teamster "feels" in his hand more closely an approximation of what the bit "feels" like in the horse's mouth.

Fig. 141) Holding lines under the hand. This position is the least sensitive and used where the greatest leverage or force is needed.

CHAPTER ELEVEN
RIGGING THE HITCH

Fig. 142) A grade draft horse hitched single to a cart using a basic brichen farm harness. Ray Drongesen driving with Juliet and Ian riding.   *Photo Christene George*

This chapter illustrates the configurations and positioning of fourteen different hitches. Actual hitching-up procedures are covered in the next chapter. The information in this chapter should serve in an unintentioned way to impart a sense of the great flexibility of true horse power. The teamster, for instance, with four horses, has the possibility of four single horses each hitched separately, one single and a unicorn hitch, two singles plus a team, or two teams. In other words, with additional teamsters to drive, the four horses can be hitched more than twelve ways, culminating in four abreast or four-up. Try to imagine taking one large tractor and dividing it into four little ones as the need arises.

In North America the team (two horses hitched abreast), is the most popular hitch with the single being a long second. In the British Isles, the opposite is true, with singles being the most popular hitch. With so many small farms taking to the use of one horse or mule, there may be a change in view in North America.

THE SINGLE HORSE

Without going into all the possible derivations in single horse harness, let's just say that the same basic harness used for teams will work for single with minor modification. First of all, if the horse will be drawing something other than a wheeled vehicle it will probably not need a braking system to the harness. A cruper harness would suffice for work such as cultivating, plowing, logging, etc. A brichen harness would be necessary for wagon or cart work or anything which required that the load be prevented from rolling or skidding upon the horse.

A cruper (plow) harness (see Fig. 61) consists of all the basic parts with the exception of the brichen/quarter strap assembly. "Cruper" refers to the strap which fastens around the tail head to secure the harness from sliding off to one side or the other. A brichen harness (see Fig. 59) includes the brichen/quarter strap assembly which functions (whether used team or single) as the braking and backing system.

The driving lines for a single horse consist of two single leather lines, 1" to 1¼" in width and anywhere from 18' to 24' in length, with either snaps or buckles at one end of each line. The bridle and hames used for a single horse are the same as that used for a team. I recommend that you have two spreader-type straps with a ring in one end and a snap at the other end. The strap should be anywhere from 4" to 14" in length. I call these "line keepers".

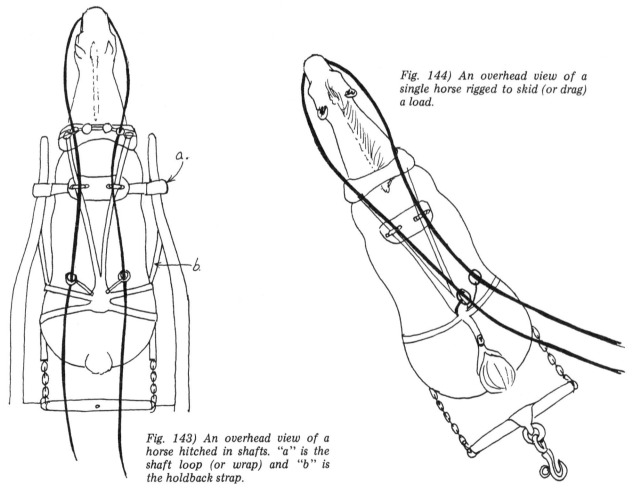

Fig. 144) An overhead view of a single horse rigged to skid (or drag) a load.

Fig. 143) An overhead view of a horse hitched in shafts. "a" is the shaft loop (or wrap) and "b" is the holdback strap.

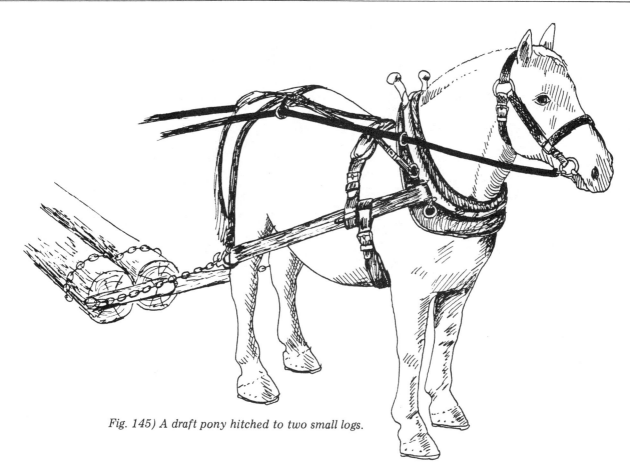

Fig. 145) A draft pony hitched to two small logs.

Whether you use a cruper or a brichen harness, the lines are set up the same. I should mention that a brichen type harness can be used for all types of work, whereas the cruper style has its limitations. Also in a brichen style team harness, a breast strap and a pole strap are used for the neck yoke assembly. In single horse work these parts are not necessary. If the horse is to be used to pull a two wheeled cart with a heavy load front of the axle center, then it will be important to make sure that the back pad is sufficiently large and clean of sharp or uncomfortable edges. A little padding in the back pad might even help. The back pad should sit right where a saddle normally would, directly behind the withers of the horse. The reason for all this concern is that with the horse between the shafts all the front weight of a two wheeled vehicle is pushing square down upon the back pad, the weight being transferred down the shafts through the shaft loops to the back pad.

In North America, teams of horses are hitched to wheeled vehicles with a single tongue or pole extending forward from the vehicle and between the two horses. This tongue or pole is attached to the horse's braking and backing system usually by way of a neck yoke. When hitching a single horse to a wheeled vehicle, the horse is placed between two poles, or what are referred to here as shafts, which extend from the front axle forward. As with the wagon tongue, when the shafts are turned from side to side, the vehicle also turns. To be of proper length, the shafts should not extend beyond the front of the horse when hitched. Obviously, there is great variation in length of shafts depending on the size of horse used. Same thing is true of the distance between the shafts. Most buggies are set up to be pulled by 1000 lb. trotting horses and a 2000 lb. draft horse won't fit between the shafts. Modifications can be made to allow that bigger or smaller horses be hitched to any vehicle.

(above) A photo of a French-Canadian draft stallion hitched, in breast strap harness, to a buggy at the Upper Canada Village in Ontario.　　　　　*Photo by Lynn Miller*

(above) A Percheron working a horse power (gear drive) which powers a drag saw for cutting cord wood.
Photo by Lynn Miller

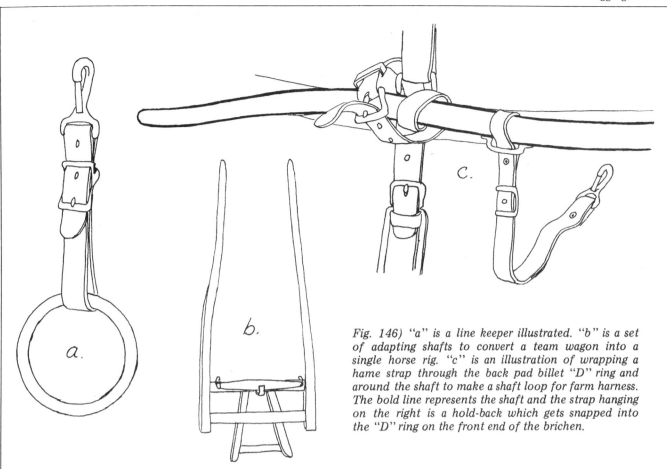

Fig. 146) "a" is a line keeper illustrated. "b" is a set of adapting shafts to convert a team wagon into a single horse rig. "c" is an illustration of wrapping a hame strap through the back pad billet "D" ring and around the shaft to make a shaft loop for farm harness. The bold line represents the shaft and the strap hanging on the right is a hold-back which gets snapped into the "D" ring on the front end of the brichen.

The harness required for a horse between shafts can be especially designed for the purpose, fancy or plain, or it can simply be a farm brichen harness with a few extra straps. The basic hitching principle remains the same. The shafts, one on either side of the horse, are held up either by passing through leather shaft loops which attach down from the back pad and over the tug, or can be strapped in the same position with two hame straps attached to the "D" rings at the end of the belly band and back pad billets (see Fig. 146c). Next, "holdback" straps are attached to the end rings of the brichen. These serve as the braking and backing system. The holdback strap is attached to the shaft just back of where the "shaft loops" go. The attachment usually consists of a metal loop fastened to the underside of the shaft. An adjustable strap, about the length of a harness quarter strap, passes through the loop and around the shaft. On the end of the strap is a heavy snap which hooks to the brichen ring.

With the shaft loops and holdback straps fastened, the tugs pass over the holdbacks to the singletree. With tugs and holdbacks fastened you want just a little slack, not much, in both. It will take a little doing for the inexperienced teamster to figure out proper adjustment of the straps. Here again, it would save time and grief to start out not only with an experienced horse but also with a harness and vehicle already set up and properly adjusted. With a four-wheeled vehicle there is no significant weight passed through the shafts to the horse's back. With a cart or two wheeled vehicle any weight forward of the axle can be expected to apply pressure to the horse's back. With a healthy, big horse and proper harness, up to 200 lbs. of actual weight is no problem. Yet it would save the horse energy if the weight could be balanced over the axle with only a slight extra ahead of the axle.

THE TEAM

The term 'team', when used to describe working horses, commonly means two animals 'hitched' side by side (or abreast). In some regions 'team' means any 'hitch' of two or more animals working together. In the southern United States it is common to hear people refer to a 'span' of mules (or even horses). Here again, depending on the particular region, span might mean two animals or it might be inclusive of two or more animals. For the purposes of simplicity and clarification this text refers to team as two animals working side by side (as illustrated here) and leaves the definition of 'span' to future campfires.

In chapter seven, HARNESS, the parts of the harness were described and mention was made of the function of team harness parts. In chapter eight, HARNESSING, illustrations indicated how to harness a horse with a team brichen harness. In chapter nine, doubletrees and neck yokes were described and illustrated. And in chapter ten, DRIVING, you were taken through the exercise of driving a team. Hopefully, the illustrations you see here will cement all that information into a solid picture of the structure and dynamics of two horses working together.

First, a quick review of the basic difference between harness used on a tongue (for a wheeled vehicle), and harness used to skid a load: When a team, or any hitch, is hooked up to a wagon or implement which rolls free something must be done to restrict the movement of that vehicle. Yes, the first concern might be how to hook on and pull the vehicle, but of equal concern must be the restraint, when necessary, of movement. Or in other words, backing and stopping the load.

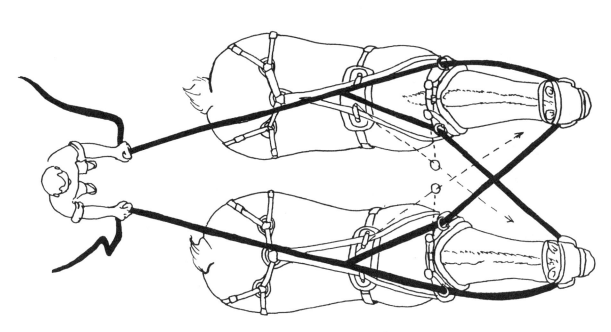

Fig. 148) Team lines — dotted line represents spreader use.

The harness for hitching to a tongue must include at the very least a breast strap. This author recommends the use of a full brichen harness including quarter straps, pole straps, and breast straps as illustrated in chapter seven. Fig. 149 in this chapter illustrates how this assembly hooks to the neck yoke which in turn fastens to the tongue.

When skidding a load, where there is no concern that the load might run up on the animals, no brichen is necessary and a cruper or 'plow' harness is adequate. There is no reason why a brichen harness, however, shouldn't be used to skid loads as well.

Lines. The driving lines used for a team are quite different from those used for a single horse. There are illustrations in chapter seven of lines and on these pages, Figs. 148 and 149 illustrate how the lines are used. As stated before, in driving horses the lines are your critical contact with the animals. Never use weak, dry or poorly constructed lines; it isn't worth the possible trouble.

With team lines, the cross check is normally a few inches longer than the main line. The main line, usually a continuous (spliced) line of leather, always passes to the outside of the team (either animal) and the cross check runs to the inside of the team as illustrated.

Setting up the Lines. With two horses in harness standing side by side, the main left line should pass through the top hame ring and fasten to the left (outside) bit ring. The left cross check passes over the animal's back, through the top right side hame ring.

Line Adjustment. (As illustrated in Fig. 148 .) With two horses in harness standing side by side, the main left driving line should pass through the ring (on top of the left side hame) and fasten on to the (outside) left bit ring. The left driving line cross check passes over the same animal's back and through the top, right side, hame ring of that left horse. The cross check then passes over to the right horse's left (or inside) bit ring. The right main driving line follows the same pattern in reverse. It passes through the top ring (of the right side hame) of the right side horse and on forward to fasten into the (outside) right bit ring. The right cross check passes over the right horse's back and through the top ring (inside left hame) and on across to fasten into the left horse's (inside) right bit ring.

Fig. 149) This drawing illustrates the neck yoke fastened to the breast straps and the end of the tongue. Note also the line setup with spreaders and in the middle, the heart, is a center line drop as described in the HARNESS chapter.

If the team, as it moves forward, walks with their heads pointing in together, check to see if the lines are set up properly with main lines running outside and cross checks inside. If this is correct, adjust the lines by moving the cross checks 'forward' at the splice. Now check to see if, when lines are taut and animals moving ahead, their heads are straight. If their heads are facing out, adjust by moving cross checks back a little on the main line. The object is to have the team walking comfortably, straight ahead. If the lines are properly

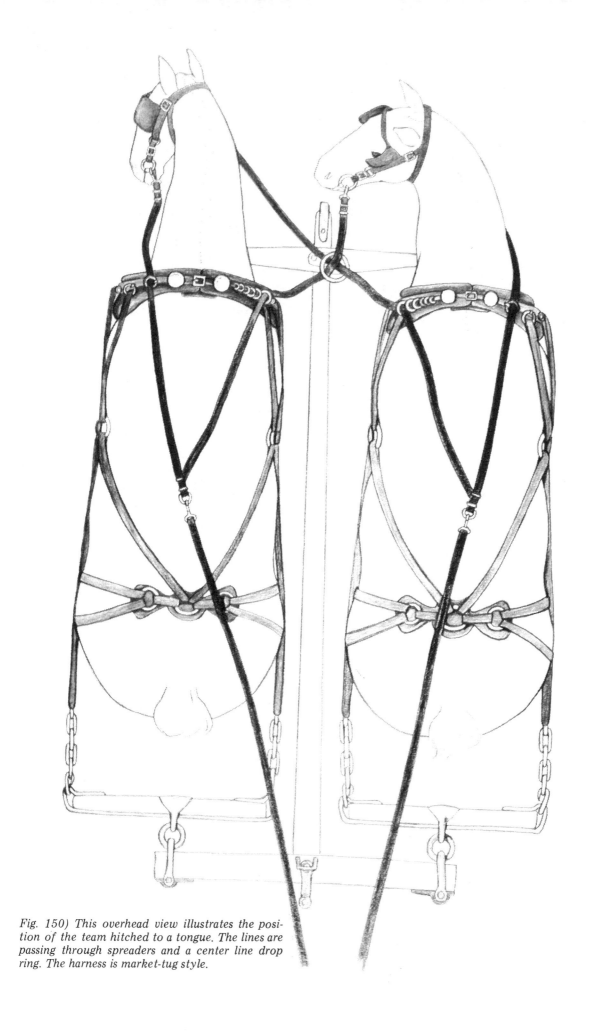

Fig. 150) This overhead view illustrates the position of the team hitched to a tongue. The lines are passing through spreaders and a center line drop ring. The harness is market-tug style.

Fig. 151) A logging team with doubletree and chain setup.
Photo by Nancy Roberts

Fig. 152) Setting up the neck yoke on the team.   *Photo by Lynn Miller*

adjusted and one of the animals insists on walking with head in or out, check the shoulder for bruises and the mouth for soreness (inside and out). Some young or green animals will do this out of nervousness and time and work are the only cures.

When skidding a load it may be desirable to have horses work close together, in which case the above described line setup is proper. In other cases, such as working hitched to a wagon, it may be desired to have the animals working farther apart. This is accomplished by the use of spreaders (see Fig. 77). Make NO adjustment in the lines. Rather fasten the spreaders to the tops of the inside hames and pass the cross checks through the end spreader rings (instead of the hame rings), see Fig.

Eveners. For team hitching doubletrees may vary in width from up to 48" wide down to 30" wide, depending on the job to do. The neck yoke should be the same width as the doubletree.

TANDEM

On the British Isles it is common to see two horses working in line rather than side by side. Such a hitch configuration is called 'tandem'. In situations where the going is narrow but that require additional horse power, this hitch may be needed. It is rarely seen outside of the show ring in North America. Perhaps one reason is that it is one of the most difficult hitches to drive. Normally, if using a wheeled vehicle, the "wheel" horse (or the animal nearest the vehicle) is between shafts and easily accessible, but the 'lead' horse is way ahead and relatively free. The lead animal must be well-schooled, quick to start, a straight mover, quick to stop, and all the while easy to control. It is extremely easy to jackknife this hitch.

The wheel horse is hitched in normal fashion with the leader's tugs hooking into the wheeler's harness, or, better yet, tugs. Ample room must be allowed so that physical contact isn't made between the leader and wheeler, (usually 3½ feet).

Fig. 153 illustrates the line setup. The teamster will have to handle two lines per hand and keep them all separate and even. This will be done in the same manner as illustrated in Fig. 167 for four head. Notice in Fig. 153 how the leader's lines pass through 'line keepers' which hang from the sides of the wheeler's bridle. These line keepers are the same as illustrated in Fig. 146 only smaller. They are normally hung from the bridle, either buckled in or snapped in above the blinders just below the ears.

The driving lines for the tandem consist of two pair of single lines. One is of ordinary length (16' to 20') and the other set is 30 feet or more depending on size of animals, vehicle and/or procedure.

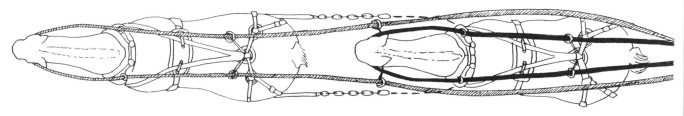

Fig. 153) Tandem hitch illustrating line setup.

UNICORN

This hitch was used in city traffic when a team was not quite enough power. Rather than hitch three abreast, which takes more road space, a third horse was hitched ahead. If the load to be pulled wasn't too big, the lead horse's singletree was hooked to the end of the tongue (see Fig. 154). If the load was substantial the lead horse's single-tree would be hooked to a cable or chain which would hang parallel to and under the tongue, hitching direct to the same pin as the wheeler's doubletree. In such cases, since an "evener" effect was not had, it was up to the teamster to be certain that all animals were pulling their fair share.

This is a difficult hitch to drive and requires the same exemplary qualities in a lead horse that are required in the tandem hitch.

The lines on the wheelers are set up the same as with a regular team. The leader's lines are set up the same as the tandem leader's (see Fig. 153).

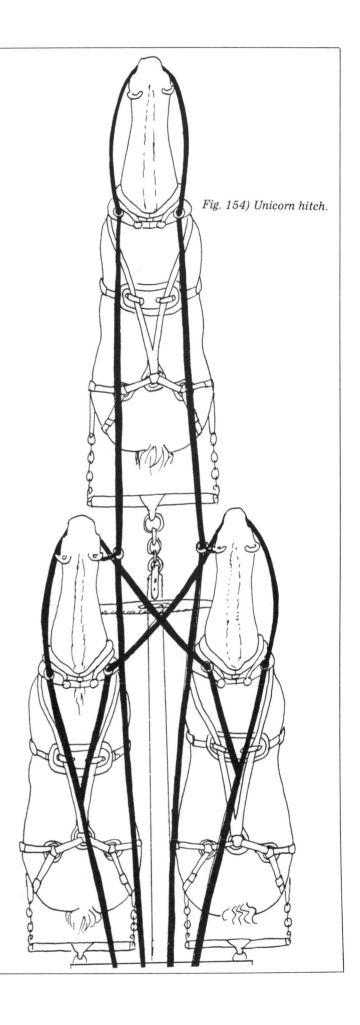

Fig. 154) Unicorn hitch.

Unicorn hitches at the last Draft Horse Festival (1981)   *Photos by Nancy Roberts*

THREE ABREAST

Fig. 158) Three abreast   Photo by Marianne Johner

This is a most useful hitch for farm field work but is rarely seen in the woods or on the highway because of the extra width. For plowing, discing, harrowing, even spreading manure, three abreast gives an extra measure of power that keeps horses in harness longer. In other words, the work might be done satisfactorily with a team, but adding another animal in the hitch means less strain on each individual. The result is that the animals are fresher at the end of the day and at the beginning of the next.

Different designs of three horse eveners are illustrated in chapter 9, HITCH GEAR.

There are several different possible setups for lines. Fig. 159 illustrates a system which requires a set of standard team lines (extra long if possible), plus two 38" long check straps. These straps can be made of line leather with a snap on each end and a conway buckle for adjustment. Or, if unavailable, a regular halter rope can be used, being tied on at the hame end. Individual animals and different circumstances may affect the position on the hames that check straps fasten. Normally they snap into the top hame ring which makes the strap run at the same angle as a line would. The way this system functions is that as you pull one line you pull two horses, the third animal being brought around by the center one. This system is sufficient and works well with trained horses. If you're using an unschooled animal, hitch it in at the center position. That way there is a line on both sides of the mouth and full control.

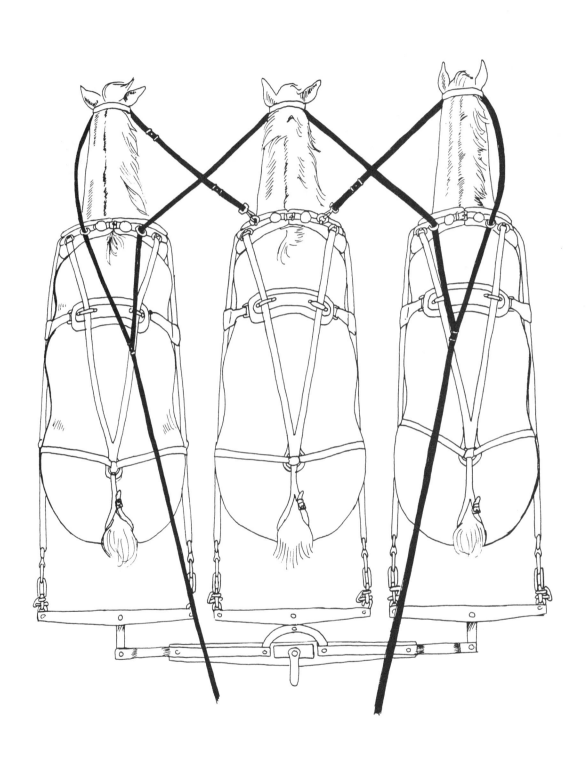

Fig. 159) One system of three abreast lines using two check straps.

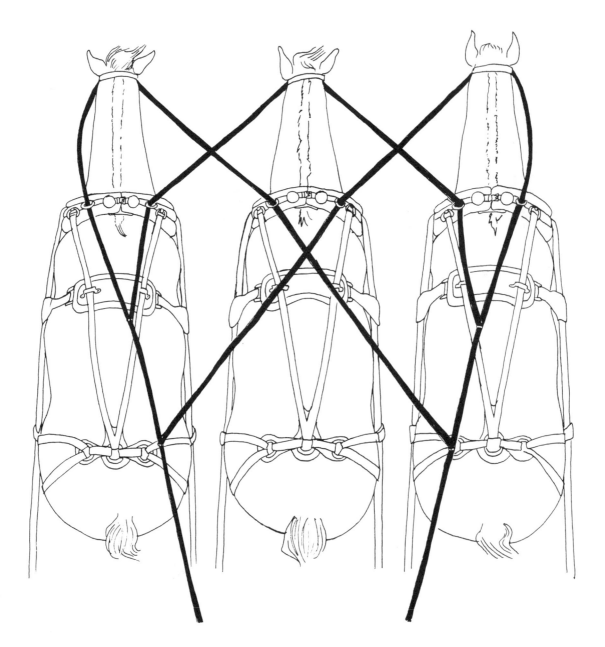

Fig. 160) A full line, three cross check, lines system for three abreast.

If you are inexperienced or have several green horses, Fig. 160 might be a better line setup. Here a set of team lines are set up with a second set of cross checks. In this way, there is true line contact with both sides of each horse's mouth.

If you have one horse which likes to move out faster than the others, put him in the middle, as it will be easier to hold him back and even.

Fig. 161) A three abreast evener at work on a sulky plow.

Photos by M. Johner

Fig. 162) Aden Freeman driving three Belgians abreast on a new style sulky plow. This is a line setup as in Fig. 159.

FOUR ABREAST

Photo by M. Johner

This is a popular farm field work hitch which will cover a lot of ground. It is important with this outfit to have long lines as when the hitch turns the outside animal will move a long way out and away. Figs. 163 and 164 illustrate two systems for lines. The captions explain those systems.

The Wilder four abreast show hitch of dapple-grey Percherons at the last Draft Horse Festival.
Photo by Lynn Miller

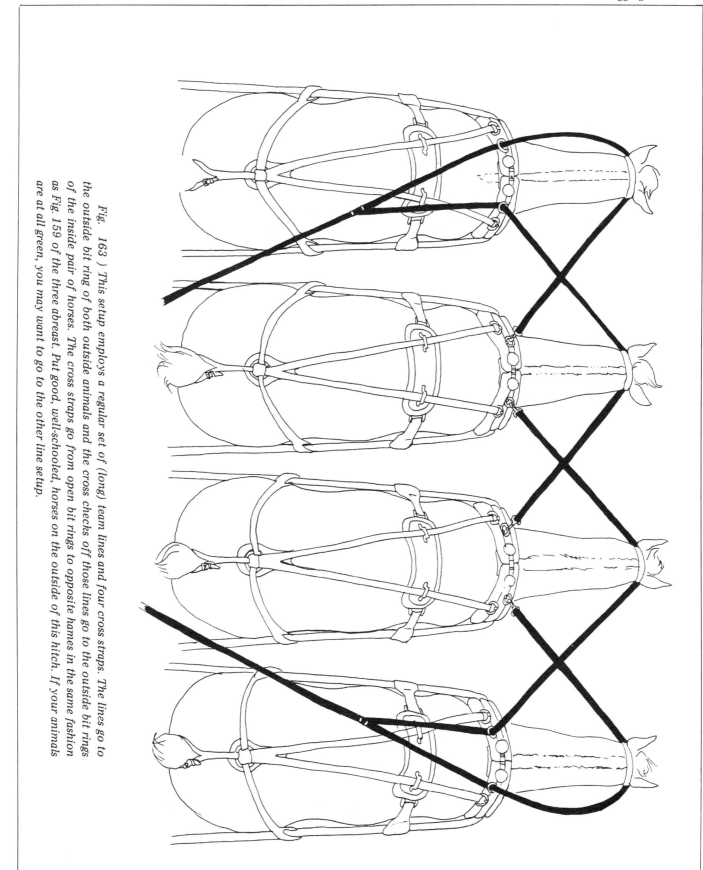

Fig. 163) This setup employs a regular set of (long) team lines and four cross straps. The lines go to the outside bit ring of both outside animals and the cross checks off those lines go to the outside bit rings of the inside pair of horses. The cross straps go from open bit rings to opposite hames in the same fashion as Fig. 159 of the three abreast. Put good, well-schooled, horses on the outside of this hitch. If your animals are at all green, you may want to go to the other line setup.

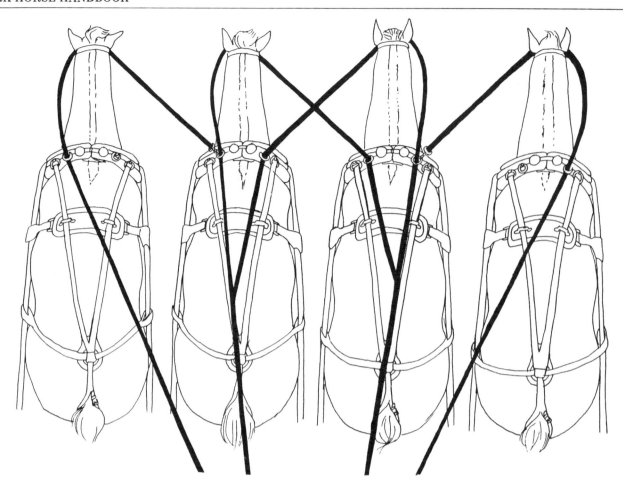

Fig. 164) This system requires the teamster to handle four lines. It takes one set of regular team lines, one set of single lines and two cross straps. The illustration shows how to set the lines up. With this system you have at least a line on each animal, but it does require greater driving skill to handle the lines. See Fig. 171 for examples of how to hold the lines.

Photo by MaryLyn Eagle

Fig. 165 & 166) Two photos of a four-up hitched to a sulky plow.   *Photos by Christene George*

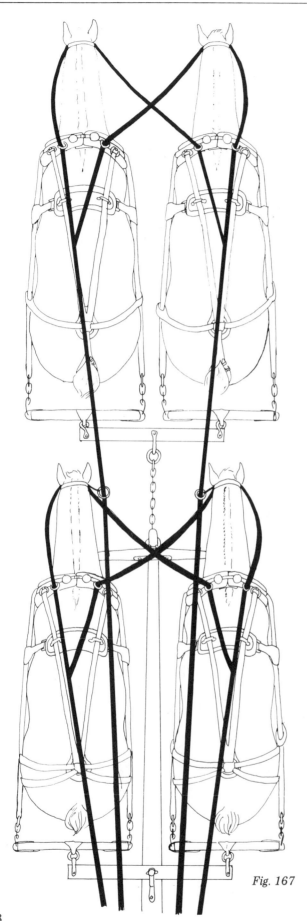

Fig. 167

FOUR UP

Working two teams, one ahead of the other, is a popular setup for transport and farm work. Obviously four horses can handle more of a wagon or freight load than a team. And for the experienced teamster, a four-up is an easy hitch to drive. It does require good alert leaders and stout wheelers. Fig. 167 illustrates a wagon hookup with conventional doubletrees, front and back. In the HITCH GEAR chapter there were illustrations of equalizing four-up eveners which are a must for heavy work. Some of the same driving concerns mentioned in the six-up discussion apply, rather obviously, to this hitch as well. Figs. 139 and 171 illustrate the principle of driving with multiple lines.

FIVE UP

This unusual hitch, employing two horses — set wide — at the wheel and three leaders, is a very effective outfit for farm field work. Because of the position of the wheel horses, the teamster has excellent vantage of the leaders and plenty of room for driving lines. On a large productive horse farm, this hitch will become most popular. The illustration caption will explain the buck-back, tie-in setup for this hitch. This "buck-back" system can be customized to work with any multiple hitch and make it possible to drive with just two lines.

Buck-back. This system works by hooking or tying in all but the lead animals. Buck-back refers to the use of a strap which fastens to both sides of one animal's bit and runs back to snap into the adjoining animal's trace chain (or to the lead chain). In this manner, the "bucked-back" animal is prevented from moving separate of the entire hitch. A tie strap or chain then hooks, preferably to a halter, (rather than a bit), and runs forward to hitch to the trace chain of the animal in front (and to the side) as illustrated several times in these drawings. There are variations of this system as shown in Fig. 182 and, if large multiple hitches see increased use, there doubtless will be many more innovations.

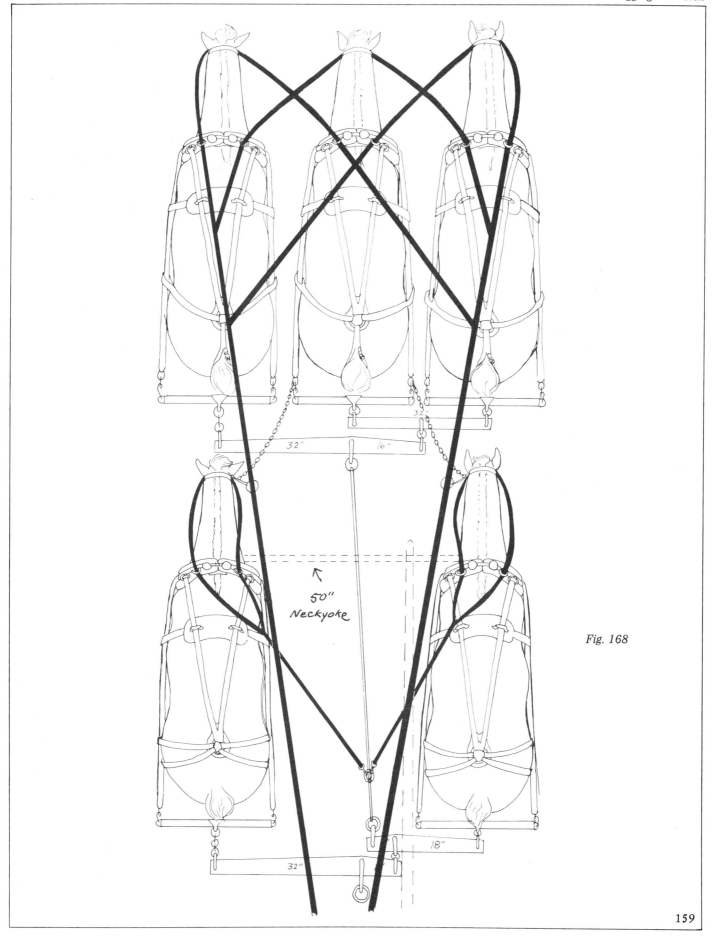

50"
Neckyoke

32"

16"

32"

18"

32"

Fig. 168

Fig. 169) Don Nagle drives a five-up hitch (as diagrammed) on a gang plow.   *Photo by Lynn Miller*

NOTES ON DRIVING MULTIPLE HITCHES

If you are using the "buck-back" system and driving with just two lines, there are some things to be mindful of with the big hitches. First of all, with the multiple hitches it is difficult to see where the lead horses are at and too easy to drive into fences or other obstacles (especially if low set). If possible, get as high a seat or platform (as safe) on your implement so that you can 'see' not only ahead of the animals but also all the rigging! Allow yourself plenty of line length because turns will draw a great deal of outside line. *(Of course, be careful to keep lines out of machinery!)*

If you are driving big hitches with four, six or eight lines, you will have to have had plenty of driving experience, because you will need the agility that comes from developing instinctive responses to situations. Having to keep more than two lines even, with PERFECT TENSION is difficult. The basic positions illustrated in Fig. 171 should be a help in keeping lines organized. One of the common mistakes made by beginning big hitch teamsters is 'holding back' lead horses and even swing horses, thereby requiring wheel horses to work harder. Watch that the tugs are all taut and each segment of the hitch is working. This is not a problem with the buck-back system but it can be when driving with full lines. While you want to allow the leaders to pull their share, be carful NEVER to allow the lines to get slack or they may tangle and it is a long way to your lead horses if you are out in the field alone.

Fig. 170) Gene Hilty drives a six-up hitched (as diagrammed) to a pull-type tractor gang plow. Gene and Donna Thomas are standing on a mounted platform board on the plow. Note the use of check straps from center horse hames to inside bit of other horses. *Photo by Lynn Miller*

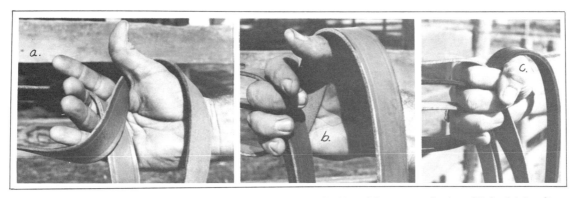

Fig. 171) These photos illustrate suggestions of ways to hold and keep organized multiple driving lines. "a" shows a four lines system with two lines per hand. In this instance the lead line passes above, the wheel line passes under the hand — up and through the palm — and over the thumb. This keeps the lines simple and untangled. "b" illustrates six lines (as with six-up). Again the lead line is above, the wheel line below (and over thumb), and the swing line is in between. "c" illustrates an eight-line system using the same pattern — lead, top; point, second; swing, third; and wheel, bottom.

If you are driving with four-up or six-up (three teams of two) hitched to a wagon and you are going to back the outfit, care must be taken not to back the lead (and swing) teams into the wheelers.

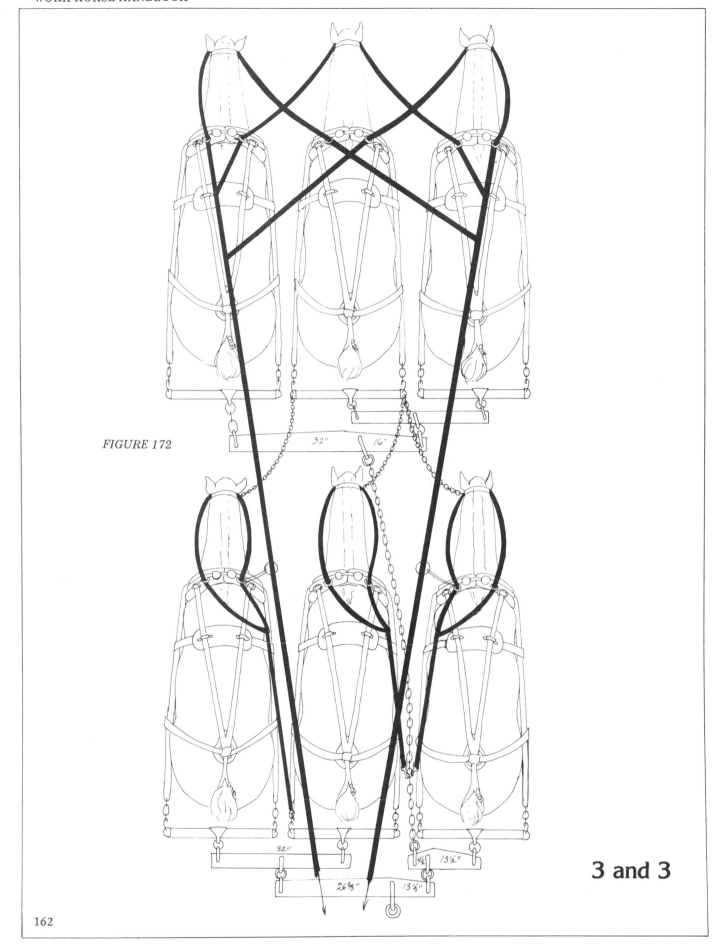

FIGURE 172

3 and 3

SIX UP

This hitch of three and three is, again, a farm field work outfit used for tillage practices. It is an easier hitch to drive than might be readily apparent. In the drawing (see Fig. 172) it might appear that this hitch has a built-in angle on the leader chain that would cause problems. With the offset three horse eveners, as all animals pull ahead, this hitch straightens itself out somewhat. There will still remain a slight side draft depending on the tool being used (i.e., plow or disc, etc.).

The tie-chains and buck-back straps function in the same manner as the five-up in Fig. 168 , allowing the teamster to drive with just two lines. This hitch can also be driven with other line systems such as illustrated in Figs. 159 and 160 or with a system on both the wheelers and leaders.

SIX UP - 3 of 2

This hitch of two, two and two is not a common work hitch because it is more difficult to drive than the six with three and three. But this outfit is the best for heavy highway hauling or wherever a narrow hitch is necessary. The middle team in this hitch is called a "swing" team. This setup can be driven with two, four or six lines. Fig. 173 illustrates six lines. Working with two or four lines will require setting up a buck-back system. If this hitch is to be used on a wagon, it will be preferred to have lines on at least the wheel and lead teams for backing control.

If this hitch is used on an implement or vehicle with a tongue the wheel doubletree (if an evener) should hitch below the tongue as illustrated in Fig.166 .

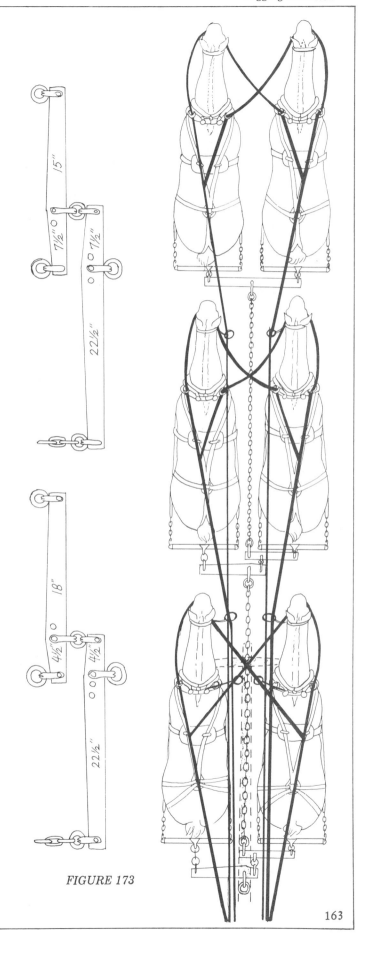

FIGURE 173

Fig. 174) Eight mules hitched (as diagrammed) to a gang plow in Washington state wheat stubble.
Photo by Lynn Miller

Adie Funk drives Doug Hammill's four-up of Clydesdales hitched by way of forecart to a combine. This Montana photo by Carla Hammill.

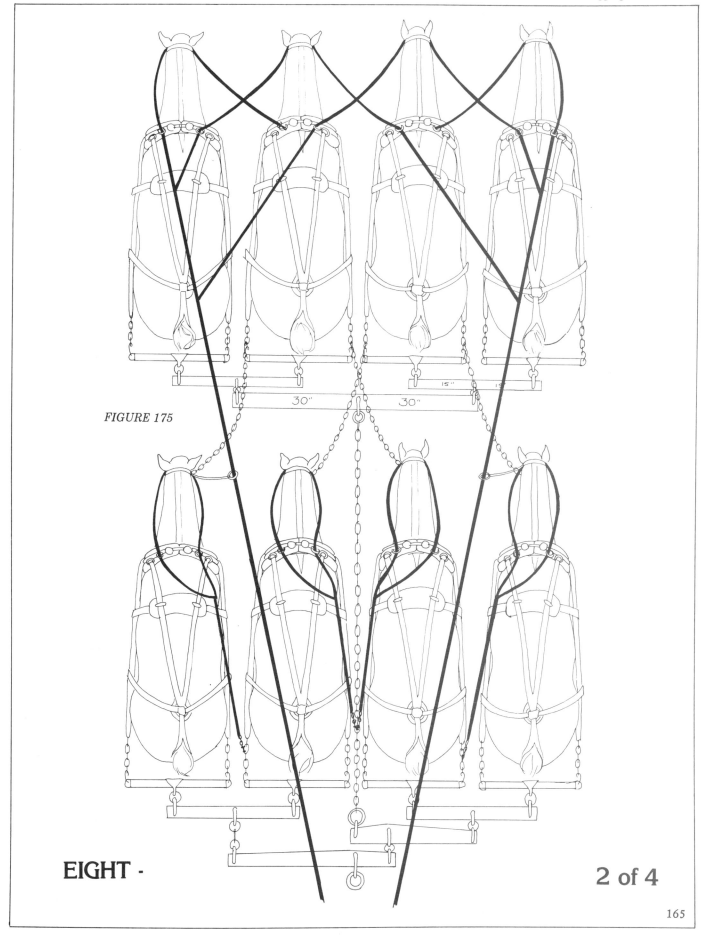

FIGURE 175

30" 30"

15" 15"

EIGHT -

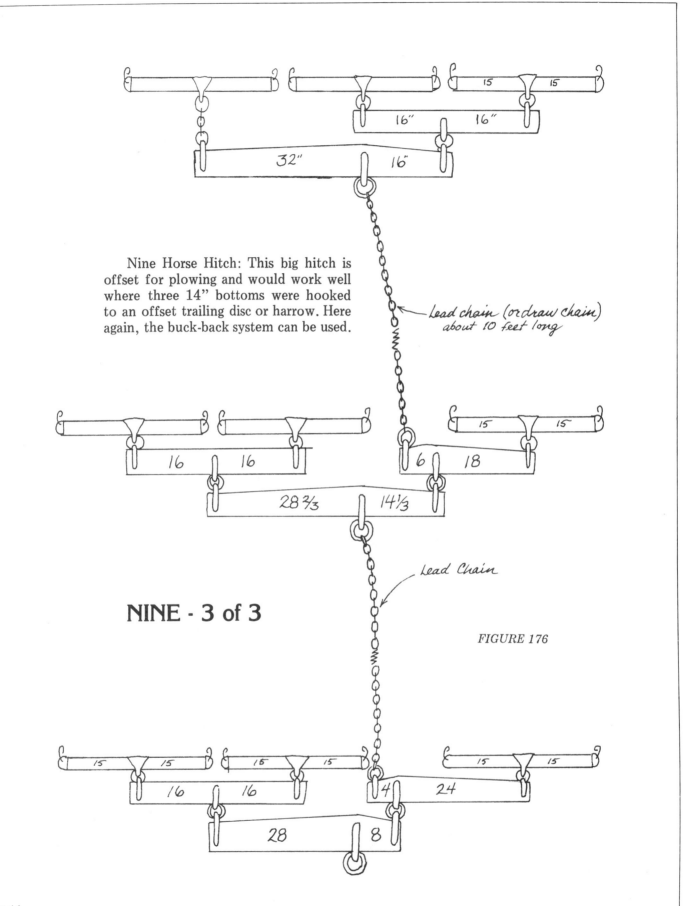

Nine Horse Hitch: This big hitch is offset for plowing and would work well where three 14" bottoms were hooked to an offset trailing disc or harrow. Here again, the buck-back system can be used.

Lead chain (or draw chain) about 10 feet long

Lead Chain

NINE - 3 of 3

FIGURE 176

TWELVE - 3 of 4

Fig. 177) Don Thomas' twelve mule hitch.

Fig. 178) The gang plow used in the above twelve mule hitch.

Figs. 179, 180, 181 illustrating the twelve mule Thomas hitch as diagrammed in Fig. 184.

Photo by Lynn Miller

Fig. 182) A closeup of the swing team of the Thomas twelve mule hitch. Note the tie chains; one going forward to a lead trace chain, one going over to the bar upright off the evener, and the outside chains running into the neighbor's hame. Also note the line keeper on the farm mule's bridle.   *Photo by Lynn Miller*

Fig. 183) The lead four on the Thomas twelve mule hitch. Here the check straps run straight across rather than back to the opposite hames.   *Photo by Lynn Miller*

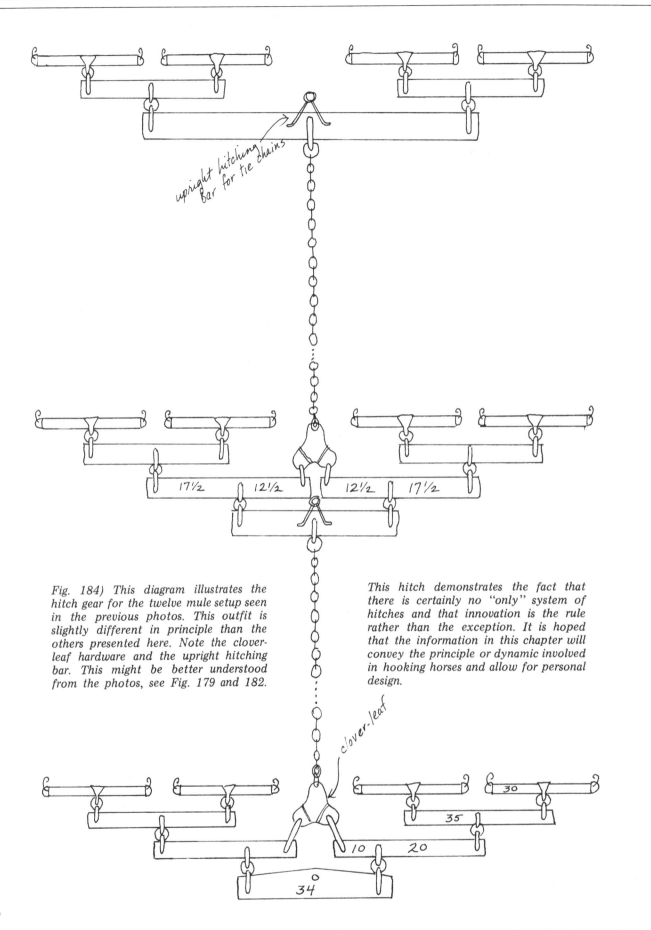

upright hitching bar for tie chains

17½   12½   12½   17½

clover-leaf

30

35

10   20

34

Fig. 184) This diagram illustrates the hitch gear for the twelve mule setup seen in the previous photos. This outfit is slightly different in principle than the others presented here. Note the clover-leaf hardware and the upright hitching bar. This might be better understood from the photos, see Fig. 179 and 182.

This hitch demonstrates the fact that there is certainly no "only" system of hitches and that innovation is the rule rather than the exception. It is hoped that the information in this chapter will convey the principle or dynamic involved in hooking horses and allow for personal design.

CHAPTER TWELVE

HITCHING UP: Approaches & Procedures

This chapter covers a wide variety of different approaches and procedures for hooking and using horses in harness. The possibilities for the application of horse power to work and transport are nearly infinite. So with the varieties of hitching possibilities. We do not pretend to cover every application and procedure in this book, let alone this chapter. The specific technologies and methodologies of logging with horses or farming with horses are deserving of whole books in and of themselves. The information in this chapter is rudimentary and should, coupled with good common sense, put you on your way.

The Single Horse: Chapters 7, 9, 10 and 11 have information pertaining to using the single horse covering harness, hitch gear and such. If you are to use a single animal to skid a load (that is to say, to 'drag' something) a plain work harness such as in Fig. 185 will suffice.

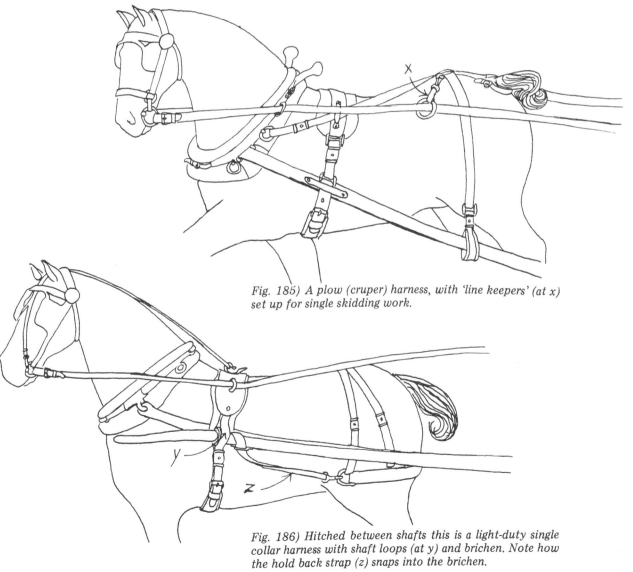

Fig. 185) A plow (cruper) harness, with 'line keepers' (at x) set up for single skidding work.

Fig. 186) Hitched between shafts this is a light-duty single collar harness with shaft loops (at y) and brichen. Note how the hold back strap (z) snaps into the brichen.

Fig. 187) A Belgian gelding hitched to a light delivery wagon. A standard farm brichen harness has been modified with extra hame and quarter straps. The hame straps were used as wraps around the shafts and the quarter straps were used as hold back straps.
Photo by Lynn Miller

Of course, start with a well-schooled horse if you yourself are green. If not possible, and both you and the animal are green, have an experienced teamster available to help with things to remember when hitching a horse to a skid load — be it logs, sled, harrow or whatever — including being careful not to ask (or demand) a horse to pull an impossible load. The best way to gauge that is to work up slowly. The animal will be able to pull an enormous load (sometimes equal or greater than his weight) for a very short bit. All-day work should be much, much less.

The drag or skid singletree should be equipped with a hook more often than a clevis (see HITCH GEAR, Fig. 118) for easy hookup to chains or rings. The best approach for hitching is to drive alongside of the tool and turn close in front so as to minimize backing up. If you do have to back up the animal to hitch, you may need to pick up the singletree and pull back on it and the lines. Try not to get the animal tangled up and worried. Remember, you are at least ½ of the team effort. After hooking, or fastening, to the implement or load, be sure to stand clear of its path as the animal pulls ahead. Be especially careful when skidding logs as they may easily roll or slide into you. For this reason it is a good idea to chain two logs together whenever they are small enough to do so.

When hitching the single horse to a cart, wagon or rolling implement with shafts, you can use a harness like that which appears in Fig. 186 or you can improvise and convert standard team work harness as illustrated in the last chapter in Fig. 122 . Hitching to shafts is a little more complex than a skid load. First of all, make sure that the animal will fit the shafts. Then, while the animals is standing, lift the shafts and line them up with the shaft loops of the horse's harness. If the vehicle rolls easily, pull it forward, carefully guiding the shafts into the shaft loops. Now, one side at a time, hook the tug into the singletree and fasten the holdback strap from harness to shaft. You may have to make adjustments initially, but after that it will be easy to hitch up. Care should be taken that both the animal and the shafts are strong enough to take any weight that may be transferred, such as in the case of a cart that is front-heavy. The shaft loops should function to keep the shafts from moving much up or down, but there should remain, for the most part, a slight downward pressure.

Fig. 188) A team of Canadian Belgians hitched (by hook) to a flat stone boat. Note how Aden Freeman has his lines gathered and out of the way.

Photo by Marianne Johner

Fig. 189) (below) This diagram shows a sled design which employs a tongue and runners. The tongue allows the team to restrain the load on steep hills and the runners allow some clearance. If wagon tire irons are used on the underside of the runners, rocks or gravel will not wear them down and the sled will start easily. Also, this setup works very well, not only in snow, but in wet grass and mud as well. There is a discussion later of how to hitch to a tongue.

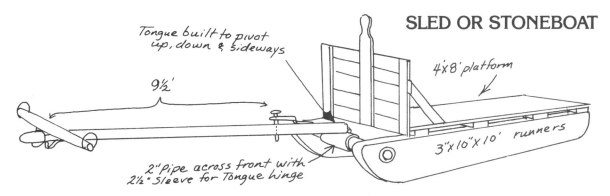

Tongue built to pivot up, down & sideways

9½'

2" pipe across front with 2½" sleeve for Tongue hinge

SLED OR STONEBOAT

4'x8' platform

3"x10"x10' runners

Fig. 189) A logging team of Percherons takes a short break. Note the doubletree hooked full out

The Team: Again, chapters 7, 9, 10 and 11 have information pertaining to the use of the team. That material covers harness, hitch gear and driving. If you are going to use two animals, hitched side-by-side, to drag or skid a load the harness does not have to include the brichen-breast strap assembly; a plow (cruper) harness will suffice. However, if all you have is a brichen harness, it will work just fine.

When hooking the team to a skid load of some sort make sure that your point of hitch is secure whether it is a clevis or hook. The most common problems come from old cracked or rusty clevises (or clevis pins) breaking when the team is pulling hard or a hook coming undone while horses are relaxing with the rigging loose. When you hook it is a good practice to have the team stand just far enough away so that the hitching is done with tugs at least strung out rather than loose. This

173

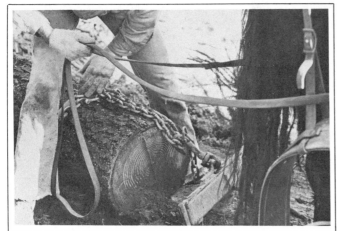

LOGS

Fig. 190) In this example, a chain is wrapped around the log to be yarded. And the hook of the double-tree is set up with an eye to where the log will go. For instance, a buried or bound up log can be started easier if the team swings to either side and rolls the log slightly before pulling ahead. And the roll can be assisted by hitching over on the opposite side so that the chain pulls the log around. You can see here how dangerous it can be and why you must always pay attention.

Fig. 191) Two logs are wrapped together with the chain in such a manner as to tighten the wrap as pulled. Where possible it is an excellent idea to put two or more logs together as this restricts some of the rolling action that is so dangerous to the teamster.

Photo by Nancy Roberts

just prevents the horses from stepping over a tug as they move ahead. Be careful while hooking not to be in a position of danger. NEVER STAND INSIDE THE HOOKED DOUBLETREE OR EVENER! Always think about where everything will go when the horses move and where you are in relation. This is certainly critically important in logging where obstacles and terrain, as well as the hitch itself, can cause unexpected movement of the log(s), maybe right into the teamster.

Remember, that as the team leans into the collar and pulls, this action can also be translated into a lift. So the shorter (or closer) the horse are hooked, the more likely they will lift the sled, or log, or whatever, as they pull. This can be beneficial in getting a very heavy load started. However, you may be hitched to a tool such as a walking cultivator, where you do not want a 'lifting' action and so the horses must be hooked farther forward.

If you are hooked to an empty doubletree, you will, of course, want to hook it long so that the rigging does not bounce off the walking animal's heels. The time to shorten the rigging, if desired, is either after hooking or just before as the animals are standing. At pulling contests you might see a "swamper" (a second person), who carries the short hitched doubletree as the teamster drives. This is done to prevent hitting the horses, because most pullers want to hook to the sled quickly, and because the horses are excited in the competition and safety is good business. If you are working (yourself green) with a nervous team and do not have an experienced teamster available to help, at the very least have a second able-bodied person there to help hold the horses or correct little problems! Avoiding the accidents from the very start will pay big dividends down the road. The more you work the team (successfully and quietly), the more cooperative they will become.

WALKING PLOWS

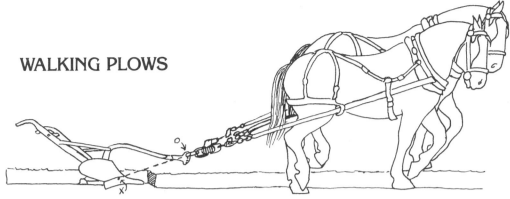

Fig. 192) The proper adjustment of the hitch is the most important factor in the operation of horse-drawn plows. In the diagram, "x" marks the center of the load, and "o" marks the point of hitch. The point of hitch MUST be on a straight line drawn from center of load to the point of draft at the collar. If the line is not straight it will cause the plow to either pull out of the ground or go too deep. If the line is straight the plow will run easily at the proper depth. The horizontal adjustment of walking plow hitches is relatively easy, provided the doubletree is about the right length and the plow share is properly set. If a right-hand plow is not taking a wide enough land, the clevis may be moved one or two inches to the right. If taking too much land, an adjustment of one or two notches to the left will bring the desired results. A left-hand plow is adjusted in an exactly opposite manner.

FIGURE 193

If you are plowing for the first time without help, it will seem an impossible procedure to master. Experienced horses, a helping teamster and a clean furrow would be ideal circumstances for the beginner. If this is not possible, try at least to have some of the first furrows started for you. If that is not possible, have someone either drive or lead the team until you have a good clean furrow.

When plowing with a team, the opening or crown furrow is the most difficult. It is best to have some understanding born of experience first. One horse will be walking in the furrow and one will walk on the land. For this reason, it MAY be necessary to make a slight adjustment in the lines to compensate for one horse being higher.

FIGURE 194

The lines are best tied together and put over one shoulder and under the opposite arm. If an accident of some sort should occur, the teamster, by tucking his head, can easily get away if one line is over and one under. The length of lines depends on the entire hitch.

To start plowing, lift up on the handles and have the team step ahead. The plow will suck down into the ground and find its proper depth without your help. As you move ahead, slight pressure on either handle will cause the plow to move to the opposite side. Increased pressure to either side will cause the plow to come out of the ground. Pushing down on both handles will cause the plow to come out. Pulling up on the handles will cause the plow to go down deeper.

The rule with the walking plow is RELAX! Let the horses pull it and go with the plow, making minor adjustments. If you're pushing, as in Fig. 193, you're causing yourself unneccesary grief. You should be comfortable, as in Fig. 194.

RIDING PLOWS

Fig. 195 illustrates the correct up-and-down adjustment for riding plows. As in walking plows, a straight line from "x" (center of draft or load) through "o" (point of hitch), to the point of draft on the collar is necessary. When hitching horses strung out, the hitch at "o" must be lower than when using animals abreast. The teamster should try to get the horizontal hitch point as near as possible in direct line between the center of draft and the center of power when the plow is running straight and horses are pulling straight ahead. To find center of draft, measure total cut of plow. Half of total cut is center of cut. Measure to left of center of cut ¼ of the width of cut of one bottom to get center of draft.

Fig. 196) Comfort to horses when plowing depends on the adjustment of horses and harness. For best control horses should work close together. Long tugs give horses more room and tend to make the plow run easier and steadier. If trace carriers are used, they should be adjusted so that they hang free. If loops pull up on the traces they will change the line of draft causing the plow to run unsteady and putting weight on the horse's backs. Ray Drongesen plows with three abreast on a frameless sulky plow in this photo.

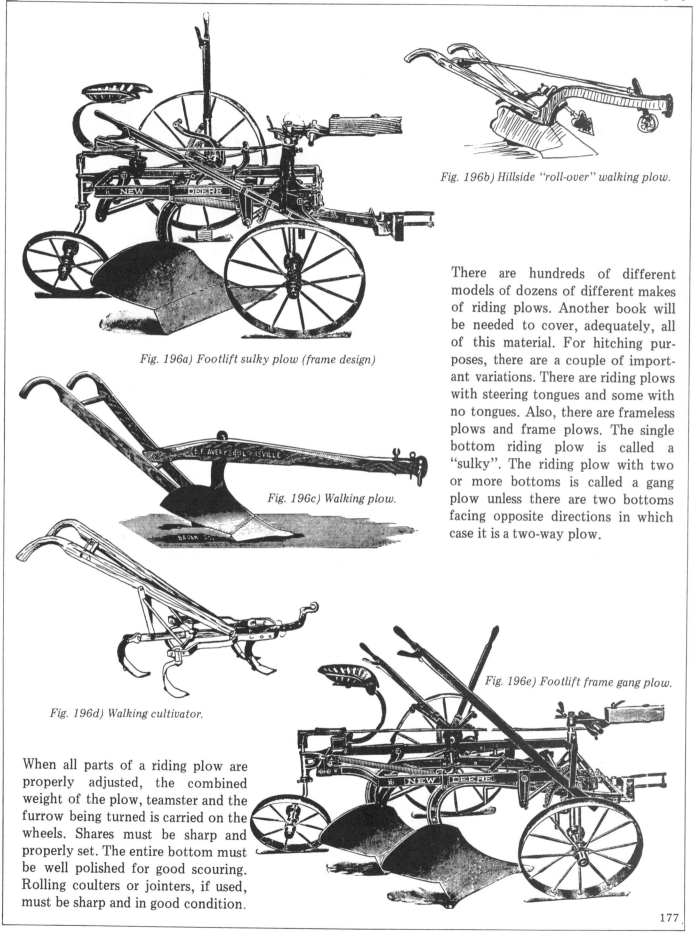

Fig. 196a) Footlift sulky plow (frame design)

Fig. 196b) Hillside "roll-over" walking plow.

Fig. 196c) Walking plow.

Fig. 196d) Walking cultivator.

Fig. 196e) Footlift frame gang plow.

There are hundreds of different models of dozens of different makes of riding plows. Another book will be needed to cover, adequately, all of this material. For hitching purposes, there are a couple of important variations. There are riding plows with steering tongues and some with no tongues. Also, there are frameless plows and frame plows. The single bottom riding plow is called a "sulky". The riding plow with two or more bottoms is called a gang plow unless there are two bottoms facing opposite directions in which case it is a two-way plow.

When all parts of a riding plow are properly adjusted, the combined weight of the plow, teamster and the furrow being turned is carried on the wheels. Shares must be sharp and properly set. The entire bottom must be well polished for good scouring. Rolling coulters or jointers, if used, must be sharp and in good condition.

Fig. 197) In this photo a team is being hooked to a (single) six foot disc. Discs are normally equipped with either truck wheels (as in this case) or with a tongue. The tugs should be hooked long when using the truck wheel disc so that the horses are not lifting the front end as they pull. Be very careful when hooking a nervous team or any team, as you will be in a direct line with the disc.

Photo by Scott Duff

Fig. 199 (next page) Here are four head hitched abreast to an eight foot single disc.

Photo by L. Miller

HARROWS

Horse-drawn tandem disc

Fig. 198) When hooking to a spike tooth harrow be sure to hook the tugs and hitch long enough so that the harrow, when drawn, does not lift on the front end. You should figure one horse per four foot harrow section, but if you have three available, they will pull two sections longer and remain fresher. Be sure that the driving lines are plenty long so that you don't "run out" of line as you make a turn.

Photo of Herman Daniel and author's Belgians by Nancy Roberts

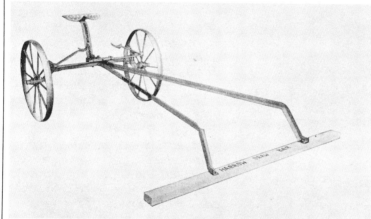

Fig. 200) A harrow cart. This implement is designed to carry the teamster behind a harrow. The two long tongues reach over the harrow and fasten into the harrow evener. The horses hook the same as before. The cart is equipped with two footrests which work on a scissors principle to turn the cart wheels so that it follows the harrow around turns.

Fig. 201 (below) Four Belgian horses abreast hitched to four sections of spike tooth harrow. Joe Van Dyke drives while standing on a board that is tied to the harrow. This, although dangerous, is the most prevalent system for the teamster.

RIDING CULTIVATOR

Fig. 202) Straddle row riding cultivator. The principles described in "Hitching to Tongues" apply to the riding cultivators. In the illustration notice that singletrees hang off of vertical bars, the bottom of which hitch direct to the cultivator beams. The singletrees can be moved up and down depending on the size of the horse. There does not want to be any lifting action with the cultivator. The teamster, as he sits on the cultivator, will find, with most models, stirrup-like foot pedals which, when pushed, will move the cultivator shovels from side to side, allowing a little flexibility when cultivating crooked rows. The handles adjust the depth of the shovels and the level.

Fig. 203) Riding disc cultivator with tongue. This implement is adjustable in width and, depending on how much angle is set, will throw soil up onto the plant roots. It is hitched to in basic fashion.

HITCHING TO A TONGUE

Wagons, mowers, corn planters and all sorts of wheel vehicles and implements are often equipped with tongues that function in conjunction with brichen harness, as a restraining, backing and/or braking system. There are some procedural considerations in hitching a team or three abreast (or even four) to a tongue which must be followed if safety is a concern.

TEAMS: First of all, check to be sure your equipment goes together, is in solid shape, and that the animals are going to fit. Next, put the doubletree on the implement and set the neck yoke alongside the front end of the tongue. If the tongue lays on a comfortable angle from vehicle to the

Fig. 204) Horse-drawn mower. About 99% of all horse mowers were designed for team use. There are few single horse mowers. The basic principle of the horse mower is simple but the actual design is sophisticated and complex. The wheels turn an encased drive axle which, through a gear box, increases speed and transfers the driving motion to a 'pitman' gear which runs an arm, and cycle bar, back and forth. Needless to say, because of the motion and vibration, parts need to be in good condition and kept well lubricated. There are many brands of mowers. This author recommends 'John Deere' and 'McCormick' partly because parts can be found. Before hitching a team to the mower, be sure that it is out of gear and that the cycle bar is up in the travel position. Use a narrow evener and neck yoke. Drive the team over the tongue and hitch as described in "Hitching to Tongue". Note in Fig. 206 that breast straps need to be adjusted short so that the tongue has the proper angle for best mower operation. After the team is

hitched, drive them a few feet to check out the hitch before actually mowing. With everything in order, lower the cutting bar carefully. (Make sure your team is attended!) Climb on the mower seat and gather the lines. Put the mower in gear and speak to your team. Keep lines taut to begin with, until everything smooths out. Mowing is potentially a very dangerous business and IN NO INSTANCE SHOULD AN INEXPERIENCED PERSON DRIVE ANY HORSES HITCHED TO A MOWER! Get some experience and help or be prepared for trouble.

MOWER

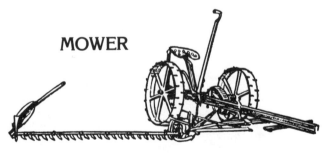

Fig. 205) When hitching to a vehicle or implement with a tongue ALWAYS hitch the neck yoke (front) end FIRST.   Photo by Nancy Roberts.

Fig. 206) The neck yoke hitched properly to a mower. Note how short the breast straps are adjusted. This is important for proper adjustment and operation of mower.

ground, the team can be driven over to hitch. If the tongue is 'stiff' (hanging in the air), or the angle originating too high, it may be necessary to either back the team or lead the animals one at a time to their positions. Let's take each of these considerations one at a time.

With an experienced team (and a helper), ground-drive the team slowly up to the tongue and ask one of the animals to step over the tongue while you turn them close in. The result should be the team in proper position for hitching with little or no backing necessary. It may take a lot of practice even with a good team. Remember that when you are ground-driving the team there is no physical restraint preventing them from spreading apart at the rear when backing. Make sure the team is standing straight before asking them to back; that will help some. There are those who actually tie the two together from brichen to brichen to prevent this 'spread'.

With the team standing in the right place ALWAYS HOOK UP THE FRONT END FIRST! Fasten the neck yoke to the breast strap-pole strap assembly and to the end of the tongue as illustrated in various places throughout this text. After the front end is hitched, hook the tugs. It is a good idea to hook both inside tugs first, then the outside tug on your side. If you are alone, be very careful moving around in between the horses and the equipment. It may be safer at times to carry the driving lines, and walk around the implement to hook the last tug.

Fig. 207 (below) Belgian team pulling rubber-tired late model ground drive (tractor) manure spreader which was converted to horse use by installing a tongue (overall length, 12 feet) and bolting on a seat. This arragement would be improved by the addition of a foot rest. Hitching to a manure spreader is the same as hitching to most wagons.

CORN PLANTER

Fig. 208) Corn planter with extra fertilizer pots. The vertical handle sets the depth of the planter shoes while engaging the seed plates into rotation. Off to the side is the row marker: with this the teamster can straddle the marked line (running directly under the tongue) and come up with straight rows. For precise work it is a good idea to hitch with a short doubletree and neck yoke. The hitch wants to be in a direct line to the planter shoe (or longer) to avoid 'lift' as can be seen in Fig. 210 below.

Fig. 209) Mowing with a team, notice how the author is sitting on the gathered extra lines to prevent tangles that would result in accidents. Care should be taken to watch the path of the mower for garbage that might cause broken equipment and wrecks. The field is usually opened in this manner with the horse walking in the grass the first round. After one trip around the field, turn around and head in the other direction, with horses from then on walking on mowed grass.

Photo by Marianne Johner

Fig 210) The author drives the late Bud and Dick on a John Deere corn planter. The lines hanging behind illustrate a very bad practice as they might easily wrap around the moving axle and cause trouble. The best results in planting corn and beans will be had from fine seedbeds of moderate moisture. Mud will clog the planter shoes. The corn planter is an easy tool to use and horses (or mules) excel in this sort of work.

Photo by Christene George

Figs. 211 & 212) Two photos of six foot horse drawn grain drills. The drill needs to be balanced over the axle or there will be too much weight at the neck yoke. Horses are hitched normal tongue fashion. The handles set the depth of the seed drill and engage the hopper screw. You can figure about 3' to 4' drill width per horse. A 12' wide drill can be handled nicely by four abreast.

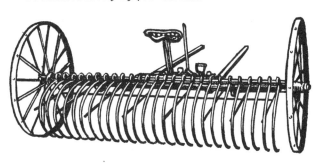

(above) Dump rake with shafts, hitch one horse. This is an obsolete implement and not recommended, as side delivery rakes are vastly superior. (above right) Grain binder setup for four abreast. Depending on the size of cut made and the draft, binders operate with 2, 3 or 4 horses. Hitching is done in the normal manner of tongue setups. The binder is an extremely sophisticated, complex machine which requires some adjustment and maneuvers while operating. This must be done while also driving the horses. For this reason, it is an impossible task for the raw beginner. The adjustments and specifics of operation must be covered in another text.

HITCHING TO THE TONGUE (cont.)

If the wagon has a 'stiff' tongue, it may be necessary to back the team, carefully, with the tongue coming in between; or to simply lead each animal to position, then hook up the lines, and then the neck yoke, and finally the tugs.

THREE ABREAST: When hitching three to a tongue, obviously two animals will be to one side and one to the other. For this reason, it makes sense to drive the single animal over the tongue rather than two horses over. If the three are to be hitched to a regular center-line tongue, a special evener will have to be used. This evener (as illustrated in HITCH GEAR) is built to hitch in line with the tongue (1/3 over) and still have all animals pull even. The design employs offset lever support to get the job done. When hitching three abreast to a riding plow such an evener isn't necessary as the tongue is adjustable and separate of the hitch which is also adjustable. So a regular three horse evener can be used. The same hitching principles apply, NECK YOKE FIRST, then tugs.

FOUR ABREAST AND BIG HITCHES: Four abreast hook the same way with tongue running in between. Principles and rules are the same. It is, of course, more difficult to back three and four abreast than a team.

When hitching multiples with wheelers (and possibly swing), on the tongue, hook the team completely before hitching additional animals ahead. The first thing to do is have lines set up and in hand. Then hitch the front end of the wheel team, then the tugs. Do the next team ahead and so forth. Have help until you've got your animals 'worked down' and a system set up for easy hitching.

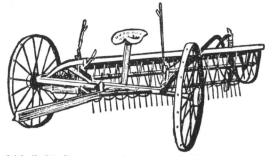

Fig. 216 (left) One type of home-made fore cart designed so that the seat is just behind center of the axle. In this way, weight on the tongue is minimized. Fig. 217 (above) A side delivery rake ground-driven with a long tongue and seat mounted. Most ground-drive tractor rakes can be modified in this manner for horse use.

FORECARTS

The question regarding availability of horse-drawn equipment (for whatever purpose) can be attacked from two entirely different angles. One, of course, is to ask what must be done to get manufacturers to retool and start making the stuff again. (This will happen as the demand grows.) And the other way is to use an adapter that will allow horses to be used with the abundant pull-type tractor equipment available. In this way, one needs to come up with one new tool. And, in this text, we'll call that tool a forecart.

For these last 30 years, horse farmers and loggers have come up with a vast array of different forecarts, the majority of which are based on a simple design principle: two wheels — weight balanced and slightly back — tongue coming direct from axle — and hitch point close to axle and under the seat. Carts like this have been hitched to by 2, 3, 4, or more horses, and all sorts of implements have been attached behind. The list includes: harrows, discs, rollers, grain drills, plows, side-delivery rakes, wagons, manure spreaders, logs, etc. Innovative horse farmers have even hitched to balers, combines, choppers, silage wagons and more. The sky and imagination seem to be the limit.

This author, using his own experience and borrowing from others, has come up with a different principle for forecarts. As pictured below in Fig. 217 this cart has three wheels (the front one steering), and an adjustable seat. It allows, because the seat is forward, for greater flexibility in implement hitch and there is no weight from the cart on the horse's neck. Dimensions are given on the next pages to make it possible for you to perhaps build

your own or have one custom built. *Some of the construction requires steel cutting and welding, which may have to be custom-done.*

The cart is built on a 4" square tubing "T" frame with used Rambler wheels on the rear axle and an offset axle bracket and wheel (off the rear of a junked side-delivery rake) for the front end. The seat, including foot rest, is a separate unit which slides down into standards, allowing for adjustable height. This works great with big hitches allowing the teamster to "see" his leaders and the rigging. The tongue slides onto the steering shaft in the same manner as a plow tongue and carries just its own weight. The hitch is adjustable up and down for different size animals and outfits. Because of the triangular shape of the body of this cart, and the steering tongue, even with four abreast hitched, this unit will turn around almost on top of itself. The frame is stout enough, and there is room enough under the seat, to handle a 5-hp motor mounted to propel a power-take-off unit and/or even a remote hydraulic system. If you add brakes this cart would be able to handle ANY tractor equipment. This author sincerely believes that the best and most immediate future for sensible animal power is within this forecart approach.

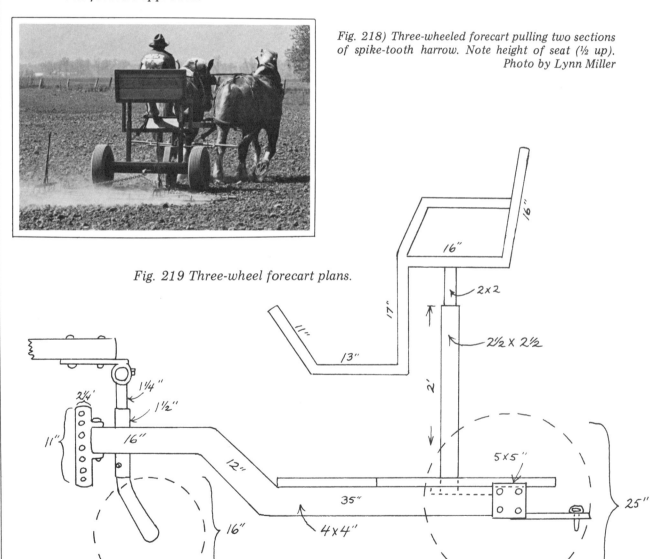

Fig. 218) Three-wheeled forecart pulling two sections of spike-tooth harrow. Note height of seat (½ up).
Photo by Lynn Miller

Fig. 219 Three-wheel forecart plans.

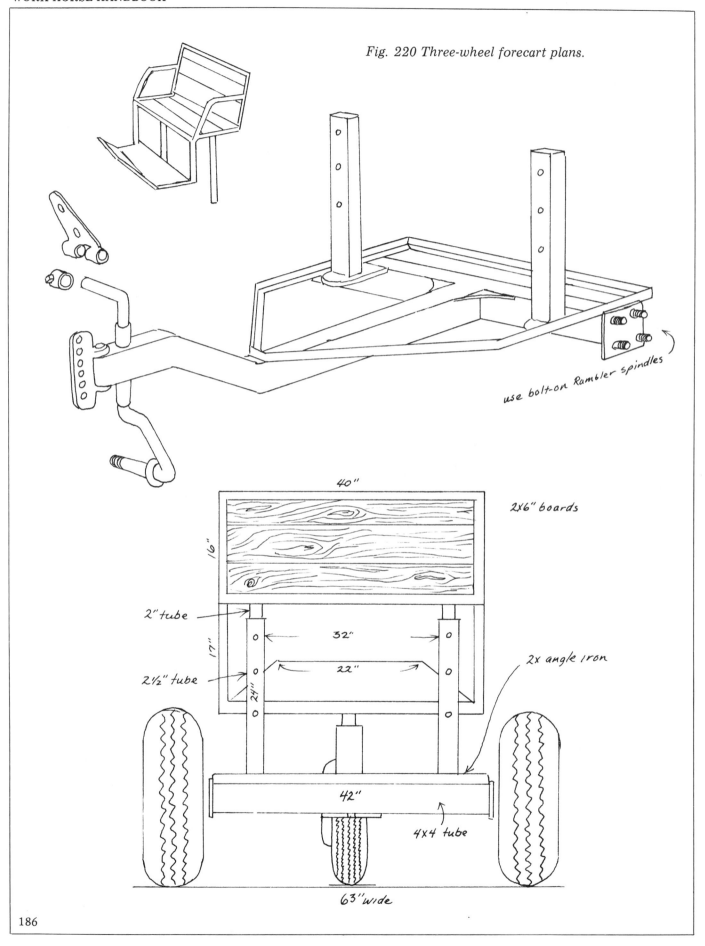

Fig. 220 Three-wheel forecart plans.

use bolt-on Rambler spindles

40"

6"

2x6" boards

2" tube

32"

17"

2½" tube

22"

2x angle iron

24"

42"

4x4 tube

63" wide

CHAPTER THIRTEEN

COST OF USING HORSES

From 1867 to about 1930 the USDA conducted studies and surveys on the animal power question and published numerous excellent, although often slanted, bulletins offering the findings to the general public. This writing draws on some of the basic statistical findings (updated) of that body of work with statistics from current practices and information from personal experience.

This writing is meant to answer questions about the cost of using horses. It also answers some questions along the way about the number of horses needed for certain acreage and vice versa. This chapter goes into some detail but it is centered around certain common practices, crops and economies and the reader may have to work out dollar and crop translations modifying the information for his or her particular circumstance and area.

In computing the actual gross costs of using horses for motive power on the farm it is important to account for many items which are not direct cash outlays. For instance, feed grown on the farm or labor performed by the farm family may not require an actual cash expenditure but they are true costs and need to be computed in. The actual dollar costs attributed to these sorts of entries are going to vary remarkably depending on the attitude of the farmer and the total circumstance. Meanwhile, persons needing to make practical decisions about the future of work horses on their farms are going to be most particularly concerned with actual cash outlay required. For this reason we will include this as a separate category.

The use of horses has certain offsets if the farmer chooses to take advantage of them. For instance, manure and the raising of colts for replacement or sale have definite values which serve to offset either the gross costs or the cash outlay. For this reason, we also include their effect by offering categories of net cost (gross costs less offsets) and net outlay (cash outlay less offsets).

There are several intangible values or disadvantages, relative to specific operations, which either cannot be computed or which we choose for the sake of simplicity to exclude. We will mention those at the close.

We must assume that the use of work horses presupposes a deliberate choice of a mixed farming system of moderate size as versus a large monocultural practice. This is not to say that horses could not supply dependable power for a large single crop operation, but rather that the true economy and practicality of the horse is best realized on a farm with various crops in rotation including crops suitable for horse feed.

Understanding and controlling the cost of maintaining work horses with the concern on the one hand of realizing maximum work efficiency while on the other hand keeping costs to a minimum will result in a greater share of produce income returning to the farmer. The fact that much of the expense of maintaining work horses is made up of feed produced on the farm makes it easy for the farmer to be unconcerned about cost. But, insofar as this has a direct relationship to the amount of commodities available for sale or feed to other stock it has a direct bearing on the total farm profit.

By USDA census, on January 1, 1921, there were 24,663,000 horses and mules on American farms. These animals had a total value of $2,255,991.00 and were maintained primarily for the purpose of furnishing farm motive power. The American Horse Council reported in the spring of 1979 that there were 8,200,000 horses in the United States. These animals have an unknown value and are used primarily for sport. The regenerative capacity of horses is tremendous and if the need arose total numbers could triple in 10 years.

The gross cost of keeping work horses is made up of feed and bedding, labor, interest, stabling, use of harness, shoeing, depreciation, and miscellaneous charges. If we subtract the offsets from this gross cost the resulting net cost would be the cost of the work performed.

From 1914 to 1918 the annual cost of keeping work horses on corn-belt farms of approximately 160 acres usually amounted to $450 to $750 per year. The average per horse per year cost being $99.21. So, obviously, the farm which could efficiently complete its work with four head of horses (160 acres) had a lower overhead (and higher return) than a farm which used seven head of horses. But there were several important differences between then and now. For one, in 1917 there were more horses available for sale and the offset value resulting from a breeding program selling horses was much less than today. That is to say that a farmer/stockman today might have 6 mares and a stallion (and growing colts) and perform the field work for less money than another farmer with 4 geldings. For the farm with available space, top consideration should be given to working mares and raising colts for profit and replacement. (And it is not necessary that the farmer raise registered purebred stock as the market for good grade work horses is excellent.)

It is important to understand the nature of costs involved in using work horses so that they might be efficiently controlled. Some of the costs are of minor importance, others of great importance.

Fig. 235 shows the categories of cost and the percentages of the total. These figures are updated from a 1921 USDA survey and are based on a 160 acre mixed crop and livestock farm using six geldings.

For the sake of comparison, Fig. 228 shows projected cash outlay on the same farm scale but with a work unit of six brood mares and one stallion.

Feed

Feed and bedding, using the numbers from Fig. 235, is the most costly category at 39% of the total. Yet when comparing Fig. 235 and 228, feed becomes an area of expense with which the farmer might have tremendous flexibility. For these two reasons, feed as a category deserves first consideration in attempts to control or reduce costs.

Under Fig. 235 there are notes showing how cost calculations were made. If you are already using horses you may find fault in these calculations. Some differences can be traced to substantial variations in climate, available feed crops and farm economies. It is, however, more likely that a misunderstanding of the horses' digestive system and the best principles of feeding for work are the root cause of many farmers' overfeeding (or, in effect, wastefully feeding) work horses. See FEEDING chapter.

Fig. 221) Good feed and feeding habits result in reliable horse power. And the beauty of it all is that the horses can be used to make their own feed. The author (left) and Ray Drongesen mowing oat hay.

Photo by Christene George

The best methods of feeding work stock should always have first consideration on a well-managed farm. The quantities of grain and hay must depend on the kind and regularity of work, the speed at which the work is performed, quality of the feed, age and condition of the horse, and the keeping qualities of the individual animals. Although the exact quantity is variable, a good, practical guide for the farmer to follow in feeding the horses is to allow 1.1 lbs. of grain and 1¼ lbs. of hay per 100 lbs. of live weight when the animal is performing moderate work. For horses at hard work the grain should be increased to about 1¼ lbs. daily per 100 lbs. live weight, but the hay should not exceed 1¼ lbs. daily per 100 lbs. live weight (unless the hay is of very poor quality).

Quite contrary to the boasts of many old-timers and not-to-be-outdone newcomers, who have the average weight of any respectable work horse at at least a ton, surveys conducted 40 and 50 years ago and personal observation over these last ten years indicate that the average weight of most of the horses which truly work is about 1400 lbs. The range is anywhere from 500 lbs. (nod to our pony friends), to 2500 lbs. per horse. By far and away the majority weigh in at 1200 to 1600 lbs. Fig. 226 shows the feed requirements of 1300 to 1400 pound work horses as an indication of what is meant.

The amount of feed required by horses varies, not only from season to season, but also from day to day. Just because four horses are being used at heavy work does not mean that all the horses should receive a similar heavy grain ration. The observant teamster will find that a certain animal may perform well and hold his weight on slightly less grain. It is the

Fig. 222) Combining with Clydesdales.   *Photo by Carla Hammill*

little daily reduction of grain that counts up for a large saving during the year. Also making individual determinations of need will assist in keeping the horse in working condition.

As the spring work season opens up the amount of grain must be gradually increased so that the horses are ready to receive a full grain ration when the heavy work begins.

Aside from the idle winter season, there are times during the summer when at least some of the horses are not working. During such periods the use of good pasture in place of the grain and hay ration is not only an economical practice, but also will have a good effect on the digestive system of the horse. If the pasture is short or poor it may be necessary to supplement to keep the animals in good flesh.

If a horse is on night pasture (an excellent practice) and worked during the day, the regular grain should be fed, depending on the nature of the work. If the pasture is good the horse will consume only a small amount of hay and if a large amount is kept in the feed manger, a considerable portion will be wasted under foot. At all times, the horse should be fed so that he will utilize all the feed put before him, which will aid directly in reducing costs by preventing waste.

Many farmers are wasteful in the feeding of hay. It is common for farmers to keep the manger filled with hay at all times. This is not only a serious waste but experts say it is also detrimental to the horse's health. The horse has a small stomach and a touchy digestive system. He cannot take care of great quantities of roughage during the working season.

If you feed too much hay to your horse prior to work it will have a bad effect on the respiratory and digestive systems, and is the cause of excessive sweating and fatigue. Only a small amount of hay should be fed to horses in the morning and noon meals; the greatest amount should come at night. It is also an excellent practice, if possible, to allow the animal to eat some small quantity of hay before placing the grain ration in front of him. The roughage in this instance acts to slow the digestion of the following grain, allowing the horse to derive more nutrients.

The use of feeds which aren't readily saleable is to be recommended. If farming practices provide a quantity of good straw, dried corn stalks or stalk pasture, their use as horse feed will help to reduce the feed expense and permit the sale of hay or its use to feed other stock. The practice of letting the horses have the run of straw stacks (if you are lucky enough to have them from threshing) or stalk fields during the fall and winter not only results in saving of more valuable feeds but tends also to make the animals more hardy and in better shape for spring work.

To obtain the best results in feeding it is imperative that rations be properly balanced and supply adequate protein for the building of tissue and the supplying of energy. The less protein in a given ration the more feed required. A little time spent in the calculation of rations enables the feeder to provide the proper nutrients which benefits the horse and can often reduce the feed bill.

Chores

The USDA 1921 study on the cost of using horses surveyed 279 farms and found the average amount of time spent feeding and caring for seven head of horses per farm amounted to 467 hours per farm (or 66 hours per year per head). On some farms the amount went as high as 125 hours per year per horse.

Chores are nearly always done either by the farmer himself or by members of his family without actual cash outlay. Some reduction in time spent can be had by having convenient feeding and stabling arrangements so that handling horses and moving feed can be done in as short a time as possible.

Depreciation

The net decrease, or depreciation, in the inventory values of work stock on the farm is a calculation of the per year value of the total cost of replacing worn out stock. On the farm which depends exclusively upon gelded horses for work there is no escaping this cost item even though it may not represent an actual cash outlay until the day of need.

One system used by some farmers to greatly reduce the true depreciation is the purchase of three year old stock which is worked until five to seven years old and then sold (in the prime of life). The proceeds of the sale are then used to purchase young stock again.

The item of depreciation can be (and is) lessened or removed altogether on some farms by the raising of colts, as shown in Fig. 228. Colts increase rapidly in value and continue to increase after broken for work, until the highest value is reached at about seven years. Thus there is little or no depreciation other than that caused by disease or injury until age seven or eight. With today's high horse meat prices and high draft horse prices, farms which use brood mares for work and to raise colts for replacements and sale are showing steady appreciation in the total value of work stock rather than depreciation.

Strong young fertile mares can be worked steadily from one week to one day before foaling and, if no complications arise, can return to work within a week. Care should be taken that pregnant mares are not required to pull extremely heavy loads under slippery conditions as a fall or wrenching slip might cause problems. Most vets, however, will tell you that a mare which is worked steadily will have a better overall physical condition which makes birthing easier. After foaling, the mare's diet must be balanced and adequate to produce both work and milk without loss of body tissue.

The best methods of feeding and care of work horses, keeping them in good condition, is an important factor in reducing depreciation charges. Overheating or overworking the horses and the lack of proper attention often makes horses unfit for hard work when they are needed most. Permanent injury or chronic disease may be the result, requiring premature replacement.

Stabling

Stabling cost concerns only that part of the building in which horses are housed and feed is stored. On farms having low-priced or solid older structures, the cost of sheltering is a small item; on other farms where considerations are urgent and expensive it is quite another thing.

A small part of calculations included in the tables are actual cash outlay.

Fig. 223) Ontario horseman, Aden Freeman, leads a Belgian gelding from the stable to work.   *Photo by Lynn Miller*

Fig. 224) Bridles   *Photo by Nancy Roberts*

Harness Costs

The maintenance cost of harness becomes properly a part of the cost of horse power. It is an item of small importance and can be reduced some with good habits of use, care and storage.

Shoeing

Shoeing and, to some degree, hoof trimming, are direct cash expenses on most farms. The cost of hiring this work done is increasing as farriers are justifiably insisting on a fair wage. Costs can be kept to a minimum by the farmer learning to trim his own horses' feet and by shoeing only those horses which require corrective or preventive work and those which must go distances on gravel or asphalt roads. Horses with strong healthy hooves will be best off if left barefoot to do field work.

Miscellaneous

This item is composed of veterinary services, medicines and salt. It represents a direct cash outlay and the amount will be affected considerably by the time and service required of the vet. With good preventive care and a well-educated farmer (in vet matters) this cost can be held down.

Fig. 225) Horses not only provide fertilizer, they spread it.   *Photo by Nancy Roberts*

Manure Offset

In computing the manure credit I used the average actual nitrogen produced by one 1400 pound horse over a year at 160 lbs. (the total manure tonnage came to 7.5 per year). At a chemical market value for actual nitrogen of $27.50 per hundred weight, the value of manure per year is about $44. Since it is difficult to sell manure, the value used does not represent a cash credit but rather a cost offset. An offset of this nature will vary in amount according to the individual manure handling practices and the relative value to the individual farmer of the fertilizer.

Cash Costs

Only part of the items discussed here can be considered as being either cash expenses or involving materials having a sale value. The hay straw and grain consumed may all be salable. Stover and pasture could be considered byproducts of the farming system and may be difficult to sell. A percentage of stabling and harness costs could be classified as cash expenses. Hoof care and miscellaneous vet expenses are most likely cash expenditures. If we total the feed, a percentage of stabling and harness ($10) and all of hoof care and vet expenses, we come to a cash cost of $401.82 per year per horse. If we adjust the total to reflect actual cash out of pocket and assume that all feed is grown on the farm we come to a total of $110 per horse.

Cost of Horsepower

The daily or hourly cost of horsepower on any farm is dependent upon the number of work horses, the cost of keeping them and the number of days or hours worked in the year. As we've shown, the cost of keeping horses can vary dramatically. In the 1921 survey, 279 farmers average 723 work hours per horse. The more horses per farm (of the same size) the fewer the hours per horse and vice versa.

Using an average of 723 hours of work per horse the average cost per hour taken from Fig. 233, costs would be $1.03 per hour (or acre). This is, of course, the high end of figures presented in this chapter. For a suggestion of the effect of the variables in cost look to Figs. 232 and 233.

Obviously, if all things were equal, the horse that worked 1,000 hours would be less costly than the horse that worked only 500 hours per year. Many types of American farming are such that some of the horses maintained throughout the year are needed only to perform necessary work during the crop season or at rush periods so that the amount of work done by a group of horses is not limited so much by their yearly capacity as by the distribution and the amount of work to be done.

The best combination of crops and procedures for a given farm may require a large number of horses for only a short period of the year, even though many of the horses are idle during the greater part of the time. The average hours worked per day or per year might be very low and still be a justifiable result of good management for that particular farm.

There are many exceptions to the cost rules we have employed here and they are only meant to be guidelines to help farmers make practical management decisions. If nothing else, the spread in possible cost numbers indicates the extent to which a careful farmer can affect his costs.

Referring again to the 1921 study, the average number of acres of crops tended per horse in different sections of the corn belt varied from 18 to 24 acres. Obviously, the higher the number of crop-acres per horse the lower the cost per crop-acres of horse work performed. But that is a dangerously simplistic mathematical distinction and serves only to indicate horses needed per acre. It should not be used as a measure of efficiency as there are far too many exceptions in this regard. One horse for every 18 to 24 acres of cropland farmed is an excellent rule of thumb for people desiring to compute future need. On a mixed crop and livestock farm with woodlot, ponds, swamps or other marginal lands, figure the amount of land in acres that is to be actually farmed and divide by 20. That should give you the number of horses you need. If you have only 20 to 30 acres, you should consider two horses as this will give you greater flexibility. If you have 40 or 50 acres, you might consider three horses as you may occasionally have a need for an odd horse plowing or as a replacement for a temporary illness. The difference of a few days during bad weather can often be the deciding factor between a good crop and a poor one. A third horse and a bigger implement can make that difference.

The economical use of horses for power is a question that must be considered in connection with the operation and management of the entire farm. The very choice of the use of horses must be made carefully. Some people are not suited for day-in day-out responsibility to livestock, and work horses must be cared for before and after the long day's hard work. Some people are intimidated by the size and strength of the horse. Many can get over this, but for those who are forever "afraid" of horses, they have no place working them. The person who would depend upon work horses as a source of power must be of strong character, patient, persistent and sensitive.

Whether or not work horses are economically efficient for the small farm depends on the farm and the farmer, or in other words, the system and its engineer.

APPROXIMATE GRAIN AND HAY REQUIREMENTS FOR A HORSE WHEN NOT ON PASTURE

FIGURE 226

(1300 to 1400 pound horse)

Period	Daily ration of —	
	Grain lbs.	Hay lbs.
Maintenance (during winter)	6 to 7	15 to 17*
Light work (light hauling and miscellaneous farm work)	13 to 14	13 to 14
Medium work (cultivating corn, etc.).	14¼ to 15½	16¼ to 17½
Heavy work (plowing, discing, etc.).	16¼ to 17½	16¼ to 17½

*Partly unsalable roughages

ACTUAL CASH OUTLAY WITH BREEDING UNIT

FIGURE 228

(6 mares, 1 stallion)

Item	7 head amount	Per horse	Approx. %	Notes
Feed and bedding	0 (2042.74 value)	0 (291.82 value)	0	Assuming liberal pasture & homegrown feeds
Chores	0	0	0	Assuming family-performed labor
Depreciation	0	0	0	Assuming raising replacements & sale of horses
Interest	0	0	0	Assuming no amortization
Stabling	105.00	15.00	14%	Assuming existing structure maintenance costs
Harness	70.00	10.00	10%	Maintenance & replacement
Hoof care	315.00	45.00	40%	Assuming only corrective shoeing and trimming
Misc. vet	280.00	40.00	36%	Increased to allow for % of foaling difficulty
Gross total	770.00	110.00	100%	
Offset —Manure credit @ 160 lbs. nitrogen	308.00	44.00		

FIGURE 229

Feeding stuff	Digestible protein (%)	Digestible nutrients (%)
Dry Roughages		
Alfalfa hay, all analyses	10.5	50.3
Alfalfa leaf meal, good	16.1	56.7
Alfalfa leaves	17.4	57.9
Alfalfa meal, good	11.8	53.6
Alfalfa & bromegrass hay	7.2	46.8
Alfalfa & timothy hay	6.6	49.1
Barley hay	4.0	51.9
Barley straw	0.7	42.2
Bean pods, field, dry	3.5	50.3
Beggarweed hay	10.6	47.7
Bermuda grass hay	3.7	44.3
Birdsfoot trefoil hay	9.5	51.1
Bluegrass hay, Canada	2.8	53.3
Bluegrass hay, Kentucky	4.8	54.8
Bluestem hay	2.5	48.2
Bromegrass hay, all analyses	5.0	48.9
Broom corn stover	0.7	45.5
Buckwheat hulls	0.2	13.9
Buckwheat straw	1.2	37.5
Buffalo grass hay	3.7	47.7
Bunchgrass hay	2.7	48.7
Clover hay, alsike	8.1	53.2
Clover hay, crimson	9.8	48.9
Clover, ladino, & grass hay	11.1	53.3
Clover hay, mammoth red	6.8	52.0
Clover hay, red	7.1	52.2
Clover hay, white	10.5	55.6
Clover straw, crimson	3.8	40.0
Clover & timothy hay, 30-50% clover	4.8	51.2
Corn cobs, ground	0	45.7
Corn fodder, well eared, very dry	3.8	58.8
Corn husks, dried	0.4	38.8
Corn leaves, dried	3.5	49.8
Corn stalks, dried	0.8	40.7
Corn stover, very dry	2.1	51.9
Cottonseed hulls	0	43.7
Cowpea hay	12.3	51.4
Crabgrass hay	3.5	47.2
Fescue hay, meadow	3.7	52.7
Flat pea hay	18.4	59.5
Flax straw	5.8	38.1
Grass hay, mixed, eastern states	3.5	51.7
Lespedeza hay, annual	6.4	47.5
Millet hay, hog millet, or prose	5.6	50.7
Milo fodder	3.0	51.1

Feeding stuff	Digestible protein (%)	Digestible nutrients (%)
(continued)		
Native hay, western mt. states	4.9	52.0
Oat hay	4.9	47.3
Oat grass hay, tall	3.4	47.4
Orchard grass hay, early cut	3.9	47.8
Pasture grasses & clovers, mixed from closely grazed, fertile pasture, dried	15.0	66.7
Pasture grass, western plains growing, dried	8.6	66.5
Pasture grass, western plains mature, dried	1.3	47.1
Pasture grass & other forage on western mt. ranges, spring, dried	12.6	67.4
Pea hay, field	10.6	55.1
Peas & oat hay	8.6	52.9
Peanut hay, without nuts, good	6.6	51.9
Peanut hay, with nuts	10.2	71.6
Prairie hay, western, good	2.1	49.6
Rye grass hay, perennial	4.7	52.5
Rye grass hay, native western	3.3	52.2
Soybean hay, good, all analyses	9.6	49.0
Soybean & sudan grass hay, chiefly sudan	3.6	50.8
Sudan grass hay, all analyses	4.3	48.5
Timothy hay, all analyses	2.9	48.9
Vetch hay, common	10.1	55.3
Vetch hay, hairy	15.2	57.1
Vetch & oat hay, over ½ vetch	8.4	52.7
Vetch & wheat hay, cut early	11.4	58.0
Wheat hay	3.3	46.7
Wheat straw	0.3	40.6
Wheat grass hay, slender	4.6	51.2
Concentrates		
Barley, common, not incl. Pac. coast states	10.0	77.7
Barley, Pacific coast states	6.9	78.7
Buckwheat feed, good grade	11.7	52.5
Corn, dent, grade no. 1	6.8	82.0
Corn, dent, grade no. 5	6.1	74.0
Corn, flint	7.5	83.4
Corn ears, incl. kernels & cob	5.3	73.2
Corn & oat feed, good grade	9.2	78.5
Cottonseed, whole	17.1	90.8
Flaxseed	21.8	108.3
Molasses, cane or blackstrap	0	54.0
Oat kernels, without hulls (oat groats)	14.7	92.0

(continued)

Feeding stuff	Digestible protein (%)	Digestible nutrients (%)
Oat meal, feeding, or rolled oats, without hulls	14.4	91.4
Oat middlings	12.7	86.6
Oat mill feed	3.7	37.6
Oat mill feed, poor grade	1.4	32.3
Oat mill feed, with molasses	3.6	37.2
Oats, not incl. Pac. coast states	9.4	70.2
Oats, Pacific coast states	7.0	72.2
Oats, hull-less	13.9	89.4
Oats, lightweight	8.5	60.1
Oats, wild	9.1	53.9
Soybean seed	33.7	87.6

Feeding stuff	Digestible protein (%)	Digestible nutrients (%)
Soybean mill feed, chiefly hulls	7.8	40.1
Sunflower seed	13.9	76.3
Sunflower seed, hulled	25.2	116.1
Wheat, average of all types	11.1	80.0
Wheat, hard spring, chiefly northern plains states	13.3	80.7
Wheat, soft winter, Mississippi valley & eastward	8.6	80.1
Wheat, soft, Pac. coast states	8.3	79.9
Wheat bran, all analyses	13.7	67.2
Wheat, mixed feed, all analyses	14.3	70.6
Wheat screenings, good grade	10.0	68.7

FIGURE 230 — NUMBER OF DAYS WORKED / COST PER DAY

	Cost per horse	50 days	65 days	70 days	90 days	100 days	125 days
A	746.52	14.93	11.48	10.66	8.29	7.46	5.97
B	401.82	8.03	6.18	5.74	4.46	4.01	3.21
C	110.00	1.69	1.69	1.57	1.22	1.10	.88

HORSE COST OF VARIOUS JOBS PERFORMED PER ACRE AND PER 10 HOUR DAY
(using 723 hours per horse per year of work performed)
FIGURE 231
The cost variables are shown in A ($746.52 per horse year),
B ($401.82 per horse year), and C ($110.00 per horse year)

	A per acre	A per day	B per acre	B per day	C per acre	C per day
2 horses—walking plow (2 acres/day)	10.30	20.60	5.50	11.00	1.50	3.00
3 horses—riding plow (3 acres/day)	10.30	30.90	5.50	16.50	1.50	4.50
4 horses—gang plow (4 acres/day)	10.30	41.20	5.50	22.00	1.50	6.00
5 horses—gang plow (5 acres/day)	10.30	51.50	5.50	27.50	1.50	7.50
6 horses—gang plow (6 acres/day)	10.30	61.80	5.50	33.00	1.50	9.00
2 horses—disc/harrow (10 acres/day)	2.06	20.60	1.10	11.00	.30	3.00
3 horses—disc/harrow (15 acres/day)	2.06	30.90	1.10	16.50	.30	4.50
4 horses—disc/harrow (20 acres/day)	2.06	41.20	1.10	22.00	.30	6.00
5 horses—disc/harrow (25 acres/day)	2.06	51.50	1.10	27.50	.30	7.50
6 horses—disc/harrow (30 acres/day)	2.06	61.80	1.10	33.00	.30	9.00
2 horses drilling grain (10 acres/day)	2.06	20.60	1.10	11.00	.30	3.00
2 horses planting corn (10 acres/day)	2.06	20.60	1.10	11.00	.30	3.00
2 horses cultivating (5 acres/day)	4.12	20.60	2.20	11.00	.60	3.00
2 horses mowing hay (10 acres/day)	2.06	20.60	1.10	11.00	.30	3.00
2 horses raking hay (20 acres/day)	1.03	20.60	.55	11.00	.15	3.00

723 hours — A = $1.03/hour
B = .55/hour
C = .15/hour

723 hours — A = $10.30/day
B = 5.50/day
C = 1.50/day

COMPARISONS IN COST

The cost of two horses mowing hay (10 hour day) on different farms where the total hours that horses are used varies

A, B, C represent management cost variables used in Tables I, II and III

Work performed per horse per year	Cost per day		
	A	B	C
Farm no. 1 500 hours	29.80	16.00	4.40
Farm no. 2 723 hours	20.60	11.00	3.00
Farm no. 3 1000 hours	15.80	8.00	2.20

FIGURE 232

COST PER HOUR PER HORSE ON FARMS WITH VARIOUS HOURS OF USE

	Cost per horse	500 hours	723 hours	1000 hours
A	746.52	1.49	1.03	.74
B	401.82	.80	.55	.40
C	110.00	.22	.15	.11

FIGURE 233

Fig. 234) The more hours a horse actually works, the less the actual cost per hour as the maintenance costs do not go up proportionately. Ray Drongesen mowing, photo by Christene George

199

FIGURE 235 Item	Amount (cash value for six head horses)	Cost per horse	% of total cost	Notes
Feed and bedding	1750.92	291.82	39	Assuming no pasture, all feed purchased
Chores	1049.40	174.90	23½	Assuming all chores hired out
Depreciation	480.00	80.00	11	Assuming all geldings with 12 yr. working life (value $1,000 each)
Interest	550.80	91.80	12	Assuming amortization
Stabling	120.00	20.00	2½	Assuming maintenance of existing structure
Harness	93.00	15.50	2	Assuming maintenance & replacement of existing harness
Hoof care	270.00	45.00	6	Assuming corrective shoeing & trimming
Misc. vet	165.00	27.50	4	Worming & misc. vet supplies
Gross total	4479.12	746.52	100	
Offset — Manure credit @ 160 lbs. nitrogen per year per horse	246.00	44.00		

Notes: Feed computed at 2624 lbs. oats per year, 1.3 tons good quality hay per year and 1.8 tons of straw per year. Chores at 66 hours per head per year @ $2.65 per hour. Interest at 9%.

Fig. 236) The actual per hour cost of work performed makes horses an excellent option for small-scale logging operations.   *Photo by Nancy Roberts.*

CHAPTER FOURTEEN

VALUE OF HORSES AS POWER

Fig. 233) The author driving four abreast hitched to a combination disc and harrow.

Photo by Christene George

This author believes that if an argument is to be made that horses are a practical, modern, power system option then advocates should be prepared to at least understand the economics involved. In the chapter, COST OF USING HORSES, formulas are given for computing the actual hourly cost of horse power relative to total investment and actual use computed against value of work performed. But what are horses worth? Not just in terms of what price to pay for them but also in terms of the future market of farm-raised work horses. And one other consideration: Does the deliberate choice to use horses open up opportunities or close them down?

If someone were expecting to use two horses on a farm and had projected that the animals would actually work 100 full days out of the year, a calculation, of sorts, might be made of the value. Just for the sake of example, let's say one of the horses is a mare and one is a gelding and that you can expect seven years of work out of each. Also, let's say that during that seven years the mare presents you with three foals. If the hourly work of the horses was worth just $1 (for the team), a day's effort would be $8 — the year's effort would be $800 in value and seven years (with no inflation adjustment) = $5,600. If one of the foals were sold for $500 the total value of that team might be $6,100. If the other two foals were kept as replacements (the original team sold at the end of seven years), it is easy to see that the value of work horses on the farm continues to grow and easily surpasses original investment. The individual can pencil out a conservative plan and projection and come up with an actual dollar figure for initial investment that would probably be higher than originally thought.

Today there is a floor (or bottom) in the draft horse market which is established by the current horse meat price. As the demand for good work horses grows and affects supply considerations (or breeding and marketing concerns) there will be a slightly higher, more stable floor to the price of draft horses, grade work horses and miscellaneous breeds such as the Morgan and French Canadian. It is the contention of this author that such a rise in price is not only justified but will improve the general economy of those using horses as it increases value of older and younger stock sold.

For those getting started in the business of working horses in harness, there should be slightly different qualifications or characteristics sought in horses. The quiet (even slow), well-schooled, sound animal will be of higher value to the beginner than will the beautiful,

Fig. 234) Work horses have the ability to replace themselves.

Photo by Nancy Roberts

Fig. 235) Any teamster would be wise to swallow his or her 'pride' and get rid of, or stay away from, the obviously "psychotic" animal. The true "runaway" horse is a killer any way you look at it.   *Photo by Christene George*

pedigreed, high-strung, young female or stallion of perfect color. And beyond that there are characteristics which will make an animal less than worthless, such as the runaway horse.

The RUNAWAY HORSE is a title often given undeservedly to animals which were forced by human incompetence, insensitivity and inexperience to "get away" at any cost. The horse, of normal brain function and memory facility, that has not been physically and mentally abused may have an accident causing him to runaway. A conscientious, patient, knowing, teamster can gradually remove that bad experience from the horse's immediate memory. The inexperienced teamster, however, can convert that unfortunate accident into a series of mishaps which would cause permanent psychological damage to the horse. This is part of the reason why the newcomer to this business needs to begin with slow, quiet, well-schooled horses that will not "blow up" with any little problem. Even so, it should be mentioned that a person of no experience, little brains and no common sense can "ruin" a fool-proof, 'broke-the-best' horse in very short time.

On occasion you will come across a truly psychotic animal with suicidal tendencies — an incurable runaway. If you've got some experience, you may want to try to break such an animal of its 'habit'. You won't be able to. This sort of beast is unpredictable and likely suffers from similar mental disease to what is seen in humans. You may think you have everything under control when 'Bang'! all of a sudden . . . . As a power source, such an animal is less than worthless. But this is not to suggest that the notion of horses as power is weak. To the contrary . . . .

Fig. 236) A sensitive, patient teamster is fully half, or more, of any working horse outfit. If the teamster does not enjoy the animals and take pride in their proper care, he or she has no place working horses. In the photo, John Male, Ontario horse farmer.   Photo by Marianne Johner

On the farm, horses or mules are an excellent power source whether exclusive or mixed with tractors or motors. And their value as power comes because of the great inherent flexibility. The limitations of intelligently applied horse power come only from the teamster's creativity. The horse in harness is not a hard, fixed, finite vibrating motor. The horse in harness is a marvelous mass of nerve ends scattered over magnificent muscles arranged on a fabulous form spirited by an unusual intelligence and acute sensitivity. If you add to that a creative, patient, sensitive teamster perhaps you can begin to see what possibilities exist.

And as far as systems go: imagine a farm with three horses that are used abreast on the plow and other tillage tools, after which two of them are used to plant crops. Three single animals are available for special little jobs and if one animal gets a sprain or is sick another can fill in. Flexible power;

And with working mares, the power source is renewable;

And their operation and care is so easily integrated into the workings of a mixed crop and livestock farm.

While speaking of their value as a power source, it is perhaps appropriate to mention the fact that they also provide fertilizer through their manure.

If we can but apply the best of advances in technology and methodology to the basic principle of animal power — all with an eye to what is appropriate — the future of the horse in harness is not just bright, it's brilliant.

CHAPTER FIFTEEN

WORK YOU CAN DO WITH HORSES

Fig. 237 (above) Dale Esgate rests his team on a turn while logging second growth Douglas fir.
Photo by Nancy Roberts

Fig. 238) Plowing with three abreast.

Fig. 239) Mowing hay with a team.

Work Done By Horses — The work which horses can do depends on their weight, their muscle tone, and their endurance. At steady and continuous work for 10 hours a day, the pull (or draft) for the animal should not be more than one-tenth of its weight. For example, a 2,000 lb. horse should not be required to exert an average constant pull of more than 200 lbs. (to 250). For a brief moment a well-trained, well-conditioned horse can pull 10 times (plus) the normal rate, exerting a pull sometimes greater than his own weight. When we speak here of the "pull" we are not speaking of the weight of the load but the actual weight of the drag. If you had a sack of feed and hooked a spring weigh scale to that sack and pulled — the pounds registered on the scale when the sack first moves will be the "pull". Obviously if the same sack is put on a wagon that rolls easily, it will require fewer pounds of pull to start the load. A team of horses can pull several ton of weight on wheels.

In measuring the rate at which horses perform work, the unit called "horse-power" is used. This is the perfomance of 33,000 foot pounds of work per minute. (One foot pound is the amount of work done in lifting one pound one foot against the force of gravity.)

Fig. 240) Gary Eagle drilling oats with a twelve foot drill pulled by four head of grade work horses. Gary farms a half section at 5,000 feet elevation in Washington state. All work is done with horses.   *Photo by MaryLyn Eagle*

Fig. 241) The author drilling grain on the flatland with a grade team hitched to a six foot wide drill.   *Photo by Christene George*

A horse weighing 1500 lbs. is able to work steadily at the rate of approximately one horse power. During a hard pull the same horse might be exerting a rate of 10 hp or more.

Weight is an important factor in determining how much a horse can pull. Feed, harness and the skill of the teamster all affect how much work horses can do. (See FEEDING and HARNESS chapters.)

The kind of road surface is a big factor in determining how much weight a horse can move on wheels. While only 25 to 50 lbs. of draft are required after the load is started, to haul a load of a ton (including weight of the wagon), on a level pavement made of concrete or asphalt, the draft on a dirt or gravel road is 75 to 225 lbs. or more per ton.

On a soft surface (especially mud), the height of wheel and the width of tire are important, as they affect the depth that the wheels cut into the ground. On a good hard, smooth surface there is very little difference in draft with different kinds of wheels.

Horses are most efficient in doing a full day's work when walking at a speed of 2.5 miles per hour. However, walking as fast as 3 miles per hour does not reduce efficiency if the animal's conformation allows for ease and comfort. It is up to the teamster to make distinction as to what is the most efficient walk for the animals used.

How Many Acres

Farms can be operated well with one good work animal for each 25 acres, excluding pasture. Mixed farming requires at least one-fourth of a farm be in pasture. This means 4, 5, 6 or 8 work animals will do all the field work on 120, 160, 200 and 240 acre farms, respectively.

Fig. 242 (above) Gary Eagle pulls a spring tooth chisel through grain stubble with five abreast. The chisel is hitched behind a two-wheel forecart of Gary's design.
Fig. 243 (below) Gary again, this time pulling a disc and spike tooth combination with five abreast.
Both photos by MaryLyn Eagle.

Fig. 244) *This is the best way to learn how to plow — with a good team and an able teamster helping. After a few rounds you may be able to take on both the horses and the plow.* *Photo by Marianne Johner*

The two horse team will:

    plow 1½ to 2 acres per day,
    disc 10 acres per day,
    harrow 10 to 12 acres per day,
    drill 6 to 10 acres per day,
    plant 8 acres per day,
    cultivate 8 acres per day,
    mow 8 acres per day,
    rake 16 acres per day,
    or do wagon work 25 miles per day.

Three horses on a farm will:
    plow 3 acres per day,
    disc 15 acres per day,
    harrow 15 to 17 acres per day,
    drill 12 to 15 acres per day,
    or cultivate (with 2 on one cultivator and
      1 on another) 12 acres per day.

Four horses on a farm will:
    plow 4 acres per day,
    disc 20 acres per day,
    harrow 17 to 20 acres per day,
    drill 20 acres per day,
    plant (with 2 planters, or doubled)
      16 acres per day,
    cultivate 16 acres per day,
    mow (with 2 teams) 16 acres per day,
    or rake (with 2 teams) 32 acres per
day.

Six horses on a farm will:
    plow 6 acres per day,
    disc 30 acres per day,
    harrow 30 acres per day,
    drill 30 acres per day,
    plant (3 teams) 24 acres per day,
    cultivate (3 teams) 24 acres per day,
    mow (3 teams) 24 acres per day,
    or rake (3 teams) 48 acres per day.

and so on.

To calculate the amount of work done, figure speed (i. e., 2.5 mph), times day's length (actually moving). Multiply resulting distance in feet by the width of the implement (i. e., 8 feet) and the result will be square footage covered. (Divide by square footage of an acre for acreage measure.)

A list of jobs that can be performed on the farm by horses include:

Plowing, harrowing, springtoothing, discing, rolling, leveling, drilling seed, planting seed, spreading fertilizer, spreading manure, hauling irrigation pipe, cultivating, mowing, tedding, raking, loading, baling, hauling hay, binding grain (including corn), picking corn, chopping silage, hauling silage, digging potatoes, miscellaneous harvest work, hauling winter feed, hauling firewood, collecting maple sap, skidding miscellaneous, and more.

Fig. 245 (above) Assorted plows 'resting' after a plowing match.
Photo by Lynn Miller

Fig. 246 (below) Lester Courtney's pony hitch at a plow match. Don't rule out ponies!

Fig. 247) A four-up doing good work plowing. Such an outfit should be able to turn over four acres in a good day's work.
Photo by Lynn Miller

Fig. 248) Gary Eagle binds his grain with four hitched abreast. Depending on equipment and conditions, you can bind between 8 and 16 acres per day.
Photo by MaryLyn Eagle

Figs. 249 & 250) These two photos are of Doug Hammill, DVM, baling hay with a team of Clydesdales hitched to a homemade heavy duty forecart. The cart is then hitched to a conventional tractor baler with a motor. This outfit can cover just as much ground as the same thing pulled by a tractor.

Photos by Carla Hammill

Fig. 251) Doug Hammill combining grain with four-up hitched to a heavy forecart which pulls a motorized combine. This outfit will cover about the same amount of ground as a tractor counterpart. This illustrates the great flexibility that forecarts give.
Photo by Carla Hammill

Fig. 252) Ray Drongesen drives the author's outfit. Here is the three-wheeled cart diagrammed in this text. The team is hooked to the cart which in turn is hooked to a tractor, goose neck, ground-drive side delivery rake. These photos on this page illustrate the future of horse-power on the farm.
Photo by Nancy Roberts

Fig. 253) Another beautiful photo of the Hammill Clydesdale-powered combine harvesting grain in Montana.
Photo by Carla Hammill

How Many Logs

It is more difficult to give even rough estimates of log skidding production with horses because there are more variables.

Depending on the length of the skid road, how hard the going is, how large the logs are, the speed of the horses and the ability of the horse logger, production may vary from one thousand to eight thousand board feet per day per team. Perhaps the most important current fact about horse logging is that, given a healthy lumber demand, the conscientious, intelligent logging operation seems to function well with horse power. It is not a get-rich situation, but it is viable.

As to how big a log can be pulled, here again the variables of weight, skid-road, horses and teamster all take effect. The teamster will "learn" his team's limitations and should do so gradually, working up to the big stuff.

Fig. 254) Jim Bower is a full-time commercial logger who uses horses. In this photo Jim's Belgian team is resting but attentive while Jim looks on. The large log is hooked with skidding tongs. One reason the future of work horses is so bright is because hundreds of young people, such as Jim, bring fresh vision and quick mastery to this subtle business.
Photo by Steve Bader

Fig. 255) Both in the woods and on the farm, horses — used to yard logs for lumber, pulp and firewood — are returning in great numbers. The predominant reason is that animal power is the most appropriate system causing little or no damage to the forest floor and young growing trees. Photo by Nancy Roberts

Fig. 256) An unusual team of Shire-cross mules went on to win the log skidding competition in the last Draft Horse Festival. Mules do very well in the woods, perhaps because their compact hoof makes them surefooted. Photo by Nancy Roberts

Drayage work and people hauling are big new frontiers for the horse power scene. Every day a new little example pops up somewhere of people using horses in unexpected but welcome ways and places. Like in California, where community parks are being maintained with horses and horse-drawn streetcars are moving people. In Oregon, where garbage, freight and people are being hauled. In Washington, where heating oil is delivered by horse-drawn wagon. In British Columbia, where Clydesdales haul a traveling theatre group. And the list goes on and on.

The potential seems wide and new ideas plus new people will keep the doors open for the horse in harness.

Fig. 257) A team of light horses draws a buggy down the road.

Photo by Lynn Miller

Fig. 258) A horse-drawn garbage compacting wagon which work commercially in Florence, Oregon, pointing the way to a diversified future for animal power.

Fig. 259) Gary Eagle takes a sled load of loose hay out to feed some cows.   *Photo by Lynn Miller*

Fig. 260) Doug Hammill uses a horse-drawn grader on Montana snow.   *Photo by Carla Hammill*

The exciting aspect of the work horse is this wonderful flexibility combined with an easily enjoyed overall character. What person isn't charmed by the sight of an oncoming horse-drawn buggy or a hard-working team in the field? Add to this the FACT that the use of horses and mules in harness IS PRACTICAL if approached intelligently and sensibly. And with that you have lots of promise. There will be more equipment and information available which will in turn improve the possibilities ultimately resulting in an even greater variety of jobs that can and will be done with horses.

CHAPTER SIXTEEN

MEASUREMENTS

GENERAL

HORSE-POWER: One horse-power is the equivalent of 33,000 foot pounds of work per minute.

One 1500 lb. horse at steady, regular work produces one "horse-power". Two 2000 lb. horses in good condition at steady work would produce three "horse-power". During a hard pull the same team would produce up to 30 horse-power.

A horse or mule at steady regular labor for ten hours per day can be expected to pull a dead-drag weight equivalent to 10% of the animal's body weight. A hard pull might equal body weight.

HITCH GEAR

TONGUES: For full size horses, figure an average length of 9½' to 10' from doubletree hitch point to neck yoke point. Add length needed to fasten to implement or vehicles. Make sure that doubletree is sufficiently ahead of implement so that turning horses will not hit or tangle. Add 6" beyond neck yoke stop. Tongues should taper from at least 2 x 3" if wood.

NECK YOKES: The neck yoke is the same length as the doubletree for the same horses. Lengths vary from 38" to 48" for wagons (or desired wide-set). The narrowest would be from 28" to 30" for use in some plow hitches and other narrow setups. Neck yokes, if wood, should taper from the center out. The center should be about 3" thick with the ends at 1½" to 2".

SINGLETREES: For full-sized horses singletrees vary in length from 26, 28, 30, 36 and 38 inches. The 36" and 38" lengths would only be used for very wide hitches, like wagons, if at all. 28" and 30" are the most common. The singletree normally measures 2½" thick at the center with ends at least 1½" thick.

DOUBLETREES: Wagon doubletrees are normally 42, 46 or 48 inches long. Narrow, plow-type doubletrees are anywhere from 30" to 40" in length with 28" rarely seen. A wooden doubletree should taper from the center and be at least 4" thick at center with something like 3" at the ends.

TRIPLETREES: 50" to 54" in length with hitch point one third over. 4" to 5" thick if wood.

CLEVIS: Are sized to fit.

SHAFTS: For full-sized horse — 28" in front, 5'6" to hold back hardware. 36" wide inside back. 100" long. See page 121 for illustration.

LEAD OR DRAW CHAIN OR CABLE: 10 foot adjustable to 12 foot.

FOR BUCK BACK SYSTEM — Tie chain = 72" to 60". Buckback strap: inside check 48", outside check 54". Main strap 106" adjustable.

HARNESS

Weight of farm harness (with 1½" tugs), approximately 75 lbs.

Weight of farm collars, 12 lbs. for 23 inch, 14 lbs. for 26 inch, 16 lbs. for 28 inch.

Tugs — vary in dimension from 1½" x 6', 1¾" x 6', 1½" x 6' 6", 2" x 6' 6", up to 3" x 6' 6".

Lines — vary from 1 1/8" x 20' to 1¼" x 20' for team lines.

Billets — average 1½" in width.

Pole straps — (sometimes called martingales) from 1½" x 4' to 1¾" x 4', some as wide as 2".

Belly bands are 1¼" to 1¾" wide

Hame straps — vary from 1" x 21" up to 1" x 36" or 1 1/8" x 24" up or 1¼" x 24" on up.

Breast straps are 1½" x 4½' or 1¾" x 4½' (doubled).

Bits for draft horses are usually 6" long, some 6½".

Trace chains are from 18" to 24" in length with 5/16" wire links. Some go to 36" with 11 links.

Hame balls are usually 2¼" to 2" in diameter with 1 1/8" opening.

INDEX

AFTERWORD

This book is the result of almost four years of effort. Granted, it has come most often in between Journal work, farm work, and travel and, until the last couple of months, was a part-time effort, but it was a bigger project than I had originally conceived. I'm a farmer and a stockman and, for over five years, made myself into an editor as I created and built the Small Farmer's Journal. But in all that time, and during the work on this book, I realized that I had no natural gift for writing. It doesn't come hard; it just comes clumsy. I have told myself over and over again that it does not matter because I am, if I do a good job, providing important information. Being still so close to this project, it is difficult for me to feel anything but terrified. I hope there is here the information that is sought and needed by so many.

As this project took shape, it became apparent that aspects of this subject required separate research, collection and publication. For example; there were over a thousand different makes and models of horse-drawn plows manufactured in the USA between 1910 and 1930! These account for hundreds of variations in adjustment and operation. There are a half dozen manufacturers of horse-drawn plows in North America today. Several other builders have expressed intentions to join the market with new plow designs. Only three of these new (or soon to be) plow makers have had products in service long enough to be tested in service. All of this material (possibly with all other horse-drawn farm implements) would be a text (or two, or three) in and of itself.

If you have any familiarity with working horses in harness you will come across names and words in this text which to you might seem misplaced. There has never been, in the entire history of the technology of working horses in harness, any homogenizing force, so cultural differences had unrestricted effect on the vocabulary of this business. There is nothing wrong with that. In fact, it should be preserved. I don't like the idea of us all speaking the same language and/or dialect. So for the sake of cultural preservation, consider the words I use as being misplaced temporary handles.

If it has not yet come across in this text, this author believes wholeheartedly in the practicality, viability and humanity of the use of horses and mules in harness. I sincerely hope that this text serves in some small way to help build the future of the work horse.

Lynn R. Miller, October, 1981

About the author: L.R. Miller is the founder, editor and publisher of **Small Farmer's Journal** an international quarterly featuring information on practical horsefarming. Since 1989 L. R. Miller has lived, with his wife and children, on a mixed crop and livestock operation known as Singing Horse Ranch. Situated in central Oregon, the ranch is operated as a research adjunct to **Small Farmer's Journal** with all field work being done with Belgian and Belgian cross work horses. L. R. Miller is the author of several other books including **Training Workhorses / Training Teamsters.**

*Copies of **Training Workhorses / Training Teamsters** and **Small Farmer's Journal** subscriptions are available. For ordering information contact SFJ Inc. PO Box 1627, Sisters, Oregon 97759 (541)549-2064*